by Two Lenz

OVERCOMING THE BARRIERS
OF SERIOUS MENTAL ILLNESS

WALKING
THROUGH
WALLS

Outskirts Press, Inc.
Denver, Colorado

What People Are Saying

Two Lenz's account of her life is an artful synthesis of the tormented reality of chronic severe mental illness, and the poignant narrative of an individual who lives it. Through her words she expresses her pain and her battles, and simultaneously her hope, her tenacity, and her quest to educate others. These elements have culminated in the creation of a work that leaves the reader with a powerful reconstruction of the concept of an individual with severe mental illness.

Her writing is eloquent and candid, and her story not only embodies her talent as a writer, but even more so her grace as an individual.

Lyn Ansher, PhD
Licensed Psychologist

Walking Through Walls is an ambitious, firsthand account of the challenges often faced by individuals with serious mental illness. Throughout the author's autobiographical journey, she also takes time to directly interact with her readers who may have experienced similar situations, in order to encourage and assure them that proper treatment can mitigate their suffering. Additionally, *Walking Through Walls* provides guidance to family and friends of individuals with serious mental illnesses. It is a moving memoir, which aspires to support and inform all readers affected by psychiatric illness, as well as introduce individuals to something they may have previously misunderstood.

Megan Leahy, Pharm D, BCPP
Clinical Pharmacy Specialist, Psychiatry

This book is much more than an autobiography. It ends up telling three interrelated stories. First, of course, it is the story of the author, a woman whose life was severely affected by her mental illness, who, through courage and hard work, has been able to reinvent herself. The second story relates to the advances that have been made in treatment, and details both how far we've come and how much farther we have to go. The third story is of how our society fails to meet the challenge of mental illness and how much can and should be done. By giving an insider's viewpoint on all three stories, there is much to learn.

Steven J. Kingsbury, MD, PhD
Clinical Professor of Psychiatry

Two Lenz's book, *Walking Through Walls*, offers an incredible insight into the heart and most importantly the mind of an incredibly brave woman. Few of us would have the courage to deal with her "realities." Fewer still would have the courage to write about them. This book is more than an interesting read. It is enlightening, frightening, and heartwarming all at the same time.

Chris Kaempfer, Doctor of Jurisprudence

Rarely does a book capture your complete attention, let alone hold it for an extended period. *Walking Through Walls* grabs your attention with a heartfelt account of a life filled with both tremendous struggle and victory. This book is a must read for mental health professionals, family members, individuals struggling with mental illness, and anyone searching for answers as to what the human spirit is capable of when faced with extreme adversity. A true triumph!

Bobby Kountz
President of NAMI of Southern Nevada

Walking Through Walls provides an intelligent, insightful exploration of the author's experience with major mental illness. The writing compels the reader's attention and remains rather engrossing throughout. *Walking Through Walls* should appeal to a variety of readers. From an educational and informational aspect, it provides accurate, first-person information about mental illness and the mental health system. Emotionally, it may be viewed as an inspirational story of a lifelong, but eventually successful struggle. Those suffering from their own mental difficulties may achieve new insights and encouragement as a result of reading Two Lenz's book.

Herbert P. Goldman, MD
Board Certified Psychiatrist

Walking Through Walls is a courageous book. It is a personal account of Two Lenz's lifelong struggle with mental illness and recovery. Her book is most certainly a special gift of hope to those who suffer from mental illness.

Julene A. Lee, RN
Registered Nurse

To My Dear Debbie,

Who has been loyal to me through 28 years of recovery.
She worked with me closely as I searched for a publisher and
strived to get my book marketed. This book would likely never
have been produced without her.

About The Author

Two Lenz has been hospitalized about 25 times while acquiring firsthand experience of the mental health system. She has sat on multiple committees pertaining to matters regarding mental illness. As a member of the Alliance for the Mentally Ill of Nevada, she earned the 1997 Nevada State Humanitarian Award.

Lenz has worked as freelance journalist and college instructor. She obtained her Bachelor of Science degree in journalism and her Master of Arts degree in sociology. In the past, Lenz has won five national awards in writing competitions, four from excerpts from WALKING THROUGH WALLS. Recently, she was an EVVY Book Award Merit Winner in the category of autobiography.

Table Of Contents

Foreword

The most shocking thing about mental illness is our limited knowledge and understanding of this health condition. People fear the diagnosis of mental illness and fear those who live with this diagnosis. The stigma of mental illness remains a major public health issue. One out of every five families in this country will be directly affected by a serious mental illness in their lifetime.

Walking Through Walls provides clear insight into the genuine pain and struggle of someone who suffers from mental illness. The book describes the stress and pressure facing a mental illness sufferer, beginning with the onset of the illness and the realization that something is wrong; moving through years battling with episodes of disordered thinking, disruptive behavior, alternating depression along with mania, and severe difficulties at home, at school, and at work. Some of these problems include years of seeking appropriate help and services while undergoing many grueling therapeutic trials with medications — some with unintended side effects. There were frequent times of coping with relapses and multiple hospitalizations. These examples reflect not only an incredible will to stay alive, but also the resiliency to continue to survive effectively.

Walking Through Walls describes landmark events and significant changes in mental health care delivery over the past four decades. Social, economic, political, and scientific developments influenced the care of the mentally ill and their families. In recent years, there have been major scientific advances. Researchers have been able to highlight several factors such as brain chemistry and the structure, functioning, and role of genes. The biopsychosocial antecedents of psychiatric medications are now available to effectively treat symptoms and assist patients in achieving a better quality of life. The understanding, support, and encouragement of the family, friends, clinicians, and others directly involved in the care of an individual with mental illness are extremely important and, at times, life-saving.

This book has a message that goes beyond the pain and anguish, frustrations, turmoil, and challenges of mental illness. This book provides a strong and clear message that mental illness can be treated and can be managed effectively. Those with mental illness can develop and achieve their full potential in life. This book can be extremely useful for mental health care providers and other clinicians, students, social workers, psychologists, nurses, chaplains, administrators, politicians, educators, patients and their families, and all those who are directly involved in the care of the mentally ill. The book affirms our belief in the beauty and dignity of the human spirit.

Rena M. Nora, MD

Clinical Professor of Psychiatry,
University of Nevada School of Medicine

Acknowledgments

Approximately 90 percent of the research and facts that resulted from efforts producing this book can be credited to the National Alliance for the Mentally Ill (NAMI). I thank them abundantly for always supporting *Walking Through Walls* with requested data that supported this book.

Other primary raw data in *Walking* can be credited to miscellaneous documentation from a variety of valid materials.

The remaining content in *Walking* came from the hearts of all those mentioned (by using fictitious names). I call this the soft data that often supported a formidable truth I have finally found myself able to share.

And I must include Krista T. in this acknowledgment for her patience and endurance guiding me through the publishing process. She was invaluable.

Karen Horton's meticulous, often brilliant editing saved me from embarrassing errors in my finished manuscript. Also, her encouragement that this book just had to be published was accepted with much gratitude.

Also, many thanks to Dr. Rena Nora for her careful editing of this manuscript to produce a much more polished product.

Accolades to my friend Christine Kaempfer, who brainstormed to come up with a great idea for the design of the cover.

Most definitely, thanks to Debbie Newsome for her wise guidance as my business manager and friend, whose ongoing solid advice regarding the production of this book and whatever other projects I come up with during my often daily erratic activities will forever be appreciated.

Finally, there was the tedious task of transferring fact to floppy disk and printed paper. Again and again, it was my smart brother who saved me from the terrible trauma of losing data.

Introduction

The mentally ill occupy more hospital beds than patients suffering from arthritis, cancer, diabetes, and heart and lung diseases combined. In addition, misdiagnosis frequently prompts incorrect treatment or no treatment at all for painfully endless periods of time, resulting in the mentally ill suffering in prisons or on the streets.

Four groups of readers are addressed in the following pages:

1) Those of you who have been diagnosed with a serious mental disorder who need to better know you are not alone in your suffering. It is important for you to have enhanced understanding that your disease does not single you out. Indeed, there are symptoms classic to many who suffer serious psychoses. This understanding will help you begin to recognize that hallucinations, delusions, and/or roller-coaster moods are not your fault. So this book is intended to be a comfort for you as you come to know you have a disease that has been discovered, is defined, and is treatable.

    You will also hopefully come to create a kinship with me, someone who has experienced and survived the focal symptoms of 39 years of serious mental illness. In the process, I hope this book will give you tools to manage the difficult days that plague you.

2) Those of you who suffer painful psychological symptoms but have never been diagnosed, while you do not know what it is that has cruelly seized your senses and brought

torment to your lives each day. Perhaps these pages will serve as a mirror that reflects the necessary insights that only others who suffer serious mental illness can recognize. In the process, you will be provided tools to help identify the source of your pain and help obtain the specific professional help needed to bring you peace.

3) Those of you who know someone or suspect a loved one who suffers from a serious mental illness, but you are not sure what that may involve. This book was written for you, a significant other who gets inside this book to hopefully look inside the mind of a person who seems to suffer a serious mental illness. Thereby, you can hopefully identify if there is possibly a major psychiatric problem suffered by that person you no longer understand. Then perhaps you can assist in obtaining crucial medical treatment for someone you care about.

   This book is intended to aid you in developing an understanding of how you can help your loved one or friend each day, and to allow you to develop an appreciation for the enormous courage required by the mentally ill to fight those daily battles.

4) Those of you, as well as loved ones or friends, who suffer no serious psychosis. Here, it is still important to understand what misery the mentally ill suffer because of the enormous stigma that pervades their world. A significant measure of compassion is due the seriously mentally ill who merit a much higher level of both respect and understanding. Though you have no one close who has been diagnosed with a serious mental illness, it is still important for the general population to learn about the painful yet courageous world of the mentally ill so that more progress can be made in quality of care and in research for better treatment.

It is difficult for most mentally healthy persons to understand how an intensely mentally ill person feels. Such lack of understanding can create cruelties of every sort, from mild impatience to brutal persecution to physical abuse. This kind of mentality cancels out crucial legislation that would provide vital funding needed for facilities to successfully treat the mentally ill, and research to discover new and better ways to identify and eradicate the cruelties of mental illness. Instead of branding the mentally ill individual as someone to avoid, you will hopefully complete this book feeling encouraged not only to feel compassion for the mentally ill but also to admire and even focus on these brave individuals to learn something about the courage behind their psychological survival.

The primary, serious mental illnesses identified by the National Alliance for the Mentally Ill (NAMI) are accepted by mental health experts. They are, from most serious to less serious: schizophrenia, bipolar disorder (manic-depression), and clinical depression. Also included, but less serious, are obsessive-compulsive disorder and panic disorder, which are only briefly addressed in this book. Schizoaffective disorder is recognized in this book as a primary mental illness, though there has been some new confusion over the years regarding the diagnostic criteria used to identify this illness. Its symptoms lie somewhere between schizophrenia and bipolar disorder in the extent of seriousness. *Walking Through Walls* will assist you in becoming more familiar with the major mental illnesses and medical criteria used to define them.

Five million American adults experience a major episode of one of these major brain disorders. More than three million children in America suffer from these disorders. (As you read, be aware whenever "brain disorder," or "mental illness," or similar terms are used, they consistently refer to "serious brain disorder," or "serious mental illness," and so on.)

Despite the extent of serious brain disorders, they are more treatable than many other physical illnesses. Treatment normally consists of some combination of hospitalization, medications, psychotherapy, and support services. Schizophrenia has a successful treatment rate of 60 percent; bipolar disorder (manic-depression) carries a successful treatment rate of 65 percent; and with major depression, 80 percent are successfully treated.

Contrary to popular belief, the seriously mentally ill are

frequently extremely talented and productive. There are famous artists and political leaders who highlight history with their valuable contributions. Dr. Ronald Fieve, a pioneer in introducing lithium to the United States (an often vital medication for those who suffer from manic-depression) and author of the classic book, *Moodswing*, names Abraham Lincoln, Winston Churchill, and Theodore Roosevelt as among those who suffered from manic-depression and succeeded in profoundly affecting mankind. Dr. Kay Redfield Jamison identifies numerous famous artists who suffered serious mental illnesses in her book, *Touched With Fire*. Author Sylvia Nasar made mathematical genius, Nobel Laureate, and schizophrenic John Nash the subject of a best-selling book, which later became the basis for the 2002 Academy Award-winning movie *A Beautiful Mind*. Likewise, various public persons have emerged in the media in the recent past few years as victims of serious mental illness.

Recognizing the abundant talent carried beneath the troubled exterior of many of his patients, Dr. Janos Marton helped establish what Academy Award-winning filmmaker Jessica Yu calls the patients' Living Museum at Creedmoor Psychiatric Center in Queens, New York. Though the "Museum" takes up only a secluded corner of the state hospital, the creations produced in this space can only be referred to as serious art.

Current research shows severe mental illness to be the result of higher sensitivity or biochemical imbalance in brain centers. It is generally thought to be mainly genetically inherited, though also environmentally encouraged. Much has been done in the last ten years to identify specific brain receptors that are responsible for specific brain disorders so that appropriate treatment can be pinpointed someday soon.

A common misconception is that seriously mentally ill patients dwell in some never-never land where pain is foreign and some sort of euphoria dominates. This is enormously false. Victims of serious mental illness most often experience both mental and physical pain that pervades their lives and destroys their reality.

Suicide is often the ultimate resort of the mentally ill individual. About half of all manic-depressives try to end their lives. About 15 percent of them are successful. With medications available to help modify the symptoms of diseases of the brain, many suicides are prevented. However, some medications create such intolerable side effects they must be discontinued. With the symptoms refusing to cease, suicide seems the only solution. I twice attempted suicide, and have become grateful that I twice failed.

The stigma associated with mental illness is encouraged by the names of some of the specific disorders. The specific labels of "schizophrenia," "schizoaffective disorder," and/or "manic-depression" are inclined to conjure up frightening visions of screaming maniacs, clasping large knives and chasing innocent passersby down long, dark alleys; until the victims are trapped and killed in gruesome manners. Such images are grossly inaccurate. When treated with effective medication, the violent mentally ill become nonviolent; and, in most cases, there is effective medication.

Still, the stigmas associated with serious mental illnesses remain. Fortunately, though "manic-depression" is the most popular label for those with severe mood swings, "bipolar disorder" has become more commonly used as a less antagonistic, more digestible term. However, "schizophrenia" and "schizoaffective disorder" technically bear no other labels. Unfortunately, other non-clinical labels (crazy, demented, mad, zany, crackpot, insane, loony, maniac, nuts, psychopath, batty, lunatic, weird, and on and on) create enormous negative stereotypes of those with serious mental illness. Such assumptions can create havoc in the lives of the mentally ill. Family, friends, and jobs (including political positions) and other opportunities in life are lost as a result of these stigmas.

Within the following chapters I attempt to provide a meaningful glimpse into my life, highlighted most specifically by my personal history of serious mental illness (beginning at age 18). This history, covering approximately two-thirds of my total years on earth, provides sincere insight into the mentally ill population and their daily struggle to survive.

If you have never suffered from any kind of mental disorder, you may wonder how the mentally ill author described in these pages could have managed to produce this written account of her dismal mental health history. It is a common misconception that if you frequent psychiatric hospitals, you are not capable of much organized thought at all. My personal effort to build words into phrases, into sentences, into paragraphs, and into chapters was not an easy task. It was a slow, tedious effort. A full nine months of grueling labor and six weeks of hospitalization were necessary to produce my first 100 pages. This was followed by a few more months of productive writing followed by two more months of hospitalization, followed by another 20 months of writing. More hospitalizations intervened between periods in which I was again able to manage the grand effort required to write, rewrite, rewrite…and complete this book. When the manuscript was finally completed, somewhere between 10 and 11 years had passed since its inception. The writing was tedious — the memories often scorching. Initially I struggled, sitting and writing for just an hour at a time, as I tried tirelessly to communicate a past full of suffering. An eventual adjustment in medication (which involved the new drug Clozaril) helped me complete this manuscript with a significant reduction in suffering. However, early on, a five- to ten-minute deep breathing/stretching break was important each half hour to one hour of work.

Let this account of my journey bear witness that those of you who have been diagnosed with severe mental illness can, when properly treated, most likely be capable of much more than unending chatter or silent despair. Let this book be proof to the mentally ill and mentally healthy alike that the label "mentally ill," which typically involves extensive brain pain, does not necessarily cancel quality of life. It can even — by involving serious mentally ill minds that think in a distinctive, often exceptional manner, plus by involving those same minds in bravely accepting productive thought and meaningful activity as realistic — remarkably enhance quality of life.

-Two Lenz

PART I:

BEGINNINGS AND PSYCHOSIS

Chapter 1

FIRM FOUNDATIONS
— SHAKY GROUND

W as I really walking through walls again? Within the darkness of my modestly furnished bedroom it was hard to tell. But, yes, it again seemed to be the case.

Only once (about ten years before), during one early, psychotic breakdown, was I certain I was walking through walls. That was in the late 1970s. I could not see beyond the wrapping of the night's darkness that cloaked my desperate form and made the walls, doors, and furniture invisible. However, I succeeded in blindly dodging all these obstructions. Most astonishing, it seemed indisputable that I was actually walking through the wall that separated my room from the bathroom.

I first sampled the various serious symptoms of psychosis during the mid-1970s when I was first hospitalized. I became closely acquainted with the intense exhaustion resulting from the manic inability to sleep. This was accompanied by uncontrollable and threatening voices and my witnessing incomprehensible, frightening apparitions (even like fiery demons). And, there was the assortment of physical pain. This often started with intense muscle spasms in my neck that eventually traveled down my back, leaving me flat in bed. It was then I was often so sure TV and radio personalities were talking just to me through the miracle of my own inner broadcasting station. I stopped eating for days after running out of food, becoming too frightened to leave my apartment for groceries (even just a block away). No wonder. People outside my window who rushed by seemed to communicate by perceiving each other's thoughts, most often critical of me. My brain typically suffered an intense inner pressure, while my body felt as if hundreds of electric wires were shooting off charges under my skin. This felt not unlike some torture technique. Ultimately, during most every breakdown, I sank into an intense depression (the counterpart of my mania). All this permeated my college career and landed me in psychiatric wards at least once a year. Through it all, I barely endured the mind and body pain characteristic of serious mental illness. My assortment of symptoms eventually supported a diagnosis of schizoaffective disorder, a clinical identification just short of that which sustained the stigma of schizophrenia.

Now it was five, no six, full days and nights that I had been nearly totally secluded in my room, only surfacing for meals. I vacillated between total mania and total, depressed exhaustion. I continuously frantically paced, no longer sure of time or space. Time had deceived me, melting days into nights into days again. Space had deceived me, convincing me I could overcome any physical obstacle. Both had seduced me, insisting I could triumph over some devious object that lingered just outside my reach. Sometimes the obstacle seemed frightening and alive (a devil, a hideous monster). Sometimes it revealed itself as a continual thought which persistently twisted itself through my tortured mind. My frantic search for relief left me weary and afraid. My constant movement caused me to be dangerously exhausted.

Despite my present extreme fatigue, I was eager to display my remarkable stunt: penetration through the solid bathroom wall. Having lost all sense of time, I called out to my roommate, unaware it was two a.m. "Jessie?"

Jessie had collapsed on her bed earlier that evening. She was exhausted from several days of worry over my tormented state while she took on all the household chores and functioned full-time as a schoolteacher. There was no answer from her room. I called out again, "Jessie. Are you asleep?"

"What?" The feeble voice from Jessie's room didn't sound like it had emerged from the lively Jessie I was accustomed to.

"Are you alright, Jessie?" No answer. I was concerned. Her limited response left me uneasy. For the first time in almost a week, I felt troubled about my attentive roommate. I had been oblivious to her week-long endurance test, taking care of my basic needs. To me, she was just around; conveniently providing meals and an audience to endless, meaningless chatter that I insisted was important enough to command her full attention.

I remembered when I first told Jessie I had a psychological disorder. She was satisfied with my acceptable appearance and normal, even articulate, communication (the result of fairly effective medication). She invited me into her small apartment to occupy a vacant bedroom and take on the responsibilities and privileges of a bonafide roommate. I occasionally displayed depression, retreating to my room for substantial lengths of time. It was then Jessie would persuade me to join her for dinner or a movie, assuming temporary depression was as bad as it could get. Indeed, her new support and my ongoing medication were enough for the first three years of our roommate relationship to mask the grim symptoms that lay just under the surface of my often confused perceptions in my suitably functional world. This world had allowed me to perform well enough while living with Jessie to cope with the scholastic stresses of graduate school and the stress of a part-time job. Thanks to some amazing brand of magic Jessie kindly delivered, it was the longest time I had been able to stay out of a mental hospital.

Now my suppressed symptoms finally revealed themselves by accelerating into a full-blown breakdown. Jessie's standing as a responsible schoolteacher was being threatened by a week-long absence from work. Her present state of exhaustion created by my refusal to allow her one full night's sleep left her requiring a good week of serious recuperation.

Most difficult of all for Jessie was her need to make the

decision to have a friend confined to a mental hospital, something she never anticipated doing. With her own health failing, Jessie knew if things continued as they were she would not be capable of helping me at all.

A wan ghost of a Jessie emerged from her room and unsteadily stood at my bedroom doorway. Barely 30, today she presented herself as nearly middle aged. "Two, we have to make a serious decision about your health." Her words were weighed down with an austere tone, foreign to our relationship. This time, my own tone was significantly more solemn. "I'm fine. Just need a little rest."

I noted that Jessie's cotton nightgown unsuccessfully concealed a shadow of the sturdy Jessie I was accustomed to.

I repeated, "I'm fine," while submitting to a less convinced tone. Jessie insisted, "But you said that nearly a week ago, and you are still pacing all throughout the day and night, every day and every night. This just can't go on."

My answer consisted of more of the same baffling babble Jessie had been audience to for the past week, sentence fragments dominating hopelessly obscure communication. However, my present prattle made one thing as clear as it had been from the beginning of my steady deterioration: I did not want to go to a mental hospital. "I'm fine," I kept insisting.

Jessie was unyielding. "I'm so sorry, Two. But, I have to call a doctor. I believe now that I can't help enough. You are just getting worse."

It was impossible for me to perceive that Jessie's heart was breaking. However, her disheveled, exhausted appearance seriously alarmed me. How could I deny her some relief? For Jessie's sake I made a grand effort and successfully halted my pacing, forcing myself into a small chair by the bed. My doctor's phone number was all too familiar to me, and I gave it to her. I surrendered information that would, again, unquestionably define me as a crazy person. Though the pending incarceration was not for criminal behavior it was still secured with a lock and key; and, for me, it had always felt like a prison.

Tears now saturated Jessie's eyelids and ran down her pale cheeks as she quickly described my behavior to my doctor. He instructed her to go to the outpatient clinic where I had been visiting him more regularly than Jessie had ever suspected.

We arrived at the clinic, a facility that had for ten years accommodated what was defined as my disability. Jessie and I were directly shown to Doctor Kline's office. The doctor viewed my haggard appearance, consistent pacing, and meaningless chatter. Confirmation from Jessie that I had not slept for at least five days promptly convinced him I was in danger of physical exhaustion (sufficient criteria for hospitalization). He quickly completed the necessary paperwork and handed it to Jessie. His instruction to her was brief and precise. "Take this to the VA hospital emergency room. I will call ahead so they will be expecting you. Two will probably be hospitalized for two to three weeks. Help her pack accordingly."

The drive back home was remarkably quiet. I was silenced by the ominous prospect of another stay in the hospital, while Jessie was hushed by the drama of the whole crisis. Once we arrived back to the apartment, Jessie quickly became busy making sure I was well supplied with what would make me comfortable for as long as was necessary. A week's change of clothes; an assortment of important items I was accustomed to for personal hygiene; and a small, cordless radio (cords could dangerously tempt suicide) highlighted these belongings.

Two brawny orderlies approached us with a wheelchair when we arrived at the emergency room. They were both eager to wheel me to the elevator and upstairs to the psychiatric ward. Jessie could not negotiate with them for more than a quick good-bye to her incapacitated roommate and friend. In an instant, she was turned from provider to visitor.

Jessie filled that role with remarkable devotion. I was unaccustomed to visits while hospitalized. However, Jessie soon assured me she would be there each evening. I would eagerly greet her at the door, knowing she would always be there at the beginning to the end of visiting hours to help reduce my pain. Not only did Jessie visit me each night, but each visit was accompanied with a gift. I was adorned with new white leather tennis shoes (great for pacing); soft, soft pajamas; anti-stress herbal shower gel;

and other gifts that provided for maximum comfort.

Hospitalization ended in three weeks as the doctor had predicted, about the time I usually needed in the hospital with medication to again proceed with my life out of the hospital after a full-blown breakdown.

Better informing Jessie of my medical past led to the necessary task of outpatient treatment that awaited me outside of the hospital. My silence about the details of my serious mental problems had to be broken. Now, able to again communicate effectively, I sat down on the living room sofa while Jessie sat across from me in the "big chair." I described to her, in detail, my history of serious mental illness; what any friend would be horrified to hear. I told it all from the physical restraints that prevented me from leaving my hospital bed, to the chemical restraints that left me a shuffling victim of my own biochemistry.

"I'm willing to take my chances." Her words astounded me. "Seems to me you have been through more than most, still coming out much more than even just acceptable. It is all very admirable." Jessie's words all provided a continuation of the comfort she had furnished while I had been hospitalized.

My roommate's acceptance, even esteem, amazed me. I speculated that perhaps it was because Jessie and I were Christians that she showed such compassion, even trust. However, I recalled my past, filled with Christians who chose not to invest their questionably spiritual temperament in my behalf. My present breakdown proved to be dramatically different. I was showered with confidence and admiration, gifts resulting from a unique friendship, characterized by extraordinary kindness and understanding.

My life began as a courtship with inevitable doom. A horrendously painful, breech birth (painful to both my mother and myself) involved forcefully turning me in the womb and using forceps to ensnare my soft, baby head as it was guided into the world. It did its share of damage. With an eventual diagnosis of schizoaffective disorder ahead of me (a small step below schizophrenia in seriousness), my traumatic birth provided a solid foundation for a troubled childhood and adolescence — all leading to an anguished adulthood. Research indicates half of all schizophrenics have problems during pregnancy and childbirth.

"Her middle name will be Two," declared my unconventional father, "and, she will always be remembered," he predicted. Perhaps, as I have visualized, my father made this decision with finger pointed upward and a voice like thunder. Whatever the zeal surrounding this declaration, my father's unorthodox choice of names was prompted by his decision to give me my mother's first name. Since I was then the second in the family, "Two" was his logical selection for my middle name. However, I was left with the distinct psychological/sociological handicap of having to remember the names of multitudes throughout my life who became easily acquainted with me; who themselves did not have names that were so unforgettable. This contributed to a kind of social phobia that somewhat highlighted young years of more significant symptoms of mental problems.

As my babyhood advanced, my mother and I struggled with more trauma. She tenderly nursed me with a bottle in a position that forced me to stretch out some tiny, underdeveloped muscles on the left side of my neck. In a few months the short side stretched out to equal the long side and I appeared balanced. The symmetry my mother's gentle efforts created saved me from a deformed appearance that would have tarnished what was already destined to become a lifetime abundantly full of a deformed psyche. However, despite my mother's persistent efforts to make my life as comfortable as possible, during adult years my neck was left vulnerable to severe muscle pain (side effects as I was saturated with antipsychotic drugs).

My mother and father formed a curious Jacqueline Kennedy and Aristotle Onassis kind of match. Mother (a professional model) was tall, slim, and beautiful; with chiseled, photogenic features. My father was a short, stocky, somewhat rotund man; Ivy League educated, and 20 years her senior. At age 47, he presented a hazardous assortment of genes for my genetic makeup: Research confirms that paternal fathers over 50 years old present a risk of schizophrenia to offspring. This risk is more than four times as high as that of offspring whose fathers are younger than 25. Though my father was not quite yet 50 and my eventual diagnosis of schizoaffective disorder was a step below schizophrenia, the shoe fit uncomfortably well.

My father was never hospitalized for mental illness. At the right times, he was truly likable. When his mood allowed, he was the life of the party. His sense of humor enhanced social gatherings my parents enjoyed with friends. Yet, his inclinations to addiction (primarily alcohol) and unpredictable, often outlandish mood swings were sufficiently characteristic of an erratic mental illness. He presented strong evidence his tarnished genes contributed to what eventually left me with a serious mental illness. A frequent and nasty temper prompted my father to be extremely violent toward my mother, such as one day pushing her fragile form out of a moving car when she chose to disagree with him; and, during one inebriated night, hitting her on the side of the head and breaking her eardrum. Soon Father's heavy drinking accompanied by physical abuse came to a final end for my mother, who worked to support the three of us: herself, Father, and me.

My parents divorced when I was three. It had not been a comfortable situation for any of us. Serious symptoms of mental illness that mirrored my father's instability first became a part of my personality during my late teens. I was never violent. However, my father's mood swings (ranging from mania to depression) eventually dominated my own life.

After the divorce and during my upbringing, Mother seldom said anything negative about my father despite his mistreatment. Those physical features she claimed I inherited from him were flattering: large eyes and a full smile (observations of a doting mother). Though my father continued to live in the same city, he chose to completely separate himself from Mother and me. I never knew where he lived or why he so completely left.

Tuberculosis struck down my mother when I was three. She was placed in a sanitarium in a neighboring state, while I was placed in a foster home. I suspected her memories of being isolated for a year with another TB patient were not fond ones. However, she did share a room with a woman who eventually became a lifelong friend. Today's treatment for TB does not require isolation and would have saved me from a lingering sense of desertion. I am left with only dark memories of my foster family. I remember two boys, twins, blond, both mischievous, who frequently teased me. Later in my life, Mother told me they were a kind family. However, I remembered only feelings of deep sadness while in their home. Without my mother, part of my personality was underdeveloped, leaving a vulnerable void where any unkindness became magnified. No matter how caring her foster parents were, a little girl who was missing her mother would only perceive strangers.

I cried at no detectable provocation for an entire year after Mother returned from her seemingly eternal hospitalization. My performance was easily orchestrated. Situating myself in the middle of a room, I commenced to sob uncontrollably. Mother tried kindness. "Darling, Two," she gently pleaded. "Please stop crying. It makes Mommy so unhappy." When those tactics didn't work, she applied a harsher tone. "Two. Now stop that crying. There is just no reason for it." Again, these irritable mood states were an indication that a serious mental illness was advancing. Eventually, they became more controllable thanks to a chubby and obnoxious neighborhood bully whom everyone called Punky. Curious enough, Punky was also an instigator of most of my compulsive crying spells. Three years older than I, he found great satisfaction making grotesque faces at me through the living room window, magnifying my crying problem. One decisive day as I walked down my front sidewalk, Punky bicycled by. As he passed, he turned and made a familiar distorted face. I did not know what prevented my tears. Perhaps it was because I was getting older. Or, maybe it is just because it was a decisive day. Nevertheless, I braced myself, held my breath, and successfully prevented myself from crying. My abuser looked back in surprise as he peddled around the corner. Soon after, considerably discouraged, he discontinued his harassment.

Preventing myself from crying was a major issue from that point on. I just did not cry. This created an internal sense of dignity I had yet not been able to achieve. However, holding in the normal tendency to cry (even on appropriate occasions) caused me to isolate myself emotionally. I eventually welcomed the opportunities when I could also isolate myself physically. This led to suffering internally from an assortment of social phobias, inviting the emergence of an even more serious mental disorder.

Mother remarried and had a son, Kenny, as I struggled through a damaged early childhood. My stepfather was a peculiar man. Not extremely handsome, he had an acceptable face, an abundance of wavy hair, and managed to keep himself trim. Though blessed with a wealth of intelligence, his high IQ did not enable him to avoid some of the damage from a childhood full of parental abuse and abandonment. As small children, he and his younger brother were often confined to boarding schools. Otherwise, his nomadic parents dragged the boys around in carnivals full of what can only be imagined as seedy, often vulgar sorts. His father was a magician, and the carnival (or sometimes the circus) most frequently consisted of home for his family. Though the thought of traveling with a circus would be a dream come true for many children, my stepfather seldom talked about his past. No doubt, his background concealed bitter secrets.

Despite a troublesome background, it was at dinner desserts that my stepfather revealed the charm that must have captivated my mother. His music and magic often followed dinner at my household. My stepfather's rich baritone graced the cleared dinner table with a vocal medley of old songs from the '30s, '40s, and '50s, most often show tunes. "Everything's up to date in Kansas City. They've gone about as fer as they could go." *Oklahoma* was a favorite of his. Or, "I'm gettin married in the mornin. Ding dong the bells are gonna chime," from another classic, *My Fair Lady*, he swore would never die.

My stepfather picked up a few magic tricks (especially card tricks) as he traveled from city to city with his magician father. My brother and I were not only audience to an assortment of magic tricks, but were occasionally (though not frequently) given the secret behind the illusion.

Tuberculosis attacked my mother again when I was six. One memorable day Mother furiously coughed up blood into the toilet while I stood by, aware in my own childhood way that there was ample reason to worry. It wasn't long and my mother found herself back in the hospital in a solitary room, hundreds of miles away. Another year passed before I saw her healed again.

Barely existing for another year without my mother created overwhelming trauma. I became vividly aware of my father favoring my younger half-brother, Kenny (his only biological son). Kenny naturally enjoyed the attention. This made me feel like a bonafide outsider. During that distressing year I became a bed-wetter. To cure me, my stepfather revealed an especially cruel side. He wielded the "shame technique" like a vicious sword, designed to wound me again and again with its brutal blade.

One hazy, particularly shameful day will always remain crystal clear in my memory. I again soiled my bed, like the night before that and before that and before that. My father solemnly told me to get a brown paper grocery bag and fill it with what he identified as necessary items: a pair of pajamas, underwear, a warm sweatshirt, and not much more. He then packed me and the brown paper bag in the car and drove me to the train station. He rested the car a short distance from the parked train cars. He then told me that from that time on I would work for a "mean old lady," helping her keep the train clean and tidy inside. It was then that I was commanded to leave the car and proceed to my new home on the train tracks. I desperately clutched my small bag of swiftly gathered essentials and was persuaded to plead, finding it impossible to communicate without tears.

"I promise I will never wet the bed again, Daddy, I promise."

However, he was unswerving. "Get out of the car...now."

Resigned to silence, I exited the car and slowly walked toward the train. After I had covered about 100 yards of train station territory, I turned to give one last, hopeless look at my abuser. I was astonished and thrilled to see him motion me back to the car. I ran wildly, terrified he would change his mind. I stopped at his rolled-down window as he asked the ultimate question.

"Do you think you can stop wetting the bed?"

I urgently promised. "Oh, yes," I pledged and I meant it with all the desperation my small, damaged heart could hold.

"Get in." He gestured to the front passenger seat.

I climbed up a mountain of upholstery and we silently drove home.

That night I slept as long as I could while balancing myself on the toilet. After dozing off to the floor several times, I resigned myself to the necessary challenge of sleeping the rest of the night in a dry bed. My efforts were futile. The next day I cowered as I ate breakfast, aware that our callous housekeeper would give my stepfather the distressing news.

"She did it again and I got a bed full of wet sheets to wash," the housekeeper snapped.

My stepfather looked at me across the breakfast table and, without a word, finished the paper and left for work. In fact, though I failed to conquer my disgraceful habit and continued to wet the bed every night for many nights to come — my stepfather never mentioned it again.

Though my bed-wetting curiously became a quiet issue, my stepfather continued to make it painfully apparent with his silence that he remained disgusted by this offensive habit. It was also obvious that he maintained in every way his preference for brother Kenny. My living on the outside of a family of two made for days full of alienation and sadness. I learned, firsthand, how other's hatred feels; a hard lesson that preceded but did not fully prepare me for the treatment and shame I experienced as an adult victim of serious mental illness.

A radiant light returned to my young awareness on the day Mother came home, healed after another year of confinement. I still recall my joy over her return. No longer would Kenny be exclusively favored. I would again exist as part of a family of four. Not angry but concerned about my bed-wetting, Mother took me to the family doctor, who instructed her to awaken me late every night to relieve myself. After a year and a half of this gentle routine, the bed-wetting stopped. What a grand day it was for my ego. Gone were mornings saturated with shame.

Immediately after returning permanently from the hospital, Mother became the dominant decision maker in the family, and she often felt like my protector. Occasionally I shudder over what a disaster my childhood would have been had my stepfather been the dominant one. I would have suffered unbearably. While favoring my brother with conspicuous and abundant acts of kindness he would have tormented me with new, brutal verbal attacks other than used up, silent tactics.

My stepfather continued to cautiously manage vocal, emotional abuse into our relationship when my mother was absent. This mental/emotional cruelty surfaced in the form of a strange variety of vicious acts. It was then he cleverly twisted my already distorted awareness with cunning conversations that left me frustrated and confused. Years later, a social worker would define it to be as "crazy-making," an activity where the abuser forces the victim into distressing and confusing conversations by administering self-centered rambling and ruthless interrogations. Most always the abuser is highly intelligent and able to cleverly, mentally manipulate the listener in an oppressive manner. This process between me and my stepfather always followed a similar pattern:

He began, "What are you going to do?" This simple question pierced my psyche as I walked past him, typically and firmly attached to his living room recliner. I was headed for the sanctuary of my bedroom.

"Going to my room," was my standard but fearful reply.

"What are you going to do there?"

Painfully honest, I could never give him a reason important enough to persuade myself away from painful dialogue. "I have to make my bed."

"You can do that later." For him there were no excuses.

"I have homework."

"This will take just a few minutes."

Indeed, it never took a few minutes, applying his distorted perception of time. What he liked to call "our little chats" felt much more like lengthy cross-examinations.

Leaning back, he sometimes voiced a philosophical (frequently theological) thought that had recently entered his mind. "You know, I believe it was the Romans, not the Jews, that killed Christ."

My awkward silence did not discourage him from successfully

forcing some opinion from me. "That sounds likely." I would answer anything to allow me to retreat to my room.

"You know. I live in a way where I never expect anything from anyone." His dark comment was typical.

His cynicism was troubling to my young mind, and I fumbled for an appropriate answer. "I suppose you are never disappointed." Agreeing with him was still the best way out.

Such discourse provided beginnings of seemingly endless conversations that came nearly exclusively from his side of the fence. My stepfather seemed to assume that I owed him my company. When any kind of convenient lull occurred, I would jump in and mention some immediate task I had to perform.

"Go ahead to your bed," he would command with a brutally blaming tone. Finally, I did successfully tear myself away, however always after my stepfather extracted major guilt from my fragile conscience. I slithered to my bedroom, feeling shame but relief to be on the other side of a solid wall.

These terrible talks started in severity from about the time I turned age ten, increased in frequency and duration as I entered my teens, and only ceased when I moved away from home at age 19. Such cruel communication took place at least three times a week.

My stepfather only spanked me once. Indeed, hunting or even hurting animals were appalling to him. A palate of cruelty and kindness, blended with playful behavior, colored this baffling man while Mother was left to administer spankings on suitable occasions.

My stepfather's contemptible "crazy-making" soon prompted me to feel consistently threatened when in the company of others. Even during simple conversations with childhood friends, I suspected something menacing lurking behind every hollow smile; possibly anger, possibly rejection, mainly residual fears left over from my stepfather's verbal abuse. To protect my fragile psyche, I became always the silent listener. My polite personality made me popular with other children. My closest friend in elementary school still remains an earnest example of my peacekeeping disposition: We never engaged in even one argument, not during all seven years of early school together.

Others sought out my friendship, knowing I was frequently available to offer quiet attention. Moreover, I was there to forgive the flaws of my friends, flaws they often refused to forgive in each other. As childhood feuds frequently occurred in the neighborhood, others must have found my kind company provided relief from their conflicts.

The more my company was desired, the more an abundance of passion for solitude and silence churned inside of me. I suffered periods of extreme self-doubt and poor self-esteem. Occasionally I discovered an opportunity to be alone. I would usually seclude myself in my bedroom. There was no stereo or TV. However, I always had a book into which I thoroughly submersed myself. Nevertheless, my isolation was frequently interrupted by a visit from a neighborhood intruder. Despite my popularity, my feeble ego failed to give me credit for my shining reputation. People's genuine feelings about me remained a painful mystery and fearful threat.

It is frequently assumed that a child's life, typically lacking the major responsibility of earning a living, is full of fun and frolic. Parents and friends would find it surprising to know the inner pain some children endure, the underdogs in a world of often angry adult power. This posture is often supported by an inherited genetic pool that early on begins to drown the young victim in a torturous muck of serious mental illness. Suicidal thoughts are likely more numerous than ever expected. With a childhood and adolescence void of sustained happiness, I occasionally asked myself, "Must life go on like this? If only it did not go on at all."

School provided a convenient diversion from my early despondency. Academic challenges appealed to me and I welcomed the quiet of a good book. It was my stepfather who unpredictably lured me into the world of reading. Quality literature, presented early in life, rescued me from total childhood despair.

Books were my stepfather's boyhood friends. He and his younger brother regularly spent entire days reading in bountiful New York libraries. Books became sacred objects to my stepfather, and this passion for reading revealed to me an endearing paradoxical aspect of his personality. *The Jungle Books,* the first selections he allowed me to borrow from his home library (which exploded with handsomely bound classics), created for me a foundation for many hours of digesting good literature. My stepfather treated his library like a collection of prized gems. There was somewhat of a ritual we exercised each time I finished a treasured volume and longed for another.

I typically emerged from the seclusion of my room where I had perched on my bed, reading into the night. "I'm finished with this one," I would say as I gently handed him a volume.

"You can go ahead and put it back in its spot," was my stepfather's cautious reply.

Once the book was back in place, I asked my stepfather for another suggestion. He paused, scrutinized the shelves, and selected what he thought would be the best choice. Sometimes he first scrutinized me, asking relevant questions. "Do you want an adventure (followed by the introduction of *Moby Dick* or *Treasure Island*)? Or, how about a mystery (and a Sherlock Holmes classic was taken down from the shelf)?"

As he left me with the final selection, I noted how he gave it a longing glance while I appreciated the emotional investment behind every book he left to my safe-keeping. I will always be grateful to an enigma of a stepfather for allowing me into his world of literature. I cannot think of anything I missed more as a mentally disabled adult than being able to read easily through almost any book. Reading was a world that became painfully foreign in my late teens. Severe mental illness created a defective memory and poor concentration, resulting in the inability to easily absorb a good book. Reading was drudgery as I later struggled through college, requiring careful note-taking for me to adequately benefit from the content of my texts.

Contrasting my stepfather's scholarly approach, Mother enlightened me in a different manner by providing me with an abundance of lessons. Mother was preoccupied with self-improvement and took on the responsibility of showering me with an assortment of classes. I can hardly remember not hearing my mother's persistent voice reminding me to "practice" something (an activity I found a multitude of ways to avoid). She paid for accordion lessons, followed by piano lessons, then guitar lessons. I also took ballet, tap, and acrobatics (a precursor of gymnastics). Mother even had me try ventriloquism and baton twirling. Though I was forever being reminded to practice something, I was never very good at anything. As my childhood retreated, so did my mother's hope I would be a prodigy.

During my later years in elementary school, Mother opened a finishing school and model agency. Modeling lessons soon became included on my mother's agenda for self-improvement. This gave me the opportunity to make some extra money as a child model and, later, as a teenage model. Unfortunately, with my ample insecurities, I felt like an exhibitionist while parading across a modeling stage. As I hurried backstage to make quick changes and last-minute makeup touch-ups I dreaded hearing my name announced by the commentator. Breezing through the curtain onto the main stage, I forced an enthusiastic walk and wide smile. I was an adequate model, but never a contented one. I was a little more comfortable in front of a camera, away from an audience. However, photo modeling still left me uneasy. Modeling bathing suits (though not nearly as revealing as they are today) was especially distressful to my modest disposition.

Mother recognized my opposition to both stage, runway, and photo modeling and did not push me into these activities. There was usually an abundance of eager young girls waiting to get a call to fill in a last-minute spot. Only occasionally (when deadlines left her desperately short of a model) did Mother prod me into filling a vacancy. I modeled my last show when I was 21 years old. Some competitive and catty co-models who jealously resented my easy access to the stage and camera (due to my easy access to my mother) became painfully overbearing.

Pets acted as major anti-depressants during my childhood. Highlighting my family's assortment of animals that came and went was an elegant, pure-bred Weimaraner named Countess. She was the shy one of the litter and was meant to be a gift for my stepfather, who had always fancied Weimaraners. However, I was the one who took Countess through doggy school, where she excelled. Eventually she won a blue ribbon when I was the one who presented her in a dog show. However, most rewarding was the affection we shared every day. We often playfully skirmished on the living room floor. Countess's satin ears flew wildly at my every lunge. After a bout with Countess I found myself exhilarated, with depression more of a remote emotion. So it was I, not my stepfather, who gave Countess abundant attention. And, so it was I whom Countess favored, taking up a good half of my queen-sized bed at night.

Already the sources and symptoms of childhood mental illness were unfolding. A difficult childbirth combined with a much older and very possibly bipolar father started the wicked wheels turning. Then a one-year separation from the family at age three to a foster home was followed by intensely irritable mood states with no seeming provocation. As my childhood progressed I became more of a recluse, even entertaining occasional thoughts of suicide.

These causes and manifestations of deep psychological distress can be added to other textbook clues in my childhood that were precursors to an adult life with serious mental illness. Included were difficulty getting up in the morning, trouble concentrating in school, difficulty making transitions, resentment of authority, and even poor handwriting. All along I knew I was different, and all along a psychiatrist would have said something was wrong.

Learning the complexities of conception and the miracle of birth was not troublesome for me (or my parents) thanks to my cousin, Lisa. Mother left this education up to my ability to digest the chapter on reproduction in a young person's set of biology books and a modestly enlightening book by Ann Landers, explaining sex to teenagers. However, my mother's efforts were preceded by Lisa's, who significantly accelerated my sex education, making sure I was well informed even before I left grammar school.

Whenever Mother navigated the 350-mile trip to visit my aunt's family, I reveled in Lisa's company. We both enjoyed our visits during childhood and into adolescence. Lisa was only three months my senior. It was her older brothers who always provided her with a generous assortment of dirty jokes to enlighten my libido. By sixth grade, I pretty well knew how sex worked. Whenever I was with Lisa, I not only enjoyed her mischievous sense of humor, but, she was always taking me on some fascinating adventure. Whether it was raiding a summer camp cabin, or stealing a dime from Auntie's purse to buy candy, or getting lost in Tijuana — we were no strangers to trouble. Usually adventures with Lisa meant eventual punishment from an adult. However, her brassy boldness produced substantial relief from my childhood gloom. I loved my cousin. Whenever we were united there was fun and excitement.

One summer came when my new teenage temperament preferred staying at home rather than traveling to spend insubordinate hours with my cousin. That was the summer I began to taste adulthood. Adolescence had intervened, initiating a new maturity. My late teens would introduce more classic symptoms of a mental illness that tarnished my twenties, giving me reason to desperately struggle through my thirties and forties to ultimately deliver a chronically restricted state of mind. But the defiant childhood summers with my cousin will always be remembered as carefree months when I was capable of conquering the world.

Chapter 2
TEENAGE PLEASURES AND PAIN

C hildhood and mischievousness with cousin Lisa slipped behind me while I advanced to my teens and entered junior high. Classes were more difficult and the new curriculum left me disoriented. Now, instead of one teacher teaching all the required subjects in grammar school, I had to cope with six different classes and six teachers every day. Never good at transitions, I required a year to adapt and start getting good grades once again.

When I entered this first confusing higher level of education, I was challenged with somewhat more sophisticated verbal exchanges with my teenage peers. The added complexity of communication multiplied my fear of social interaction and introduced considerable self-doubt. Still, I remained polite, practicing a tortured, youthful patience — wanting to run away but never wanting to offend. I tormented myself as I endured the obligation of attentive conversation with others. I lived as a prisoner of my own goodwill, always preferring solitude to threatening and persistent talk. I even found it nearly impossible to look a person in the eyes when conversing (and still do). This curious characteristic was one of my more specific, early, textbook symptoms of severe mental illness.

Again, I made no effort to seek out friends and, again, they seemed to seek me out. My musical abilities (thanks to Mother's lessons) made me the center of attention at parties. I was fairly good at playing the guitar, and led party sing-alongs in the '60s, back when folk songs were popular. Slumber parties provided eager audiences, although my teenage impatience to grow up often dampened the good times. I longed with great anticipation for the time I would drive a car and do my own clothes shopping. How little I knew. How impossible it was for me to predict the struggle adulthood would bring.

Good fortune came my way in eighth grade when Sandy sought me out, since I probably would never have targeted her as a potential friend. Sandy was exceptionally tall and seriously self-conscious about her height. This created a persistent posture problem: She consistently stooped. However, her poor posture and glasses did not discourage potential boyfriends as much as her contentious personality. Indeed, our negative relationship began with her harassment of me on campus and at parties. This did not provide a good foundation for a friendship considering that I could not easily accept criticism or rejection. But, when Sandy discovered I still could not resist laughing at her jokes, she decided to find me charming.

Sandy had a brilliant sense of humor that succeeded in removing much of my depression. For me, she was a savior who brought laughter into my life. United, we created two discipline problems who, together, constantly disrupted our classes. We both managed to create a silly, giddy mood state that made it nearly impossible to establish and maintain a learning environment. Still, our grades were excellent, so teachers did not know what to do with us except persist with "unsatisfactory" for our "cooperation" grades each semester. Our parents were blind to these indications of poor behavior. As long as our grades remained outstanding (always A's with a few B's) then references to a few discipline problems did not much matter to them.

My church provided another vehicle that successfully prevented weeks of potential despondency. Mother was responsible for keeping me active in a religious environment. Attending church each Sunday provided an emotional lift that sustained me through the following six days until I could again ask God to once more carry me through the next week. My stepfather was less spiritually dedicated and attended church much less frequently.

At eight years old I was officially baptized. My bishop asked me to present my first brief talk in church. My stepfather patiently coached me to memorize a two-minute speech that began, "A euphemism is the substitution of a mild word or expression." I do not remember anything else about this talk. However, I am convinced my stepfather reveled in succeeding in using me to show off an abundant vocabulary in one so little.

My church leaders were suitably impressed and continued to occasionally request that I speak to the congregation. I was also moderately involved in the ample selection of other youth activities. There were summer camps, holiday parties, dances, and concerts.

Therefore, God was no stranger in my young life. However, I consistently harbored doubts over the validity of my mother's choice of religion. As a result, my occasional messages from the pulpit escaped the evangelistic fury of other's lay sermons, but presented more of a generic perspective. An example is a short talk I gave in my early teens about how you can find God in nature. An excerpt is as follows:

Nature is basic. There is nothing synthetic about it. It is directly God's work, and this may be why, if we look hard enough, we can find many of God's truths in nature.

God tells us if we follow his laws we will be able to accomplish what seems the impossible. Salmon and migrating birds recognize this and, no matter how difficult it is to swim upstream to their spawning grounds or how long a flight it is to the South, both the fish and the birds are following basic laws of nature — and both achieve what, at first, seems the impossible.

E. H. Chaplin once said, "Hills, valleys, seas, and constellations are but stereotypes of divine ideas appealing to, and answered by the living soul of man."

All nature is a vast symbolism. Every material fact has within it a spiritual truth. Nature and wisdom always say the same.

I pray that we may learn God's truths by appreciating the beauty he created, and, I say these things in the name of Jesus Christ, Amen.

A rare religious discussion took place one day between Sandy and me by way of hidden class notes. Notes were not unusual, but religion was not integral to our relationship. Sandy seldom revealed a serious side. My Christianity and her atheism created a conflict that inspired Sandy to write a rebuttal to some zealous remarks I made one day about God:

"Two, You don't understand. First of all, you 'know' there's a God, don't you? Well, just as strongly as you know there is one, I know there isn't. I mean, it's something you feel, not something you can research into and find the answer. If I half-heartedly believed in God (who?) then I could understand why you would want me to look into it to 'find the answer.' (Barf.) But I have my answers. Why don't you explore atheism?

Sandy"

This type of somber interaction was rare between the two of us since Sandy's wit dominated our relationship. It kept me lifted to the emotional altitude that enabled our friendship to endure. Laughter highlighted nearly every conversation. With teenage Sandy's assistance, I avoided seriousness that only brought me down to my own inner young and troubled reality.

Aside from such occasional flights into seriousness, I laughed with Sandy all through junior high years and into high school. When the daily sobriety of learning ended, I looked forward to the happiness provided by Sandy's company as she would cover the enormous grayness of my world with her colorful cleverness. Hilarious remarks tumbled from her like bright acrobats, dominating center ring. My daily depressions made hopelessly lifeless a large space of each day; but Sandy's humor left me wonderfully alive every hour I was with her.

However, I remained totally unaware throughout our

relationship of where Sandy's amazing brand of energy and her occasional struggle with depression came from. At least her chronic depressions were likely genetically transmitted from her seemingly depressed father. An eventually diagnosed adult, bipolar Sandy would, at age fifty, conclude all the mania and depressions—and take her life.

Campus fame highlighted my high school years right from the beginning. My energy level was just beginning to climb. As a sophomore, I campaigned and won a position in the student senate.

I encouraged Sandy to do the same, and she also won her campaign, enabling us to share the school senate chambers together. I remained active in student government all during my high school years. I also became photo editor of both the campus newspaper and yearbook, Junior Class Treasurer, Treasurer of the Girls' Athletic Association, and a member of the Honor Society. I was selected as a community "Youth Forum" (an event sponsored by the local newspaper) finalist to provide the summary of my discussion group's conclusions (a speech that was printed in the city newspaper). These experiences and the popularity they provided boosted my fragile morale. My young but withered ego was furnished considerable security by my noticeable place on campus.

So did this micro but, for me, magical high school habitat seem so important even monumental? That golden, high school frontier that I happily discovered provided both protection and isolation from the outside world. Family, friends, and acquaintances projected my fame on campus as potential fame in the world, beyond student senate meetings and speeches in student assemblies. The blind assumption was that because I had achieved so much during those three years, everything would always fall into place for me.

My senior year found me especially absorbed in extracurricular activities. Both Sandy and I again ran for student government offices, and Sandy became Student Body Secretary while I was elected Student Body Treasurer. My fellow students would frequently find me rushing from one project to another. I was compulsively busy and my "other than classroom pursuits" took me away from more responsible efforts to make good grades.

However, my intense involvement in extracurricular activities was not as much by choice as by necessity. I felt an intense need to move. More mania was on its way and only beginning to require intense physical activity. Though my final grade-point average was not as high as Sandy's, who graduated in the top five in our class (earning a comfortable scholarship), I managed to make "Most Outstanding Senior Girl," and graduated 19th in a class of about 350 students. No one questioned that I would be successful for the rest of my life.

Mental illness continued to more and more subtly creep into my life during high school. It was ominous when at the near end of my junior year I hyperventilated in a physical education class. I had become temporarily depressed by the academic and social pressures of high school and was willing to take drastic action to escape. So I faked a health problem.

Not sure what to do with me, my teacher sent me home. My parents were both at work, and I was grateful for my quiet bedroom where I could huddle in bed, away from humanity, for the rest of the day. Though I had never done this sort of thing before, I did not recognize this as a significant loss of control. It was incomprehensible to me how this degeneration would ultimately dominate my life, eventually rendering me insane.

Bitterness crept into my personality about the same time the hyperventilation episode occurred. This was not an emotion familiar to me. Until that time, during my teenage years, I was capable of elation (many thanks to Sandy), sadness, empathy, compassion, even some anger. However, bitterness was not a emotion my heart was accustomed to. It was clearly revealed in the following poem:

Simply a Poem

Yesterday I fell out of love,
The clock said two p.m.
And I said, "It will be some time
Till I fall in again."

Today I passed a lonely child.
"World, you'll have to wait.
I've got my love all scheduled now
For a later date."

Catastrophes were a new and favorite subject during what was fast becoming a dangerously dismal adolescence. My poem, "The Conqueror," exposed a teenage consciousness that brought to light the increasing personal inferno that I was finding more and more difficult to conceal. It read as follows:

The Conqueror

One
    Two
        Three
            Four
                Five
                    Six

Seven million shallow cracks.
Seven million broken backs.
The sidewalk's here. The sidewalk's gone,
Measured sections, stretching on.

All around the city looms;
Shopper hurries, auto zooms.
Colossal building, reaching high;
Up and up, to scrape the sky.

Walk—don't walk, red light—green;
Must protect man from machine.
Policeman stops to warn another,
Must protect man from his brother.

Honking horns, flashing lights,
Noisy days, louder nights.

Dented beer cans, broken glass;
Then—without warning—
A blade of grass.

It rises from a tiny crack
To execute its planned attack.
Form is frail, but will is strong.
A rustle is its battle song.

Monoxide fills polluted air.
Sunshine's gone, replaced by glare.
Winter, slicing cold, arrives.
But it thrives. But it thrives.

Nature plants more grass around
The hardened bit of manmade ground.
Then, larger plants rise to meet
Sewer pipe and blackened street.

Slowly, slowly, cracks give way.
Foundations weaken, bridges sway.
Buildings creak, highway rumbles.
Then—suddenly—the city crumbles.

Cloaked with silence, deathly still.
A laughter rises, tones that chill.
Victorious nature mocks the place
That dared throw concrete in her face.

Mononucleosis assaulted me during the second half of my senior year. Many people can pinpoint an event that marks their growing up. For some it is a specific birthday and others a religious ritual. Of course, many remember themselves reaching adulthood at their high school graduation. I grew up the day I contracted mononucleosis. My family doctor, not a psychiatrist, failed to recognize this viral infection as a typical predecessor to many serious mental disorders.

Though I had continued a pilgrimage of peace throughout junior high and into high school, my timid soul (full of unexpressed fury), finally exploded, and more visible symptoms of mental illness manifested themselves. It was especially during my last semester before graduation when significantly more pathological characteristics became detectable to those who knew me well. My deteriorating psychological condition created casualties along the way. I began to lose the high regard of those around me. I was changing and it was my good friend, Sandy, who first seemed to notice. An unusual letter from her revealed a gentleness she rarely displayed:

Two, I certainly hope you feel better tomorrow. I don't know what's come over you. It's like you are a different person! You are no longer that person I knew way back when. Your outlook has changed, your standards have changed, and (yes) you have become unbearable to be around! Where is that friendly smile, that twinkling eye, that vivacious glow you used to possess? I hope this change is only temporary, because it certainly would be a shame to break off such a unique friendship as ours.

I hope nothing has happened to you that I am unaware of. I hope you have no great mental strains causing this sudden change in you. If you do, I am willing to listen. Yes! Pour your troubles out to me. After all, what are friends for if not to help each other in times of sorrow.

I'll bear with your little whims (as I always have) and stay a friend to you as long as you want me.

Don't worry about me. If I can survive my many emotional problems, I can get along in this troublesome world! Oh, no, I agree. Your problems are much larger than mine. As they say in Germany, "Do (familiar form, of course) bist meine freunden!" which means, "You are my friend."

I'll now bring this letter to an end, and hope the best comes of it. Good-bye.

Your friend always
Sandy

31

It was near the end of my senior year, and while I visited Sandy at her home within the quiet of her bedroom, I mercilessly told her I wanted to end our friendship. I gave no reason for this threat because there was no reason except that it was a textbook symptom of an unstable mind. She was visibly hurt.

"Why, Two?" she tearfully asked. "What have I done?"

I stood like steel over her uncommonly timid form. My answer was so inappropriate I do not even recall what I said. However, I do remember my decision to end our friendship persisted, providing me with a sense of power, having made such a dramatic and damaging decision. The next day I was full of apologies, not knowing what had gotten into me. However, I found myself daily giving Sandy more ultimatums that our friendship was over, sheepishly apologizing the next day, then repeating the process at a whim. This yo-yo behavior probably left Sandy both confused and ultimately angry; leaving her heart raw and guarded and, eventually, unable to endure the inconsistencies of my behavior—cruel indications of an unstable mind.

My symptoms escalated: The periods of self-doubt and poor self-esteem intensified. As my last school months progressed, I felt more and more rejected. While my social and academic successes on campus continued to somewhat support my ego, the advancement of my mental illness was relentless. Though my hyperactivity provided an inner energy that quickly propelled me all over campus, during the last semester of my senior year I was stopped in my tracks with mononucleosis. The negative symptoms of some serious mental illness were becoming larger and larger, greater and greater. My personality was no doubt evolving into something less and less appealing.

I lost Sandy's friendship by the time I was 20, a friend any sane person would find it impossible not to treasure.

Losing Sandy punctuated for me a friendless existence that underscored every tormented day for what seemed a millennium. However, it would soon be that major symptoms of a serious mental illness left me lame to almost any quality of life.

Chapter 3
SUBSTANTIAL SYMPTOMS EMERGE

During the summer following graduation, I began working as a lifeguard and swim instructor (the most lucrative job I had ever held). I remained living at home to save money for college in the fall. I initially approached this opportunity to accumulate money with optimism. My relatively positive frame of mind during these early days of employment under the sun motivated an attempt at humor:

A Lifeguard's Ten Commandments

1. Thou shalt have but one pool before thee.
2. Thou shalt not be a graven image (but a happy, smiling lifeguard).
3. Thou shalt not take the name of the Lord thy God in vain or use any other naughty, obscene language; for the angry parent will not hold him guiltless.
4. Remember thy day off, to keep it holy.
5. Honor thy manager that thy days may be short upon thy deck.
6. Thou shalt not yell with an angry, uncontrolled voice at thy public.
7. Thou shalt not commit tardiness to thy respective guarding position.

8. Thou shalt not steal thy fellow lifeguard's suntan lotion.
9. Thou shalt not bear false witness against thy dear public.
10. Thou shalt not covet thy neighbor's tan.

Despite my initial efforts at comedy, I separated myself from my coworkers. I spent my breaks away from the staff, avoiding any conversation, friendly or otherwise. However, I made sure I did take my turns watching over a wild assortment of mainly unruly children. Lunch was always eaten by myself, some fast food consumed in the privacy of my car. My self-imposed estrangement presented a combination of comfort and alienation. Before my first month of summer work had passed, I started suffering from recurring headaches that hammered my temples. A medical encyclopedia cautioned that the headaches could indicate the presence of a brain tumor. In a mild panic, I had X-rays taken, which revealed my brain had no tumors. Though these results brought me some comfort, the headaches persisted without another diagnosis.

I continued placing myself on the outside of the social circle created by the swimming pool staff. It seemed apparent to me that I was disliked. I amplified my perceptions of the staff's resentment by identifying any negative glance or tone as a malicious gesture focused just my way.

Even more serious, I began to suspect that I was not totally concentrating on the job. I found it difficult to focus on one thing for very long. I dreaded children drowning all around me while I stood in a daze over my assigned area of pool, preoccupied with my thoughts. A near double-drowning finally occurred in my area, and I actually did not notice. A young boy carrying his sister on his back wandered over into the deep water and could not stay afloat. Another lifeguard performed the impressive double rescue that was my responsibility. My display of incompetence left me even more an outcast, and I agonized over my ineptitude until the summer's end.

Happy when that summer was over, I began the challenge of higher education by enrolling in a local college. My plan seemed sensible: I would attend an affordable, local campus for the first two years where I could complete the basic courses required of most students. Then, I could transfer with a well-deserved scholarship to a prestigious, out-of-state university where I could earn my degree.

My headaches, however, continued and my childhood fear of people resulted in an even greater beating. I could not concentrate on anything relevant to earning good grades. Lectures all seemed obscure. Professors loomed in front of the lecture classrooms like vultures, ready to snatch my future away with failing grades. My hands trembled as I attempted to take legible notes. Reading and comprehending texts quickly became more and more impossible tasks. As my headaches persisted, each instructor's words seemed to lose their meaning after a sentence or two.

Much of my terror involved a deep dread that other students despised me. Every laugh or whisper seemed directed at me. Every person's expression seemed to accuse. With every minor frown from my parents, I absolutely knew they hated me. It seemed indisputably true that they wanted me out of the house and, so, out of their budget. Soon, I became more and more convinced everyone I associated with detested me. My entire world of acquaintances seemed to shun me at the slightest provocation.

Then mania began. I felt a ball of desperate energy throughout my body. While passing other students walking from class to class, I had a great need to run in order to release this inner energy. Yet, I refused to succumb and look like a fool. How peculiar it seemed to want to run so badly when running had nearly always seemed like such a strenuous thing to do. Containing this energy created a force inside of my abused psyche that produced a need to explode.

I continued my childhood pattern of attending church. Growing up, I had depended on my faith to provide weekly relief from depression. I craved even more relief from this new, greater agony, but now I only saw the church as a threat. My former church leaders now appeared as monsters behind the pulpit. During services, I was sure I was the center of their angry attention. As my paranoia progressed, my faith seemed to cause me more and more suffering. Instead of bringing spiritual comfort, my new religious environment appeared vicious and hostile.

Without the comfort God had always blessed me with, I began to develop theological ambivalence. It became hard for me to make up my mind about once largely clear religious issues. As my head pounded and my heart could only feel fear, I wrote the following poem, "Analysis":

Analysis

Perception enters spinning head,
Not too sure of what's been said;
Teasing super ego so,
Answers wonder where to go.

Fear intervenes—it forms a wall
Blocking infinite lengths of hall;
Vaguely, hardly, all along,
Insisting what is right and wrong.

More confused and frightened each day before the first barrage of semester exams, I dropped out of school. I began to frequently seek solace in my bedroom. Within these walls, my greatest comfort was to pray on my knees for help while yearning for relief from a pain that was beginning to manifest itself in what seemed like every molecule of my body. After a time not even my room protected me from an angry God, who disapproved of me as He hovered and watched me pray. It seemed the more I spoke to Him the more distorted and terrible my relationship with Him became. I fluctuated from fits of crying to an overwhelming exhaustion that left me sprawled across my bed or lying on the floor. My parents left me pretty much alone, certainly unaware of what anguish was occurring inside my room.

My second semester of college arrived. I tried working on a part-time basis while taking a couple of classes. Walking across campus now was even more frightening. I was terrorized by the thought that someone I knew would see me and kindly interrogate me into confessing I was a semester behind everyone else. This fear quickly evolved into the conviction that everyone could detect there was something seriously wrong with my mind. My paranoid self felt "Inside Out," another poem I desperately penned:

Inside Out

Mankind tries, but cannot hide
Fashioned feelings, stitched inside.
Life's episodes, sewed-up dreams,
Must be displayed like finished seams.

A quiet tear, a sudden jerk
Is memory flaunting handiwork.
Subtle jokes and comments shout,
As people live lives, inside out.

Because I couldn't concentrate on my texts, passing exams became impossible. Exams were the critical instruments that measured academic progress. I was in a humiliating bind. During my second college semester, I managed to summon enough courage to take the necessary exams and passed my two classes with average grades. However, they were certainly not up to my high school standards. The quality of work performed in each class was inferior. In fact, the academic world eluded me to such a degree that very little began to make sense. My confusion was expressed as follows:

Limits and Limits of Logic

My mind is melancholy.
My heart throbs full of glum.
This student just decided
Ten parts result the sum.

Logic's luminous lines
Seal in all unanswered thoughts.
Then, shut out soul's creations.
A thinking mind now rots.

A steakhouse owner provided a part-time job. Unfortunately, it presented me with the impossible task of learning to operate a cash register. My efforts to adequately absorb the information provided by my supervisor were futile. The cash register loomed in front of my trembling body as an enemy, bent on destroying my job and my reputation. I quit after two weeks before I lost both.

Desperate to have some kind of explanation that provided answers and perhaps even comfort, I visited the family doctor. He had delivered me into the world and followed my medical history up through the years. Now it was time for him to enable me to handle the life he gave me. His gentle demeanor had always been reassuring. I was counting on him for a cure.

I described to him the inferno my world had become. He kindly asked me to give him a word that described the way I wanted to feel. I knew immediately that word was "peace." Each minute I battled an interior war where I became a giant casualty. The sweetness of "peace" was all I longed for. There had been too much mental bloodshed, and I was tired of the battle.

The doctor hypnotized me and provided the pivotal suggestion that when I said the word "peace" to myself I would not feel any of the familiar inner horrors. After leaving his quiet office, I tried this solution as I interacted with the peril of daily living. However, there was no relief and there was no peace. I felt only confusion. It was the 1960s, and Vietnam had created the "V" hand gesture, labeling it as "peace." I was bombarded with friendly peace signs from everywhere, and my doctor's remedy, to my great disappointment, quickly lost its potency. The too, too universal word "peace" did not succeed in making the magic I needed to be healed.

With two semesters of college behind me, I began finding nearly everything a great effort; a stark contrast to my animated mania and an indication of a serious clinical depression. It was exhausting forcing myself to awaken every morning, only to barely attain the stamina to endure another excruciating day. Whenever I would put the necessary effort into accomplishing something meaningful I would only fail. This pattern persisted for three more semesters of starting school and dropping out, starting school and dropping out, and starting school and dropping out again.

Somewhere during these increasingly erratic efforts at higher education, I moved away from home. It seemed appropriate that, at age 20, I should be on my own. Though I had developed a fear of my parents, I strongly suspected they ultimately could not fail to love me. Therefore, I wrote the following reflections on my "Need to Leave":

A Need to Leave Home

When their love becomes confining
And their giving a burden
We need to give away;
Then a need to leave happens.
With intense struggle
To put distance
Between sheltering closeness;
We need to grow,
Honoring further away.
Sliding under their love
To come up on the other side,
We need the separation;
Distance, solitary, still caring.
Golden space between contains
Devoted years of gentle teaching.
We find new honoring,
Identifying with the wisdom.
So we make decisions, adult.
We accept responsibilities, mature.
We find new freedom,
Sometimes lonely and unsure.

When their love becomes supporting
And their giving a blessing,
We find a new needing.
Then our freedom becomes joy.

Though both my parents were against my moving out of the house, I had come to assume they preferred that I leave. My mother expressed their feelings in the following poignant letter:

Dear Two,

As I reflect back on our conversation last night, I am sorry we were unable to convince you to abide by the rules of our home. (We had exchanged a conflict over how late I stay out.)

Daddy and I do appreciate your desires to be independent. Why do you think we want you to have an education? It is a parent's privilege and pride to assist their children to grow up and be independent. We have always wanted the best for you and perhaps, as you have mentioned, corrected too much. It was certainly because we care and love you and no other reason.

As an honest parent to you, as you are honest to me, I find I cannot tell you it is right to go to work on five hours' sleep. (A pattern I was unsuccessfully attempting.)

I hope you save this letter and five or ten years from now you will probably smile and say how foolish you were about some things at 20 years old.

Daddy and I love you for your good moral and honest values. We are proud of your strong faith in the church. We pray you will always stay close to the church and kneel daily to thank your Heavenly Father for the many blessings he gives you; that you will pray sincerely for his guidance when you are troubled.

You have worked hard these past few summers and we have also been proud of that accomplishment. We would like you to continue school to give you more security for the future. This is your choice to decide.

Regardless of what you do, please know we love you and want the best for you. We are always here to help you when you need us.

Love always,
Mother and Daddy

Despite this confirmation, I still questioned my parents' sincerity.

I moved in with a family who was renting out a room.

This move lasted just a few weeks. The family's two children refused to stay out of my room and my belongings. They terrorized what comfortable living arrangements the parents attempted to provide.

I moved out of this miniature combat zone and into an inadequate apartment, better described as a shed at the rear of a trailer park. It consisted of one room, a sink, a small stove, and a midget refrigerator. I kept my clothes on a rack next to my bed. I had to leave my tiny room to shower around the corner each morning in a drafty stall without warm water. Morning showers became tortuous when winter arrived. It had been my original (and I thought noble) goal to live in a state of poverty to withstand, firsthand, what this kind of hardship involved. The experience was what I had vaguely suspected. However, I was not tough enough to endure the substantial discomfort. I was soon ready to move out and in with a roommate under more comfortable circumstances.

My first roommate worked for the federal government as a secretary, a position most would perceive as held by a solid personality. My immediate description of her was "peculiar." Her abundance of makeup caused her to resemble a clown, and she was obsessed with tidiness and cleanliness. The fringe on the living room carpet was always kept straight. If I left any minor debris on the kitchen counters she would erupt in an outrage. I have since learned her extreme preoccupation with maintaining meticulous surroundings was probably the sign of an unfortunate, compulsive obsessive problem. However, at the time, she just appeared eccentric.

I soon settled into a full-time job as a photo-lab technician while trying again to earn a few more college credits. Again I failed at college. I decided it was time for a change of tactics. Instead of trying work and school together, I thought I would try one at a time. I settled down to just making a living full-time and saving for college as I had done that first summer out of high school.

My full-time salary was initially appealing, but I soon became overwhelmed with my familiar depression. Awakening each morning was a phenomenal feat. Brushing my teeth took immense

41

energy. Climbing one flight of stairs repeatedly at work every day demanded an extraordinary effort. I was devastatingly unhappy.

Soon this distressing mood swung back into mania. Such mood swings would eventually become painfully typical, highlighting every lifestyle I attempted. Mania was primarily characterized by speed: I hurried wherever I went. Details slowed me down, so they were overlooked and I often left them out when they were most important. The quality of my judgment was decreasing. I frantically needed to change the circumstances that had been dealt me. I began a new effort.

First on the agenda was to escape my meticulous roommate, a chief source of stress. I purchased a small trailer. It seemed a good idea to make payments that would result in ownership rather than just pay rent for an apartment. My new home provided a tiny kitchen table, bed, and bath. Though it was three years old, it was in good condition. My parents gave me permission to park it in their driveway until I found a modestly priced piece of land.

Even before a short time had passed, I had one especially undesirable day at work. I was asked to develop pictures of my employer with some VIPs. The results were sadly spoiled images, the supreme faux pas of my short career as a photo-lab technician. Before anyone had a chance to fire me, I was out the door. I desperately packed a meager bag, leaving the newly purchased trailer and my car in my parents' driveway. I then started hitchhiking to see my remote high school friend, Sandy, who had moved over 2,000 miles away. Why I assumed she would take me in despite my earlier ostracism can only be explained by an escalating mental illness. Though today hitchhiking is primarily an activity left to those who live on the streets, this was the early 1970s, a time when independent hippies (even from affluent homes) hitchhiked to escape from oppressive institutions. However, the element of danger was ever present. I left only a brief note behind me:

Dear Mom and Dad,
   I quit my job today. I'll notify you soon as to my whereabouts. I'm okay. Don't worry. I'll send you trailer

payments soon. Meanwhile: 1) The trailer and all it contains are yours; 2) my car is yours to sell, and all necessary papers are on the trailer table with a 50-dollar check to the insurance company due in the mail any day. The sale of the car should provide all necessary money to pay you what I owe in repairs.

The remainder of this farewell consisted of a few other odds and ends that needed to be attended to. It ended with a gutsy request to call my employer with confirmation that I quit.

Though Sandy and I had become estranged from each other, I hoped she would again accept me into her life. Only distance and Sandy made real sense anymore. I had attempted to achieve and failed again and again. I knew something was seriously wrong with my mind. It was clear any treatment for recovery would leave my parents impoverished from medical bills. It seemed to me the only sensible solution was to run away to some better place where a friend would again make me laugh and people did not know my failures.

Chapter 4
A DESPERATE ESCAPE

An irresponsible lack of fear and an abundance of desperation hitchhiked with me to Sandy's along with a small bag of basic necessities and my guitar. Traveling over 2,000 miles via thumb up for truck drivers (I was advised they gave the safest rides) was an effort that seemed absolutely necessary at the time. I had run out of ways to try to achieve at home. The only alternative involved accepting plenty of expensive psychiatric help that would bankrupt families with greater finances than mine. Something was overpowering my life. It seemed I could only escape by leaving my home, the scene of the struggle.

The truck drivers proved to be as safe as I had been told. My first "Good Samaritan" offered me $15 for a bus ticket home. The only truck driver who made a pass at me was quickly made aware of his confusion over my discreet moral values. Why this episode didn't terrify me, I can't say. I can only blame my actions and feelings during this journey on the poor judgment that accompanies severe mental illness. My lack of fear was uncanny. I recall standing by the road in the dark one night, waiting for the next truck. Large forms lurked behind me. I guessed they must be cattle and refused to let their presence frighten me. I carelessly resolved not to reflect on the dangers of my long impulsive journey, believing that more fear would only entice danger from others. The only time I remember feeling real fear was when the truck I happened to be riding in passed a troop of Hell's Angels. They were a vicious-looking pack and prompted me to realize how lucky I was to have been picked up by a truck before I had been required to thumb along that ominous route. Perhaps it was my psychotic attempt at mind control over the drivers who plucked me from the pavement, or perhaps it was my mother's prayers that delivered me, without harm, to Sandy's apartment in less than three days.

A letter from my mother did beat me to Sandy's door. It reflected the love and fear she must have felt:

Dear Sandy,

Two is on her way to see you. It was a very sudden idea, apparently, as she seemed happy and content this past week since she bought her trailer. Something has happened that she didn't want to talk about to us, her parents. We are particularly concerned as it appears she left with just her guitar and what clothes she was wearing. We had a telephone call from a Bishop Snow, who, in turn, had received a telephone call from a church member who had picked Two up on the highway in Utah. She told him about wanting to visit you. Two is 21 and can go where she pleases. However, we are very concerned about her personal welfare and safety with hitchhiking across country. She may contact home if she needs money or anything. Please tell her we love her, and for her not to worry about being nagged at when she contacts us. We know she can do what she wants to do even though we may not approve. We all have to learn with experiences…and I just pray her experience will not harm her. Many of us try to learn by running away; and we do not solve our problems this way.

Sandy, please feel free to call collect when you hear from Two. (Phone number.)

Much love,
Two's parents

Upon arriving on Sandy's doorstep, I immediately sent a telegram to my parents:

> All's well had an incredible and enjoyable journey am with Sandy will write immediately Love Two

Sandy had chosen to live in a college town made unique by its plush forest terrain and accented by occasional waterfalls. Her four-room apartment was decorated like that of a typical student, though she was exclusively a secretary at the local Ivy League university. Avant-garde posters covered her apartment walls. The landscaping was inhabited by lively squirrels that scampered up lofty pines outside.

Though Sandy had been away a short time, she had developed a new identity. Her self-esteem had become elevated to such a degree that she confidently enjoyed the frequent company of a handsome physics grad student. I was delighted with the positive change in Sandy. However, her new self-reliance put a gap in our relationship that added to the familiar alienation I had been feeling from my escalating symptoms. We had become like strangers.

Sandy was remarkably generous. She did not hesitate to loan me her little Volkswagen, invaluable in traveling the steep hills of her little town. However, my careless frame of mind persisted, and the inevitable happened: I had a car accident. These circumstances soon prompted another telegram to my parents:

> Emergency I had an accident with Sandy's car today please wire the deductible 100 dollars for insurance will repay you when I receive my first paycheck thank you love Two.

A money order for a hundred dollars arrived in the mail nearly immediately.

Soon my emotional inconsistencies were demonstrated to my parents by means of a brief letter. The following are excerpts, reflecting the type of communication from a sufferer of a manic phase:

Dear Mom and Dad,

I'm writing to you instead of speaking to you on the phone because I don't want to hear a lecture or an argument concerning the decisions I've made. I've decided to go into veterinary medicine, which takes only six years. It will take me the rest of the year, working two jobs, to have the money. My high school grade-point qualifies me for admittance if I have the capital.

Right now, Sandy can't afford college. However, with my help she will be able to. I'm saving enough to also buy an older, three *or* four bedroom home and restore it. Sandy will help me renovate and in return will get free room and board. That way, we will both profit and be able to go to school.

Love, Two

An ex-student with a history of multiple college dropouts and with the inability to hold a job and save a meaningful amount of money would not likely be able to carry out such industrious plans. Indeed, I had not even consulted with Sandy about my ambitious agenda. Reality was becoming more and more obscure as I became desperate to change my life.

Sandy showed kind hospitality for a while. However, the inevitable day arrived when the relationship between Sandy and me became hopelessly strained. The pivotal episode was when I used too much of her shampoo. No doubt, it was an uncomfortable collection of minor problems such as this that persuaded Sandy to insist on my either sharing rent or moving out. However, my diminished funds combined with fear of another failure on the job presented an immediate predicament.

Initially, I was perplexed over what to do next. But my dilemma was brief. A young woman I had met back home had mentioned thinking she might like to join the military. She had informed me of the educational opportunities (especially the GI Bill) the military provided. I had quietly snickered. Everyone knew the military accommodated loose, unprincipled women, only there to keep up the men's morale. Now, as I pondered my options, joining the service seemed a reasonable alternative.

As I trudged the steep hill to the recruiter's office, a current swing back to depression made everything a major effort. I could taste the sweet, syrupy courtesy as the hulking, persuasive female recruiting sergeant reviewed her list of enticing advantages that lay ahead for me should I "sign up." In her congenial (and suspicious) way, she described an attractive package: free food and shelter…and a free education after I left the service in three years. The highlight of the package was the GI Bill. It would provide enough money to at least pay for an undergraduate degree. It would allow me to work little or not at all while attending a university away from home. It was a captivating thought; after three years of serving my country, a complimentary education would be waiting for me by means of an academic red carpet.

I signed the paperwork and watched my mild-mannered recruiter transform herself from an amiable friend to a dictatorial superior. No longer did she speak in gracious suggestions. Now I was given abrupt orders to appear the next day for testing. The IQ and skill tests, vehicles prepared for the masses (including those who had not even completed high school), were a minor challenge. Also, I imagine because my symptoms had not become full blown, whatever psychological tests I took were general enough to prevent me from not appearing psychologically fit. All my scores convinced everyone in uniform in that small recruiting office that I could handle the military. It was the Vietnam era and an assortment of men were being recruited. I became a member of this group, and slid my way past the recruiter and into a group of new enlistees.

After this small cluster of questionable personalities accompanied me in a brief enlistment ceremony, I was flown to a basic training post. I then boarded a bus with about a dozen new female recruits. We sat strangely silent as we were transported to a menacing, new experience. Maybe our silence was due to the unfamiliarity with what lay ahead. More likely it was because of our dread of what we imagined might lie ahead.

The evening my fellow collection of recruits and I reached our destination, we were lined up in a holding barracks where a drunken female sergeant staggered and slurred her way through a welcome speech. The next day we were transferred to our training barracks and collectively became Company C. Eight weeks of basic training was explained and presented a sinister agenda.

Shortly after entering the military, I wrote home:

Dear Family,

Tonight I'm on CQ duty (Charge of Quarters). I just completed a bed check and no one is AWOL (Absent Without Leave).

Interesting, the contorted positions some people assume when they sleep. One especially poignant example is that of one woman who fell to sleep while writing a letter. Her pen was still poised in her hand and the paper was next to her cheek.

I was the head of my detail today. We really worked. Lawns were trimmed and mowed, hall floors were waxed and buffed, and latrines were made spotless. (I have had to get used to calling bathrooms latrines—a crude adjustment.)

This morning we were told to police an area. I looked forward to what I assumed was a new position of authority. We all ended up picking up trash. These new policing methods are original.

I've finally mastered my shoe shine. I get a glass shine now, almost every time. It's taken me a good two weeks to adjust to the routine (with the help of a special blessing from the church priesthood). I'm even beginning to like the challenge and, especially, the truly unusual people I meet.

Someone is sounding "all is well" on a bugle outside. I hope that message is true for this barracks. I'm prone to panic and, being on CQ duty, I would be responsible for any problems.

Last week our platoon marched in parade. One girl in front of me, rather than using the regular stance, enthusiastically swayed to and fro to the music and snapped her fingers to the beat. It was hilarious, especially from the rear. Rumor has it that this young woman is now out of the service with a dishonorable discharge.

Love

Two

Not long after this positive letter I began having serious problems with my new environment. I discovered something I never detected in myself: I highly resented authority. A letter home reflected this resentment:

Dear Dad and Mom,

Yesterday, we had 15 hours of straight KP and it was miserable: I had garbage duty. According to Private Dinkle, a girl from a Kansas farm, garbage detail smells just like a pigpen. We scrubbed the insides of about 30 garbage cans. It was nauseating. Then, in the afternoon, I cleaned leftovers off of plates. The coup d'etat was when we were ordered to peel some bad bananas before we threw them away. When I asked why, we were told the extra trouble was because the pigs that ate these leftovers did not like the peels. I actually was ordered to peel bananas for lousy pigs.

The military is unbearable. I'm convinced its organization is all wrong. We are made to think we are the scum of the earth, bodies to be clothed, laughed at, harassed, and greeted as a group rather than as individuals. I am expected to obey orders without question. No wonder when people leave the military they have lost all personal drive and ambition. Required to sacrifice faith in themselves and their own thinking ability, they end up machines, only able to carry out defined instructions.

Despite the misery of KP and other details, it would all be endurable if it weren't for my sergeant

Oh, the harassment! I've had difficult teachers and bosses, but no one ever got to me like Sergeant Winelli. It's impossible to block out the fear. It is a constant companion, especially for me since I'm the sergeant's favorite victim. This harassment is something I wake up to, feel as I eat meals, and sleep with. That woman's eyes grind into the back of my head. They are everywhere and can't be escaped. I feel like I'm continually being watched. If I don't graduate in two weeks with the rest of the company I'll desert; and the military will have lost what entered as an optimistic, capable worker. I've never worked harder with the result being abundant personal abuse.

I'll write again soon.

Love
Two

My defiant manner was referred to by the sergeant as an "attitude." Soon, I found great satisfaction in returning the icy stares of this company sergeant, instead of meekly turning my eyes away (her usual response from a new trainee). Sergeant Winelli was a huge woman, large-boned and a good six feet tall, with 18 years in the military. She managed to reduce the size of those who dared attempt to challenge her staunch military bearing. Retaliating against my rebellious behavior in her standard way, Sergeant Winelli frequently singled me out for harassment. I was often taken out of a marching line to demonstrate whatever drill she was teaching at the time. If my performance was flawed, I was harshly berated in front of the entire company. The final blow was when she insisted I cut my shoulder-length hair a couple of inches, "to meet military standards for women." I went over her head in protest to the captain, who said my hair was fine in front of the whole company during a class session.

A hushed fury burned from the sergeant's every pore as she took me into a room by ourselves and communicated raw fear into my quaking form. First silently towering over me forever, she then told me she would have me recycled through my eight-week basic training for eternity if I ever went over her head again. The experience, combined with all the former harassment I had endured (and, perhaps, usually deserved), left me with a sense of shell shock. In a kind of daze I walked out of that room, changed into civilian clothes, walked out of the barracks, and discreetly walked to the post's exit, ready to easily attract rides to a neighboring state.

After a few hours of fortunately safe travel in a couple of commercial trucks, I turned myself in at an Air Force Base where two military police escorted me to a women's barracks. I was treated with considerable kindness. The women expressed compassion when I told them about my version of my basic training experiences. They had stories of their own terrible weeks of basic training and I reveled in their sympathy. They gave me free access to the refrigerator, and I saw the first TV shows I had seen since "signing up" five weeks earlier. Though only a few hours long, it was a true vacation that gave me the time I needed to recuperate from my sergeant.

The following morning, two military police again escorted me, this time off the base and to the nearest bus station. The anticipation during my ride back to my basic training post was horrifying.

When I arrived back at my Company C barracks, I braced myself for the fury of a sergeant who I was sure found it incomprehensible that a basic trainee would go AWOL. Instead, I was immediately surprised at the lack of anger or hostility expressed by the sergeant. She displayed the most remarkable poker face I had ever seen. I was treated with indifference, almost as if I wasn't there.

However, some retribution was inevitable. The next day I was ordered to the captain's office. This officer's already petite frame was made all the more diminutive by the massive desk that stretched several feet in front of her. She seemed to immediately like me and appeared to be surprisingly amused by my misconduct. I was disciplined with what was called an Article 15. Here, the captain had full legal freedom to punish me in any way she chose, while avoiding sending me to a military jail or kicking me out of the service. For going AWOL, her Article 15 put me on restriction for two weeks and provided a mild reprimand. Apparently, the captain had been informed of the sergeant's abuse and felt somewhat sympathetic. She told me the sergeant had been given orders to discontinue any harassment. That accounted for the sergeant's poker face. I felt like I had escaped manslaughter.

The captain sent me down to the young and ambitious

lieutenant, who made me very aware that she had little sympathy regarding my brief vacation. She indicated to me the military was her life, and my AWOL defiled what was, to her, holy ground. A battery of tests had been ordered to see if I was psychologically damaged by the sergeant's treatment. The result was a diagnosis of manic-depression. However, the lieutenant's officious manner communicated a coldness that left her unfeeling regarding my troublesome mental state. It was the consensus by my testers that the enormous stress experienced by the typical basic trainee would probably produce some kind of abnormal psychological state in anyone. The notion was that once I completed oppressive basic training my symptoms would quickly disappear.

However, because my previous performance had been exceptional (good class scores and nearly flawless inspections), I was given the option of leaving the Army or staying in if I chose. My immediate choice was to stay in. The college education the three years in the military would provide me was too attractive to give up.

My strangely lenient treatment for the unthinkable crime of going AWOL in basic training was soon followed by a letter from Mother, which provided her own brand of reprimand. It read as follows:

> Dearest Two,
>
> I just finished talking with your captain. You are very lucky she is being very lenient with your AWOL. I hope you take your punishment with the right spirit and know you have learned something worthwhile from this experience. You don't want blight on your past good records.
>
> Honey, when you feel this disturbed please feel free to call us collect. Sometimes, just talking to someone will help you make a better decision. You just can't run away now, dear. You have made a strong decision, and I pray you will take on a better attitude. You have a marvelous opportunity to strengthen your character and knowledge in the military. Take advantage of it.

Daddy said if you can tolerate the petty things in basic training, you can cope with the larger problems when you are out of basic training. Where is your sense of humor? Is it so difficult to follow the rules?

If you are disturbed, ask for counseling. You can have so much from the army by asking. They try to take care of you, but they are not there to baby you. I know you are sensible. Use your intelligence, Two. You have many different personalities around you now and this will only strengthen your own character. You be you. Don't copy anyone that you do not admire. I am grateful the Lord watched after you and please lean on the Lord to help guide you to do what is right.

We all love you and, again, do not hesitate to call us.

Love again,
Mom and Dad

So, it was back to my basic-training schedule. Continued military stress began to introduce some curious results, even without the sergeant's abuse. During those last four weeks of basic training, I found my perceptions undergoing a peculiar alteration. Everyone I saw and spoke to appeared as animated caricatures straight out of the comics. Instead of serious trainees, they were amusing personalities that I frequently found difficult to take seriously. This odd phenomenon was contrary to any other social intercourse I had dealt with before. Fear was no stranger to me, but continual comedy was a foreign event.

The sergeant's new benevolence resulted in no more overbearing orders and no more hostile glares. I was now treated as a nonentity. I concealed a curious admiration for her capacity to obey her superiors. Her 18 years in the military had drilled into her brain a stimulus/response pattern when it came to following orders. She was a soldier with a mission and that mission was to obey. Aided by my new, puzzling, even comical sergeant, the remaining weeks of basic training became much more digestible. I refrained from looking her in the eyes, and she refrained from looking at me at all. Why I escaped being recycled (where I had to start basic training all over again) was a mystery to me. Some of the other company trainees resented this leniency. When I graduated with my original company, I was not the most popular private on post.

Prior to graduating from basic training with Company C, I wrote the company's graduation song, which was sung during the final ceremonies. I was surprised to detect a hint of admiration from the sergeant for my musical abilities. However, I was not surprised at the frequent hostile stares from the young, zealous lieutenant. The captain still indicated a measure of affection as her stern expression broke into a smile more than once when she looked my way.

Graduation from eight weeks of basic training was followed by AIT (Advanced Individual Training) where our little band of trainees would learn the skills they originally signed up to pursue. Individual members of Company C were flown to their respective army posts to undergo this more specialized, second phase of the training process. My choice AIT was Medical Lab with my training post located 900 miles away.

The new accommodations were less than acceptable. The barracks were bug-infested, and we were warned not to roam the post at night (at the risk of rape or some other assault). My medical lab classes became a hopeless struggle. Though I had passed the elementary exams in basic training, I could not concentrate on lectures in advanced training. I found what the instructors lectured and wrote on the board to be incomprehensible. It was all about blood—red corpuscles, white blood corpuscles, and platelets—for me an obscure blur. During the third class, we were divided into partners to take blood from each other's arms. With my lab partner's permission, I quickly chose to be the first to take blood rather than give it. All seemed to be going fine until I forgot to remove his tourniquet before removing the bursting red syringe. This proved to be a messy mistake, while the blood was given plenty of room through a bulging blood vessel to escape through the puncture I so confidently inflicted. Blood splattered everywhere, and my partner immediately turned a pasty white as his eyes glazed over. I was sure he would faint, but he remained conscious. He escaped having to take blood from my arm, which left me enormously grateful.

My ultimate response was just to stop attending med lab classes. I spent a couple of class days out of class hibernating in the library until I was finally called into the company major's office.

Major Kindel was a sophisticated woman by army standards. Her stylish hair and refined manner provided a curious contrast to her archaic army uniform. She heard my story and was sympathetic. Her mild chastisement included the comment that she probably would have also gone AWOL if she had been me. I was given another (necessary) Article 15 but only suffered her merciful reprimand for again going AWOL (what my skipping class was called). The dialogue ended with her encouraging me to attend Officers' Candidate School. To my relief, I had been spared a second time for a somewhat serious offense. This communication with my superior officer had even ended with a compliment! It was the second time that an officer had showed benevolence.

I transferred out of medical lab.

A clerical position was my next assignment, where I battled in vain the details of desk work. I was in charge of scheduling televised training classes. The television crew was exceptionally nice and I even dated a couple of them. However, my errors accumulated as the days progressed. Painfully discouraged, I slept in a couple of mornings. Two more AWOLs were added to my sadly tarnished record. Still, I remained assigned to this confusing job. After three more incompetent months, I made the ultimate mistake of forgetting to schedule a news show that the post commander watched religiously every day.

The next day I found myself at attention in front of the personnel sergeant's desk awaiting a new assignment. After a brief interrogation, the sergeant discovered that I was a qualified lifeguard and swim instructor. Within a day, I was transferred from the scheduling desk to a swimming pool, where I worked as a lifeguard in my new uniform: a red, white, and blue, starred and striped, bathing suit.

I performed my shift alone, with no higher rank hovering over me. I was the first female to be given this job in the history of the post. (It was 1971 and women were being given more opportunities in the military.)

My good fortune seemed uncanny. I had gone AWOL four times during my first five months in the military before landing my pre-trained position as a lifeguard. I had been given only three Article 15's, while penalties were lenient in almost every case. There are those who believe in angels. My shoulder carried at least one, and I appreciated the company more each day.

My persistent resentment of military authority continued to gnaw at me emotionally, physically, and mentally. Emotionally, I felt anger and depression. Physically, my bones actually hurt from stress. Mentally, I suffered from what I suspected was severe psychological pain. To retaliate in my bitterness toward military protocol, I devised a vengeful disguise. Identifying myself only as "the bronze dove," I discreetly placed bits of poetry in conspicuous places for the officers to discover (on windshield wipers, etc.). The typical verse was as follows, and nothing less than hostile:

Our Strength, Our Glory

Hail the military mind,
With its properly spaced, filed and categorized
FL's, DD's and DA's,
And its cold stone discipline to constant schedule and
abrupt order,
Shining through static glare from two slits of eye
That must have shone with love…once.

Hail the military bearing;
Still and formal, starched and pressed,
Noble, proud, and brave,
Donned in all-colored medals for such amazing
courage,
Afraid only to reach out when love is offered,
For fear to bend a crease.

Soon I got tired of the emotional wear and tear from being found out after a few months of indulging in sharp poetic license. Or, perhaps my aesthetic enthusiasm dampened over being so malicious. I stopped writing the poetry.

I continued to work without stressful supervision each day, carrying only the responsibility of guarding skilled adult swimmers. I found it nearly effortless to succeed at work. Previously, it had seemed a millennium had elapsed since I felt any sense of accomplishment. Now, suddenly, I was a success—even a post celebrity—being the only female lifeguard.

After a few months as a lifeguard with the rank of private, I earned a rank of specialist four, which was comparable to the rank of sergeant (without carrying the particular leadership characteristics). Teaching lifesaving techniques to classes of GIs became my next assignment. I had managed to earn a rank that exceeded that of all my students and was considerably self-conscious of my elevated status. My resentment of authority left this position difficult for me to comfortably adjust to. My elevated rank left me giving orders rather than generously sharing knowledge. In addition, with my thinking and concentration skills still problematic, teaching required an adjustment that took substantial effort on my part.

However, after a couple of classes graduated with their lifeguard certificates, I began to settle in as a comfortable teacher instead of superior specialist. My students seemed to appreciate my rare orientation to rank. Even without employing the force of rank and preferring to share knowledge, the gawky young GIs presented no discipline problems. Admittedly, my students' sergeant contributed to this flawless behavior. Sergeant Campbell was a former giant (Olympic), heavyweight wrestler, whose method of discipline was taking disobedient GIs behind the nearest barracks and administering his distinctive style of punishment. Sergeant Campbell did not bother with Article 15's, satisfied with his own discipline. My GI students were not completely naturally well-behaved angels: They were petrified into strict obedience.

My charmed lifeguard position provided frequent occasions for brief conversations with those who visited the pool. One GI who stayed in my mind prompted me to wax poetic. I was inspired as follows:

A Nice Place to Visit

Today, I met a GI New Yawker,
A big Irish kid,
Eighteen and just back from Nam,
He rapped on the rice patties
And Central Park,
Of slanted eyes and Spanish Harlem.
In a divinely impersonal, big city manner,
Through an easy smile, words came and came rapidly,
About war crimes and hooky in Times Square.
About a street gang and fights erupting over concrete
  squares.
About friendly fire and company buddies down from the air
  lift.
The GI New Yawker put in to go back to Nam,
But Personnel said no and gave him an early out instead.

I never saw combat, and my primary assignments, lifeguarding and teaching, made my tour of duty comfortably uncomplicated. However, my three years in the military were riddled with internal trauma. Outrage overshadowed my military experience. Whatever mild opposition I had to authority in my relatively obedient lifetime was accentuated in this new totalitarian environment. I had escaped from my home in desperation, with a mysterious affliction in my mind and heart. Now, my original fear and pain merged into an all-encompassing anger over having to take orders. My body absorbed my fury in a curious way. As was the case at home, I continued to crave release from my interior (even manic) whirlwind urging me to run from place to place. I resolved this need, even avoiding the inevitable embarrassment frequent running would create, by energetically traveling everywhere at a rapid walk and accomplishing most tasks quickly (though often carelessly). As time progressed, I developed a peculiar sense of imbalance, where one side of me actually felt heavier than the other. I feared serious maladies such as multiple sclerosis and other crippling diseases. Apparently, the stress in my body was so intense it played havoc on my spine. Later, I was to learn a somewhat progressive scoliosis of my cervical spine contributed to this sense of unevenness in my body. This loss of symmetry would fade away during low-stress periods, which dispelled any feared major maladies.

A daily sadness that wore me out emotionally permeated my every waking hour. My body told me that to reduce the constant physical activity and hurt in my heart and brain and to restore a sense of physical balance...I must exercise.

So, I swam numerous laps each day. Each workout enabled me to absorb the stress of my frantic rage and created a temporary sense of physical and mental integration. I had not yet learned the positive effect endorphins (physiological chemicals created by exercise) can have on the body, including their ability to reduce depression and rage. I was also unaware that swimming was excellent exercise particularly for me, helping restore some of the symmetry my spine seemed to lack. I only knew that I must swim.

When only six months remained of my army experience, my dream of completing a college education (my exclusive reason for joining the military) prompted me to return to a clerical job. Transitions had always been difficult. It, therefore, seemed important to regain a familiarity with desk work as I attempted to adjust back into higher education.

Despite my early efforts at opposing the system as a lifeguard and swim instructor, I had managed to arrive at work nearly every day. However, my general hostility toward authority persisted for the duration of my tour of duty, and the resulting stress gnawed on my mind and body, making every day an endurance test. Though my outward appearance revealed minimal strain, my inner environment of flesh and bone and nerve produced more inner chaos every morning. I had come from a civilian place that introduced me to anguish and grief, then placed myself in a military world that provided a new, more profound suffering. I felt oppressed in an organization that was never aware of (indeed, never cared to understand) the trauma it had required me to endure. Some revel in the authoritarian milieu the military presents. However, nearly from the beginning, it had become apparent the military and I were not compatible. My exterior resigned to regimentation, while inside I was in daily combat with my surroundings. I had functioned as an enigma, managing to exist in an organization that never seemed to even suspect I steadily fought a private battle that showed no mercy and promised no peace.

PART II:

DIAGNOSIS AND TREATMENT

Chapter 5
LABELS — AND STIGMA'S DECEIT

My new military desk job took me out of the sunshine and into a drab office and beside a merciless sergeant who frequently afflicted me with detailed accounts of his gory combat experiences and repulsive sexual conquests. His disheveled appearance (even in uniform) added to his distasteful behavior. I complained to the lieutenant in charge several times. No changes were made. The sergeant knew just how to manipulate the new, young, frail-looking lieutenant, and I was made to bear stories of violence and pornography on a daily basis. Finally, I went over both their heads, hoping that the colonel would provide relief from the sergeant's vulgarities.

Instead of giving support, the colonel verbally attacked me. His weapons were a stony stare and loud, staccato tone of voice. He charged me with having it too good and still being nothing but trouble. I do not know if "having it too good" referred to my two-and-a-half-year job as a lifeguard and swim instructor, but I am fairly certain that "trouble" alluded to my early collection of Article 15's.

I cannot recall just what words were spoken, but very few were from me. Instead of attempting to remedy my plight of severe sexual harassment, the colonel (who had succeeded in frightening me into a meek silence) sent me back to the office, where I continued to endure the vulgar sergeant and the anguish his presence created.

My redeeming regular swimming, which had purged my days of painful stress, was no longer convenient. Simply by not working near a swimming pool, I neglected the daily workout that had held my nervous system together. The quality of my work reflected that of a confused and abused soul; even more than had my first army office job two years before. It was not a healthy situation.

I had lived balanced for two and a half years in a sustained manic anger, ready to topple over into grief. Now there was only one direction to go—downward. I fell into a deep depression. When the moment came, it was not difficult to give up. I awakened one morning and found it impossible to endure even the thought of another workday full of dreaded sexual harassment. I discovered an obscure place on my bedroom floor to sit and wait. Sitting in the darkness that covered my apartment, I knew that from that time on everything would always be different.

The lieutenant found my apartment by the middle of the day and persuaded the manager to unlock the door. I was huddled in a dim corner of my bedroom. I sat quietly, staring through the lieutenant to the other side of the room. No doubt it was a distressing scene to all who viewed my listless form. The lieutenant called an army psychiatrist to examine me in my apartment, then in his office. He concluded that I required hospitalization.

My first experience in a mental ward lasted two weeks. My hospital was appropriately nicknamed Chambers. Its walls were thick and menacing. Besides frequent pacing, I occasionally indulged in ward volleyball that took place on a convenient patio to which patients and staff had exclusive access. Both the initial doctor and I failed to recognize how sick I really was. It appeared to him that I was only experiencing a brief depressive episode that would require a short period of rest and observation. I had one visit with the head psychiatrist, who was, more dominantly, a colonel. It was my only therapeutic session with a psychiatrist in that hospital and strangely devoid of compassion. The colonel's office was as barren as his expression. The session occurred in a cold and rapid manner.

"You need to realize you are not the only one who is suffering in this world," commanded the colonel. "People suffer and you just have to accept that."

"Yes sir," I declared through clenched teeth.

I don't recall most of the 15 minutes I took from this psychiatrist's day. However, what I remember is the distressing essence of these brief, introductory words: I just was not trying hard like a good soldier. When I left this hospital, two weeks in a mental ward had been added to my medical records; a fact that would blemish my life from that point on. My existence had become flawed with a stigma that was overwhelming. I was no longer simply a perplexing person. I was crazy.

Stigma can be defined as a mark or brand of disgrace, deserving more attention in this text. The stigma associated with mental illness in our culture is especially severe and involves particularly heartless judgment. This stigma involves the banishment of individuals whose sicknesses are considered frightening and distasteful. Those who suffer are often assumed to deserve their illness. The mentally ill live in a society that carries a profusion of misconceptions about a serious brain disorder, which has nothing to do with the choice of the mentally ill and everything to do with basic biochemistry.

Just a note here on statistics: because of the length of time it took to write this book, the figures given therein may not, at times, be as timely as would be ideal. I believe it can be safely said that in most cases, most statistics are within five years of accuracy.

This stigma can be regarded as all the more outrageous when we consider how pervasive mental illness is. For every person suffering with muscular dystrophy, 40 suffer with schizophrenia. Though more specific statistics are not available for muscular dystrophy, it is useful to know that research monies spent per patient come to about $203 for cancer, about $88 for heart disease, and about $7.35 for schizophrenia. Of all the corporate and private foundations, only 1 percent ever subsidizes research in the mental illnesses.

The mentally ill have carried with them a legacy of abuse and misuse from stigma pervading the medical field. In London in

1620, Bethlehem Hospital for the mentally ill was nicknamed Bedlam by Londoners who visited there to be entertained. From 1900 to 1925, the patient had to be thoroughly stabilized before being discharged from the hospital. Outpatient clinics were basically unheard of. From 1920 to 1950, the rise of the lobotomy occurred (and brought a Nobel Prize to its inventors). The 1950s, 1960s, and 1970s were the eras of the misdiagnosis. Now that we are in a new century, pure necessity due to the size of the population of mentally ill has ushered in a major concern for funding research and treatment.

A recent study asked respondents which disability groups were the most/least acceptable. Most acceptable were those with visible handicaps (lame, etc.). Next on the list were the blind or the deaf. Next least acceptable were ex-convicts, the retarded, and alcoholics. The mentally ill were in last place. A dramatic example of this bias occurs in Kenny Fries' book *Starting Back*, a collection of essays describing the struggle of the disabled in overcoming their disabilities. Of the 37 separate accounts of battles with serious disabilities from paralysis to blindness, not once is serious mental illness mentioned.

The stigma of the mentally ill is reflected in what so many who suffer call home. Jails contain more seriously mentally disabled in the United States than state mental institutions. Around two times as many mentally ill live in shelters and on the streets as in state mental hospitals. Literally thousands are store-housed in dilapidated adult homes and nursing homes.

Another recent study reveals that of all health insurance policies in the United States, just about 37 percent allow inpatient coverage for mental illness (with the coverage being meager). Insurance covers any other ailing organ of the body when illness strikes. However, when illness strikes the brain, total coverage is usually not available. Though just as many suffer from epilepsy as from schizophrenia, epilepsy is fully covered by health insurers. Meanwhile, thousands of schizophrenics need to rely on public assistance for lifesaving treatment. Typical are two major health insurance plans in Washington DC. One requires those hospitalized with brain disorders to provide about a $150-a-day co-payment while requiring no such payment for others needing inpatient care. Insurers argue that premiums would increase drastically should they include the mentally ill in those they cover. However, the National Institute of Mental Health researched current coverage and utilization and found for an added annual cost of around $6.5 billion, yearly savings in indirect costs and general medical services would total about $8.7 billion. Therefore, the national net economic benefit would be about $2.2 billion each year. In other words, not adequately treating the mentally ill costs more in repeated hospitalization, costly medication, and perpetual outpatient services. Better to initially make the necessary investment and do the job right.

It has all been a terrible trial. Today, it is an ongoing effort to encourage politicians to focus on legislation that favors the mentally ill. Their constituents cannot seem to see past the stigma mental illness carries. Those with mental disorders are often treated with contempt. There are even caregivers who find it difficult to separate the disease from the person. For them, the mental illness embodies a moral issue—not a medical one.

Contrary to being incompetent, many of the mentally ill are high achievers. Through the years, major political leaders such as Abraham Lincoln, Theodore Roosevelt, and Winston Churchill suffered from manic depression (documented in *Moodswing*, by Dr. Ronald R. Fieve, MD, 1981). They mainly suffered quietly, but we know from their journals that they, indeed, suffered. Serious mental illness has not been endured exclusively by major national leaders. High achievers in the arts who participated in a current study by Dr. Kay Redfield Jamison (who wrote *Touched with Fire*, 1993) revealed that a significant number of the notably creative suffer from serious mental illness. Results indicated nearly 20 percent of all imminent British poets suffer from bipolar disorder (requiring minimal hospitalization, lithium, and/or ECT—electro-convulsive shock therapy); and about 28 percent of imminent British playwrights and novelists suffer from serious depressive illness (requiring medication). Also documented by Jamison were writers Leo Tolstoy, Lord Byron, and William Blake (and many more) as individuals who were manic-depressive and can also be recognized as brilliant writers. Today, many well-known people have come forward as having suffered serious mental illness.

Services for the mentally ill have never been adequate. The high cost of the new medications is a cause of great concern. However, the (at least) $1,000 per month price on Clozaril (generic name, clozapine) is nearly identical to the customary treatment for AIDS (where the cost is typically not questioned).

Some typical effects of stigma on the mentally ill are that sufferers do not seek needed help for fear of being labeled crazy; non-equitable medical insurance continues to flood the market; and the psychologically disabled become lonely people. Long-term results of stigma are reflected in the unavailability of group homes that provide places for them to stay once they leave the hospitals. It is a miracle when a group home for the mentally ill is able to exist in a neighborhood. Misconceptions sweep through neighborhoods while stigma does its work. People may even be sympathetic but still not want to live near the mentally ill.

The provision of daily structured routine under the roofs they are allowed to occupy is vital for the mentally ill. This routine helps them keep their minds occupied with practical living instead of delusional thinking. Also, most of the mentally ill must learn or relearn the basic skills needed in day-to-day living and in acquiring quality relationships.

One answer that has worked throughout the country is the clubhouse concept. Instead of providing 24-hour care, this facility acts as a daytime clubhouse where those who are experiencing mental illness can come and meet others suffering the same diagnosis. Some choose to help take on house responsibilities like cooking, producing a newsletter (along with other public relations efforts), maintaining the building and grounds, or providing transitional employment. Recreational activities are also provided, especially around holidays. The Fountain House in New York City stands as the model clubhouse from which clubhouses throughout the country have emerged.

For every person who is diagnosed with mental illness and is placed for any time in a psychiatric ward, the first hospitalization is pivotal. It is this hospitalization that transforms the typical self-concept of a responsible citizen into a personality with an abundance of uncertainties. Can I cope with school? Will I be able to fall in love and marry? Am I capable of raising a child? Is there hope for me in the working world? And, the biggest question of all: What will people think of me if they know I have been in a mental hospital?

Despite the devastating badge of stigma, sharing your history of serious psychiatric problems can create hope and direction for those who harbor the secret of mental illness in their lives or in the lives of those they love. Realize that those to whom you choose to reveal your disability are, like you, victims of a culture that perpetuates stigma. However, never demean a person who chooses not to disclose their mental illness. This is indeed a courageous act for the discloser. It can involve a tremendous amount of risk-taking, which can leave the one who discloses devastated.

The National Alliance for the Mentally Ill (NAMI) identifies six major mental illnesses. These illnesses have been labeled as significant in that they carry with them major symptoms and, therefore, major stigma. Five of the specific afflictions are schizophrenia, bipolar disorder (manic depression), major depression, obsessive-compulsive disorder, and panic disorder. In addition, more current diagnostic criteria used by psychiatrists, psychologists, and social workers identify schizoaffective disorder as a major mental illness. Over the years, at various phases of my mental illness, I have been diagnosed (and so labeled) with five different major mental illnesses. The clear conclusion: I was a victim of misdiagnosis.

I was first christened with schizophrenia in 1974 (I was 24), the most seriously debilitating of the mental illnesses. Less than half of all persons with schizophrenia receive adequate care. Most who develop this serious mental illness do so between the ages of 16 and 25. My first clinical symptoms appeared at age 18. One person in a 100 is diagnosed as schizophrenic. That means if no one in your family ever had this disease, the chances are 99 out of 100 you won't suffer from it in your lifetime. However, you have about a 90 percent chance of developing schizophrenia if you have a sibling who has schizophrenia. Major symptoms can include the following:

- Delusional thinking—disconnected and confusing language
- Poor reasoning, memory, and judgment
- High levels of anxiety
- Eating and sleeping disorders
- Hallucinations—hearing and seeing things that exist only in the mind of the patient
- Persistent false beliefs (e.g., that others are controlling their thoughts, etc.)
- Deterioration of appearance and personal hygiene
- Loss of motivation and poor concentration
- Tendencies to withdraw from others

My second diagnosis was bipolar disorder (also called manic depression), which I was subsequently labeled with in 1978. I was age 28 at the time. This disorder is typically thought to affect at least 0.8 percent to 1.5 percent of the population (depending on the type of bipolar disorder being diagnosed). If left untreated, about 40 percent of untreated victims of bipolar disorder will abuse alcohol or drugs; and 60 percent will experience divorce. Bipolar disorder usually begins in adolescence and continues throughout a person's lifetime. It very seldom begins after age 35. Major symptoms occur during either manic or depressive phases. During a manic phase, the following symptoms can occur:

- Boundless energy, enthusiasm, and a need for activity
- Decreased need for sleep
- Grandiose ideas and poor judgment (delusional thinking)
- Hallucinations
- Rapid, loud, disorganized speech
- Short temper and argumentativeness
- Impulsive and erratic behavior
- Rapid switch to severe depression

Depressive phases of bipolar disorders can involve the following symptoms:

- Delusional thinking
- Difficulty in sleeping
- Loss of interest in daily activities
- Loss of appetite
- Feelings of worthlessness, guilt, and hopelessness
- Feelings of despondence or sadness
- Inability to concentrate
- Possible psychotic symptoms
- Suicidal thoughts and even actions

Bipolar disorder is more treatable than schizophrenia, so I was relieved to be given this diagnosis even though it was four years after I was diagnosed as schizophrenic.

Major depression carries the symptoms of the depressive phase of bipolar disorder, without manic symptoms. About three to five percent of the population will experience this severe, recurrent depression; some as frequently as once or twice a year. One in 15 men and one in five women will experience major depression. Each episode may last more than six months. As many as 74 percent of all suicides are thought to be caused by severe depression. Of those suffering from bipolar depression or major depression, 80 to 90 percent can be substantially helped with treatment.

About ten years ago, I was diagnosed as having schizoaffective disorder. As many as 20 percent of those with severe mental illness may have schizoaffective disorder. The best way to identify the symptoms of this mental illness is as follows:

- A nonstop period of illness
- At least two weeks of delusions or hallucinations where there is the absence of prominent mood symptoms
- A manic or mixed episode (involving both depression and mania)
- Possible presence of just major depressive episodes

Therefore, schizoaffective disorder can be categorized as somewhere between schizophrenia and bipolar depression. This is my present diagnosis, and this is probably what I have always been.

I also display symptoms of obsessive-compulsive disorder (though, in my case, they are mild). Nearly one out of every 40 people in the United States is a victim of this disorder at some point. Symptoms often decrease with age and can include different degrees of the following:

- Disturbing/compulsive thoughts, ideas, urges, impulses, and/or worries
- Purposeless, repetitive behaviors (compulsions)

Panic disorder is suffered by 2 to 5 percent of Americans who most often first experience it in their early twenties. If a person has four or more uncontrollable panic responses to nonthreatening situations in a four-week period, they are identified as having panic disorder. Nearly 3.5 percent of the people in the United States will experience this disorder during their lives. I had a few panic attacks near the beginning of my disease, in my early twenties. However, they disappeared in my mid-twenties. Symptoms of this disorder can involve the following:

- Uncontrollable panic responses to ordinary, nonthreatening situations within a four-week period
- Specific phobias (irrational, involuntary fears)
- Hot or cold flashes
- Choking or smothering feelings
- Racing heart
- Trembling
- Chest pains
- Faintness
- Disorientation
- Feeling of impending death

My military breakdown and subsequent hospitalization created a transformation in me as well as others. Stigma lurked around every corner. I was no longer viewed by my army superiors with the confidence that I could provide a meaningful contribution to the military. I had only three months until my discharge date. I was placed in a nothing, clerical job.

A typical day of work involved 30 minutes of elementary paperwork. During the rest of the time, I attempted to read for personal edification. The individual words managed to enter my mind. However, the phrases they formed failed to be comprehended by my wounded consciousness. So, most of the day I sat reading and re-reading, trying to make sense of an abundance of spare time. The lack of meaningful activity that now characterized my life resulted in more stress, so less rest, and more anxiety.

My suffering soon took on a new dimension once I left the hospital. I had not been given medication, and now I began to hallucinate. Verbal hallucinations assaulted me in the form of voices that appeared to emanate from the minds of others in the office. These workers even seemed to be communicating to each other through the voices coming from inside their heads. The words emerged as brutal conversations behind my back and about my lack of sanity.

Then, as my psychosis evolved, visual hallucinations appeared in the form of images of others in the office as they continued activities when they left the room. When someone exited, I was convinced I perceived their actions outside the office. Was I seeing through walls? Like the thoughts I heard from others, the visual hallucinations were a vicious result of a rapidly escalating psychotic disorder. The hallucinations were so convincing that it did not occur to me they were illusions. Real time passed slowly with profuse psychotic activity appearing and sounding around me. The others in the office appeared so calm. They did their work so casually and routinely. Didn't they see the chaos?

Desperate, I went to the female major of my company and begged her to discharge me from the military. She was an impressive-looking woman, fastidious (even attractive) in her uniform and her manner. Surely she would be reasonable. I told her about my agonizing environment, which was becoming impossible to endure. She quietly listened while showing a strange mixture of compassion and rigidity. The conversation went back and forth. Words were punctuated with abundant bouts of weeping from me. However, I failed to convince the major to discharge me. I was sent back to my personnel desk and waited three long, confusing, psychotic months before I was honorably discharged.

I went home for the summer before starting school in the fall. Perhaps it was the security of being home that made the hallucinations disappear. But, my new sense of safety was not enough to silence the uproar in my damaged mind.

A peculiar new agony began. Obscene words and images regularly invaded my brain. They were especially unusual since I had hardly ever read or watched vulgar materials. Now, whatever emerged was some lewd television program, movie, or magazine that I had somehow, sometime, unconsciously absorbed and stored somewhere inside. In moral agony, I wondered how this subconscious rubbish could dominate my thinking. The most sensible conclusion I could draw was that I was mainly suffering from fallout due to the upsetting working relationship with the vulgar sergeant who had victimized me in the army with his crude conversation.

School began in the fall and I succeeded in being there (a small church campus that was 600 miles away from my hometown). I rented a small room from a woman whose husband was gone for the semester. No doubt, her expectations were that I would provide an element of company and security. I was a sad disappointment. I mainly secluded myself in my little room attached to her home. Between my seclusion I attended classes. Again, full-blown hallucinations haunted me. This time they arrived as a combination of lewd images and fierce demons. I prayed for them to stop and voraciously read the Bible, barely comprehending the words.

The painful images bombarded me from various directions. Again, it seemed that I could perceive the thoughts of others I saw on campus as they hurried to class. Again, they seemed to be able to communicate to each other with their thoughts; and, again, their cerebral conversations seemed redundant. I was the center of a universe that was determined to destroy me. I carried this torment down corridors and into classrooms. I shouted out allegations to students as they walked to their classes. I walked to the front of a class in session and stood beside a professor as he lectured, staring at the students before me. After about a week of this behavior, I was detained as I walked through the administration building, and was firmly escorted to a car that would carry me to my second mental ward. I offered no resistance but simply acted as I earnestly believed Jesus Christ would act: I fully cooperated on my way to my cross.

This, my second breakdown, was different from the first. Recovering would mean encountering the worst sustained pain I had ever known. My head felt as if it would explode with a pressured, inflamed ache that refused to subside. I was desperate to escape this second, painful prison. Using all the cunning my crippled mind would allow, I did what I could to appear as normal as possible. Most people believe that the mentally ill are not capable of useful thought. My circumstances in this second psychiatric ward prompted me to demonstrate otherwise. The most effective way I found to seem sane was to associate myself with any normal people I had access to. This resulted in my working with the cleaning staff. I spent as much time as I could associating with them. Washing filthy bedpans and mopping contaminated floors presented a minor price to pay for possibly escaping from my confinement.

After two weeks of this strategy I was released to go home.

Two breakdowns now paved the way for a total of 39 years encompassing somewhat over 25 more hospitalizations. I would know psychosis as I struggled to suppress voices and disregard hallucinations; while I seized brief, intermittent periods of functional peace. I would just manage a Master of Arts degree, and lamely trip through a thwarted career. The frequent agony I suffered was often similar to what I had always imagined torture must be.

My serious psychotic breakdowns most often began with some kind of stress that evolved into agitation and anxiety. This induced racing thoughts and vivid images in my mind. With all this mental interference, I found it incredibly difficult to concentrate on reading, on writing—even on conducting a simple and sane conversation.

The symptoms then became externalized, the racing thoughts turning into voices, the vivid images into hallucinations. My body engaged in intense activity, most often occurring in February—the darker, winter months when less healing sunlight caressed my consciousness. Later, I learned I suffered a certain amount of seasonal affective disorder, where mental/emotional problems were more inclined to occur during darker months when nature did not provide as much sunshine to reduce depression. Eventually, the breakdowns began occurring in a less predictable manner. These breakdowns also brought fewer, though still some hallucinations. They were replaced with more dominant mood swings: a repulsive anger (mania) and a frantic agitation (depression).

When depression occurred, I initially confused others with my desperate manner, like that of a despairing animal; futile in its search for food, or water—or love. Then I would begin to fear. My safety was threatened in the form of a terrifying sensation that I was falling down a deep well or off a high cliff into a fatal abyss. This perception convinced me each time that, should I hit bottom, I would surely die. With the fear, an intense anger from deep inside of me would reveal itself and no doubt caused others great alarm, especially those who were familiar with my peace-loving personality. I often became appalled that I was capable of so much fury.

An often immediate euphoric, though deceptive perception to having each negative breakdown was the positive belief that I was learning a new, profound truth. I felt exceptionally wise, productive, and superior to everyone around me. Once, while in the hospital, I believed I carried the extraordinary knowledge that the city's water was contaminated. Needing a reality check, I even called the local water district using the ward payphone to warn them of this calamity. They were kind enough to patiently let me know how carefully those things were monitored and that I was safe.

Each time, after an adequate hospitalization when I became closer to a recovery, deep insights were soon recognized as distorted and quickly forgotten. I could then identify this intense and unfulfilled energy as the nature of a psychotic breakdown, the departure from reality and the loss of truth.

Initially, I found it impossible to recognize when a breakdown was pending. Psychosis was new to me and crept up—intense, hideous—eager to devour my sanity. The nature of mental illness is that you are unaware you are mentally ill. The part of the brain that puts you in touch with this reality does not function correctly. A common result of this denial is refusal of medication. It was, therefore, easy for me to initially disagree that something was wrong with me. I found myself vainly trying to make sense of the strange experiences psychosis presented. Not surprisingly, my early inclination was to decline to seek exceptional help.

My breakdowns accumulated. However, my early denial was replaced by the acknowledgment that I could not recover on my own. I became more familiar with the warning signs that a full-blown breakdown was eminent. I was then able to contact my doctor for a change in medication that would hopefully keep me out of the hospital. Or, when I allowed my symptoms to escalate to a more extreme degree, I became more inclined to personally contact my current doctor for permission to be hospitalized. As I became a wiser psychotic, I became more and more aware that ignoring these warning signs would escalate my psychosis and hurl me into agony.

Therefore, the trick was to detect the early clues that kept me out of the hospital. Once the cruel momentum reached a certain point, those who cared about me could only hope I would acknowledge the situation was out of my hands and that I would agree to accept hospitalization. I eventually became a professional patient, seasoned enough to usually become able to recognize when I became captive inside my true, cruel prison—outside of the hospital and inside of me. I was left with a pain that left me solitary from others. But, to detect the early clues—that was the trick. It was then I was convinced I was severely mentally ill. And, it was then that I was most likely to turn back to God with due diligence.

Chapter 6
DOCTORS –
CARETAKERS OF THE MIND

Psychosis is brutal when it attacks. It requires treatment from a competent psychiatrist who can provide medication(s) that will remove or at least modify the symptoms. Instead of exercising their skills in surgery, psychiatrists become experts at probing the brain without scalpels.

Psychiatrists' formal education is substantial. First, they complete four years of undergraduate school, focusing on the sciences. Then they invest four more years in medical school, after which they carry the title of doctor. Then, after devoting three to five years to completing a psychiatric residency, they may choose to spend three to five additional years working in a fellowship to finalize a specialization (forensic medicine, geriatrics, child psychiatry, alcohol and substance abuse, etc.). Next, to practice psychiatric medicine, they must pass a written test in the state in which they reside. To become board certified by the American Board of Psychiatry and Neurology (crucial though not required, national certification), they must pass another written exam and then an oral exam. This usually takes one to two more years of preparation.

A young intern who once assessed my case confided to me that he suspected many of his classmates decided to specialize in psychiatry in a quest for their own sanity. Perhaps that explains why so many of my psychiatrists have appeared eccentric to me. Or, perhaps, a bizarre personality is contagious; a vocational hazard for those who fearlessly choose to daily communicate with the mentally ill. Whatever the reason, this young doctor and his classmates chose to heal with words and chemicals instead of blades, with the common result being some psychotic fallout.

Some practitioners are good and some are bad as in any profession. The tragedy remains that great suffering and possible suicide can result from the care given by an incompetent psychiatric physician. It is no secret that stigma exists in too many psychiatrists' offices and degrades the quality of treatment.

However, historically, psychiatrists do not deserve all the blame for frequent error—often misdiagnosis. Their primary diagnostic manual, The Diagnostic and Statistical Manual of Mental Disorders (DSM), has been altered over the years to such a degree that confusion is inevitable. The first DSM was published in 1952. Since that time, three revisions have been provided to mental health experts; the most current and comprehensive edition (DSM-IV Text Revised) was published in 2000.

The first doctor who treated my mind was Dr. Fields, my family doctor, responsible for delivering me from my mother's womb into what had become a confusing and chaotic world. I was desperate for some relief and decided that this doctor owed me after introducing me into the environment in which I was now being terrorized. Dr. Fields had aged through my childhood and adolescence but was still an attractive man. Now, he was confronted with a young adult who presented to him an asymmetrical personality, one he had never before witnessed in his faithful patient. He was a kind doctor, but, unfortunately, he was not a psychiatrist and so was unaccustomed to fine-tuning assortments of antidepressive and antipsychotic medications. Likewise, he was unskilled in administering the psychotherapy so crucial to my recovery.

My first hospitalization, five years later, revealed my next practitioner of mental health. This time, he was the army psychiatrist whom I met during my first hospital stay in the Post psychiatric hospital called Chambers. This doctor incorrectly assumed his superior rank of colonel qualified him as superior in healing the minds of his military inferiors. The rigidity of rank conflicted with the necessity for compassion, a conflict that could only prove painful to me.

Leaning back in his chair, with both military status and massive furniture dividing us, he asked me a few rote questions that I mechanically answered. His tall, trim form produced a punitive, officious tone that disciplined me in true military style for being silent and weak. Expecting kindness, I instead had been chastised for not understanding what I had certainly already discovered: Life was not easy. After I quietly absorbed this oppressive session, I left the office angry and terrified. Indeed, the man I had just spoken with had the power to determine how long I stayed in the hospital and what treatment I received.

Strangely enough, unusually good fortune is my best explanation for my first breakdown and hospitalization occurring while in the military. Ahead of me was necessary costly care provided by mental health specialists in and out of veterans' hospitals. However, the VA covered this cost since my mental illness experienced in the service was deemed "service-connected" soon after I left the military. This helped me to avoid an exceedingly dangerous homeless life on the streets. It took only a year out of the military for me to be designated as having a bona fide, 70 percent, service-connected disability. This decision was based on the premise that the military had significantly enhanced a serious mental illness while introducing me into some highly traumatic training and work environments, culminated by a stay in a military mental hospital. Ahead of me was necessary care provided by mental health specialists in and out of veterans' hospitals and without cost, enabling me to avoid impossibly expensive private psychiatric care and often painfully inferior state hospitals. I was also, soon after my first try at college outside of the military, provided with an on-the-job training program and modest monthly stipend, which saved me from the disgraceful and dangerous homeless life on the streets.

My madness was first given a name by a doctor in a VA hospital who felt it important to immediately provide a specific diagnosis. He was a resident doctor, in the process of completing the four years of medicine that would enable him to progress to private practice. This fresh, slim, new resident had begun to master a different technique: Instead of being cruel, he was indifferent. I am still not certain whether his cruelty or his indifference left me in greater pain. This young resident flashed in and out of my life. In a matter of seconds he swished me into a private office and gave me my diagnosis:

"You are schizophrenic."

"Schizophrenic" echoed through my brain like a final judgment. It was stated quickly, with a poker face and a voice void of emotion. I was then hurried out of the young doctor's office, and he left forever. He was tall, and imposing, and professional. He had no idea how this misdiagnosis would terrorize my life for the next four years until the less severe diagnoses of manic depression (bipolar disorder) was made. Later, schizoaffective disorder was determined. Whatever diagnoses the future held, none would terrify me more than schizophrenia.

Another psychiatrist who treated me in my early years of psychosis was a Dr. Cline, who had both her medical degree and her law degree. On the rotund side with a convenient short haircut, she presented a nonthreatening appearance. There were diplomas hanging all over her spacious office. Dr. Cline exuded a gentle empathy coupled with a clinical preciseness, and had a gift for prescribing the best combination of medications. She managed to reduce the amount of pills I took as much as was possible. This resulted in substantial relief since uncomfortable to painful side effects were consequently reduced. Sessions with her convinced me she cared. They usually began with a question wherein she simply asked what would almost always be a complicated question:

"How are you doing?"

My various specific responses escape my memory, but they must have usually involved the latest description of symptoms of depression or mania; or sometimes accounts of hallucinations and indications of delusions. Though I also do not recall her specific words, I remember the doctor typically providing her own brand of psychotherapy (often involving questions about my childhood), and sometimes making a necessary change in my medications.

"This prescription will help to relieve your depression (or agitation, or anxiety, or paranoia, or whatever my current symptom(s) might involve)," reassuring words that did not always prove to be true.

Should the treated pain remain, the doctor would try something else. As a Veterans Administration outpatient physician she would occasionally send me to a VA hospital for treatment after deciding that my psychotic suffering had gone too far. Each time she gently managed to convince me with carefully selected simple words that my reality was dangerously distorted and that I needed the hospital to recover.

"You need to be hospitalized for a little while, Two. Can you be ready to have us fly you to a VA hospital by tomorrow?" (At that time there was no local VA hospital.)

Hospitalization was not especially difficult for me to accept under these circumstances. Despite my false sense of reality (which included an abundance of denial), I trusted this doctor and perceived she was genuinely concerned about my health and probably right about the necessary treatment/hospitalization. She shared with a select few an honored place in the prestigious *Who's Who*, well deserved since not many VA outpatient doctors did as much good for me.

Dr. Cline eventually retired. It took about ten more years for the VA to provide me with another good psychiatrist. In the meantime, I endured grossly inferior care. Other outpatient doctors were notorious for rushing me through treatment, offering a few phrases for therapy and just managing to fit in a prescription for some medication. It seemed to be their goal to process as many patients as possible in a given period of time. They would crowd their days with treating people who were desperate for words of encouragement and hope, however, usually too sick to make any demands. So their patients were content to have their complaints appeased with a few words and a few pills.

Hippocrates, the father of medicine, felt effective medicine was too complex for the patient to understand. The medical world has come a long way. In the 1970s, a quality doctor/patient relationship was beginning to involve patients having more of a voice in their treatment. Psychiatric care was becoming more patient-centered. Today, guidelines for good, patient-centered psychiatry involve:

- Mutual respect and trust
- Patients feeling they are being listened to
- Patients needing to prepare a list of issues, which they can bring along to every appointment (including a daily health log)
- Doctor and patient agreeing to a course of treatment
- Doctor and patient being aware of the patient's legal rights
- Patients being aware of what the doctor is putting in their medical records
- Patients taking the responsibility to comply with treatment

During my many years of being a patient, I have identified (with the help of the National Alliance of the Mentally Ill) three basic skills that a good psychiatrist must possess: 1) interpersonal communication skills (involving solving personality issues that may occur between the doctor and the patient); 2) technical skills (involving the ability to correctly diagnose and treat the patient); and 3) supportive skills (involving the ability to instill trust and hope in the patient). Interpersonal communication is the skill identified by patients as most important. Eighty percent of all malpractice lawsuits are filed due to patient complaints concerning communication failures (not medications given). Patients are typically more compliant (take medication properly, eat right, exercise, attend appointments, etc.) when there is quality, interpersonal communication from their doctor.

A patient's reasonable expectations of the quality of psychiatric care involve that patient asking important questions early in therapy. These questions include the following:

- What is my diagnosis and the nature of my illness?

- What has caused my illness?
- Are there any tests or exams you would recommend?
- Would you recommend an independent opinion from another psychiatrist?
- What treatment do you think would be the most effective?
- What medication(s) might you be suggesting?
- How do you monitor medications, and what symptoms indicate the medications should be altered?
- What are the side effects of the medications you propose?
- What do you propose will be my length of treatment?
- What will happen if I stop taking my medications?
- Can I get pregnant safely during treatment?
- Are there any over-the-counter medications I can take?
- Are any other medications I am presently taking all right?
- Are there any new recommendations for treatment that apply to me?
- Will my treatment program involve services from other specialists (neurologists, psychologists, social workers, etc.)?
- What are the risks and benefits of your treatment?
- How will I know I am responding to treatment, and how soon will I know this?
- How do I contact a doctor in a crisis?
- What happens if I miss an appointment?
- Who do I want the doctor to communicate with concerning my disability (family, friends, etc.)?
- How can my family be involved in my treatment program?
- How much will my treatment cost?
- How much expense will my insurance cover?

Crucial questions such as these can prove to be vital to the patient experiencing maximum recovery. If the patient does not include them in the therapeutic process, inferior treatment can result. However, they are often difficult for the patient to ask since the mentally ill often carry with them nonresistant personalities and the tendency toward gullible over-compliance. Assertiveness training from a mental health practitioner can prove crucial to helping the patient secure his or her rights in and out of the hospital.

I became jaded by the long line of VA doctors who treated me so callously. The following dialogue is typical of the "care" from these doctors:

"How are you doing?" the doctor would begin, with head buried in my medical file. (Vital eye contact was often absent.)

A typical, desperate response might be, "I'm terribly agitated and depressed. I just don't know what to do."

Without much more questioning, the doctor would normally reply, "I'm going to change your medication,"(with no mention of side effects).

Desperately needing some kind of comfort and guidance, I might say, "My supervisor and I had an argument. I don't know how long I will have this job."

As if I were talking to a lifeless corpse, the doctor would reply, "Try this new medication for a while and see how it works. Come back to see me in a month."

It was not unusual for me to leave the offices of such doctors more distressed than when I entered.

One noteworthy exception to this norm of VA incompetence was a female outpatient doctor who was hired to run the outpatient mental health clinic I frequented. Dr. Harding held the title of Chief of Mental Health. Her small, sturdy frame housed a large heart. After years of poor psychiatric treatment, it was also no wonder I initially asked this new head psychiatrist a collection of questions concerning her qualifications, which she patiently answered. She did not seem to mind my interrogation.

Despite a tendency toward absentmindedness, Dr. Harding appeared to use exceptionally good judgment in treating her patients and her staff. Kind diplomacy highlighted her management style. However, she displayed an assertiveness that kept incompetence out of her clinic. In a short time, Dr. Harding staffed her professional territory with a collection of excellent mental health specialists.

Genuine, personal concern was clearly communicated by Dr. Harding. She even bothered to carefully check my medical history before initially treating me. This approach was a relief from the myriad of doctors who had always first taken about an hour collecting relevant medical information from me about my life. This always seemed to make little sense to me. What carried more credibility: the written records of previous doctors or the ramblings of a psychotic?

I soon became deeply impressed by Dr. Harding's skills. She was nearly always right about what words or medications would work best. I can so clearly see her now, typically leaning forward, focusing intensely into my eyes with her "tell me everything" look. She astutely listened as I completed describing all my symptoms. This alone made her exceptional. Too many of my other doctors had hardly taken their eyes from their notes as I sat emotionally purging myself before them. Dr. Harding absorbed every word I labored to pronounce, and persuaded me that my words mattered. Furthermore, I was relieved to talk with someone so exceptional at convincing me she liked me.

The ultimate gesture of true concern occurred when Dr. Harding gave me her home and cellular phone numbers, and made sure I knew how to contact her personally when she was out of town. This was unheard of among psychiatrists, in or out of the VA. I learned I was not an exceptional recipient of this generous display of kindness. Some other patients also benefited in this way from her extravagant treatment. Soon, overwhelmed with patients, Dr. Harding found it prudent to refer me to another doctor in the clinic.

Dr. Miles was brilliant. Besides having taught at a prestigious medical school, he had been employed by a nearby state's VA hospital for ten years. His knowledge of medication was remarkable. He was clinical but not cold. He knew the best questions to ask to obtain an effective idea of what kind of care I needed.

Initially, I felt a great degree of confidence in his expertise. He was cautious in making medication changes. However, I had always been ultra-sensitive to medication and required extra attention. Therefore, this doctor found it necessary to make more medication changes than he found comfortable. My helpless resistance to some sort of significant improvement added to an increase in this doctor's patient load. He was, fundamentally, an excellent doctor. Therefore and understandably these circumstances created in him an angry frustration. His manner and tone became abrasive and distressing. My confidence in his ability to treat me then began to diminish. I was finally allowed to change back to Dr. Harding.

Unfortunately, like Dr. Miles, too many VA doctors suffer from an overload of patients. The result is overwhelming and creates inferior treatment. However, regular work hours (eight-hour days and weekends off), no danger of liability over poor medical decisions (without the necessary malpractice insurance), ample job security (without the constant threat of losing patients), generous retirement packages, and medical coverage attract many good doctors to the VA. Unfortunately, it seems the good doctors who find the VA so initially appealing eventually become cynical as they treat their quota of hundreds of veterans, especially those who fake disabilities so that they might acquire increased disability ratings. The greater the professed disability, the greater the monthly disability payments—and, too often, the greater the lies. Many an earnest VA doctor inevitably becomes cynical over working with counterfeit illness.

I once asked a new psychiatrist how she liked working at the VA. She was surprisingly candid with me.

"There is the good and the bad," she confided. "The good is that I am able to treat a variety of mental illnesses, which makes things interesting. The bad is probably about 50 percent of my patients are faking it to increase their disability ratings."

It was only two weeks later that this doctor transferred out of the VA and into a nearby children's clinic.

Therefore, with so often an overload of fraudulent patients, VA doctors find it difficult to maintain the caring attitude needed to sustain quality medical care. As a result, too many veterans receive poor medical treatment. For me (with too few exceptions) this has meant during the 33 years since my first diagnosis much too much of an abundance of ineffective VA inpatient and outpatient care.

After residing in a few VA hospitals, I noticed that the doctors in the psychiatric units practiced their own brand of medical care. Four out of the five military hospitals I was placed in were all learning hospitals connected to nearby medical schools. My practitioners often presented themselves in teams of threes. Each team was comprised of an intern (one year out of medical school), a resident (a second-year graduate of medical school), and a senior physician (a highly qualified psychiatrist).

The intern, not yet a full-fledged doctor, was often assigned the tedious job of interviewing me to obtain my medical history soon after I was admitted. This wearisome procedure took one to two hours, a fatiguing interaction that usually took place in the privacy of my hospital room. I am not sure who found it more difficult to endure, the intern or myself. I was often not sufficiently lucid to recall the current president's name, much less remember when I first suffered psychotic symptoms. I never quite understood why the doctor in charge did not just refer to my medical records. Certainly, they would more precisely reveal my years of mental illness than questioning me at a time I was being hospitalized for severe psychosis.

Since around 1994, a new computer system has allowed medical records to be transferred in a timely manner from VA hospital to VA hospital.

The resident was the main doctor to whom I had access, though I soon discovered this access was painfully limited. This person could be officially referred to as "doctor" since he/she had finished the required four years of medical school. The resident was finishing out the necessary four years of residency to continue on and become a full-fledged, board-approved psychiatrist. This was the doctor who had the most influence on my recovery. Nearly all patient/doctor communication transpired with the resident, and it was the resident who was responsible for nearly all medication adjustments.

The senior physician (in charge of the unit) occasionally arrived to check the status of my recovery. This doctor was usually older, had completed a full residency, and had practiced psychiatry the longest (often including some time in private practice). The senior doctor usually had final say-so over my treatment and, ultimately, my release from the hospital. Unfortunately, these doctors were seldom around to talk to. They usually preferred relying on the nursing staff, intern, and resident to make me relatively well and to inform them when that happened. When the senior physician did appear, the visit was usually so brief and impersonal that it was frightening.

Confining themselves inside offices, concealing themselves from the lines of patients who waited in the halls outside, my assigned resident doctors nearly always made themselves as scarce as possible. They were continually hurrying, mysteriously slouching with heads down while rushing down hallways, seeming to want desperately to avoid patients' questions and complaints. The only precious time available for their attention was the daily few minutes they talked to me in their offices or visited me in my room.

My tormented inner-self frequently asked the simple but obvious question, "Do these doctors really care about healing my mind?" I was not sure whether they were just too busy with paperwork or whether they merely became overwhelmed with the pain that surrounded them, as patients desperately pressed forward for some treatment that would bring them comfort.

After several VA hospitalizations, I became aware that the best way to communicate with my specific resident doctor was to carefully write down my daily symptoms and hand them over as soon as this doctor entered the ward each morning. It was crucial to stop my doctor before he or she could speed by and plant him- or herself behind a closed office door and a desk piled high with patients' charts. Soon after initially entering the hospital, I would carefully stand by the front door early in the day to identify the best moments available for catching and giving my resident doctor my necessary information. When I discovered that time, I was by the front door when the doctor arrived each morning.

My scribbled notes were probably only briefly scanned. However, I am convinced they provided a valuable source of information in addition to the brief daily moments the doctor allowed us to spend together. Any communication I could manage was crucial to the doctor in determining what medication changes were necessary. Such changes were critical to me since they established the level of pain I would need to endure for the next 24 hours.

The three private non-VA hospitals where I received treatment varied in their quality of physician care. They were made available while I was in transit to some convenient VA hospital that, at the time, had no beds available. It seemed that when the psychiatric ward was part of a general hospital, the doctors again appeared to be hidden away. When the ward was part of a psychiatric hospital, the doctors were more visible. I was then usually assigned just one full-fledged psychiatrist who typically also ran a private practice. This category of doctor more often listened carefully to what I had to say, expressing substantial respect and concern for my welfare.

The non-VA doctor would typically start with the textbook, introductory question. (I choose to make this hypothetical psychiatrist male, though the gender is only hypothetical.)

"What is going on with you today?"

My reply was often a report of the effectiveness of the medication he had prescribed for me.

"The medication has reduced the fear, but I am still really depressed." Other details were often included.

Our interaction would then begin to become more specific.

The doctor might ask, "Is the depression any less than when you were admitted?"

Sensing the doctor's genuine concern and the relevance of his question, I would usually find it easy to offer an answer that made the most sense to me. "I don't know. It is hard to figure that one out."

Another appropriate question from the doctor would follow. "How about your roommate (in the hospital)? Are you getting along better?"

The doctor had actually read my medical chart and was aware of issues regarding my individual progress, more specifically, that I was having trouble with my hospital roommate—a byproduct of my current breakdown.

I might answer, "Well, she talks less lately, and that makes it better for me."

Then, displaying both sensitivity and compassion, the doctor might say, "I know trying out these new medications is tough, but if you can just hold out a couple of weeks I think the depression has a good chance of going away."

My sincere desire to exit the hospital was typically revealed in closing remarks that would include, "What can I do but try? If there is any chance of relief, it is worth a try."

Sensitive to my pain, and painfully aware of his own limitations, the doctor might end the session with, perhaps, the most comforting words that could be offered. "You are going through a tough time right now, but, believe me, there is light at the end of the tunnel. You will get better."

This, though cliché, encouragement provided a profound boost to my morale. Oh, the gift of hope. It was usually at this point that the doctor had reached the limit of his immediate effectiveness. I had valued his candidness and concern and had found it easy to willingly answer his questions. I most often left this doctor's office, gratefully more sane than when I entered.

Typical of most psychiatric patients, I soon learned how to screen out the bad doctors. I desperately sought out doctors who displayed kindness, encouragement, and a talent for listening. These were doctors I could trust with my fragile psyche and, as a result, I responded better to their treatment. The crucial trust was not always there. There were doctors whose egos were too frail (or, perhaps, too large) to allow them to listen to suggestions from their patients who were familiar with what medications worked well for them in the past. These doctors hesitated to communicate with other doctors and discuss other possible treatment options. They understandably prompted me to occasionally take my own initiative to solicit help from additional doctors, and so acquire a second opinion. Selecting the proper medication is both a skill and an art, and more than one opinion is sometimes advisable with such a complicated science as psychiatry. Fortunately, opinions were sometimes sought outside the VA system when the resources for special testing or a second opinion were not available.

Increasing mental pain chased and repeatedly captured me as I progressed through life. I became more and more desperate for psychiatrists who were gentle with my heart and attentive enough to listen to and hear my symptoms so that the best medication could be prescribed and the best psychotherapy provided. When such doctors were available, I was grateful. They seemed to appreciate my genuine, open-minded ability to listen and benefit from carefully thought-out treatment. Fortunately, I was able to now and then obtain access to this sort of doctor. Unfortunately, these healers were rare caretakers of the mind.

Chapter 7
PILLS AND POSSIBILITIES –
WITH PAIN ON THE SIDE

A n ongoing assortment of medications would grace my plate, prescribed by whatever doctor who happened to be providing treatment. These pills were meant to reduce the original symptoms. However, they could not cure the disease. As the Food and Drug Administration (FDA) now stands, there is no drug that can cure serious mental illness. There are only drugs available that can sometimes treat the symptoms and hopefully make the patient's days somewhat more comfortable.

However, this benefit should not be dismissed as irrelevant. A significant measure of recovery does occur primarily from the successful use of medications and verbal therapy. The treatment success rate (that is, treatment where the patient's symptoms have been reduced or even temporarily eliminated) for schizophrenia is 60 percent, for bipolar disorder is 80 percent, and for major depression is 65 percent. Heart disease has a treatment success rate that only ranges from 41 percent to 52 percent. A study of all medicated psychiatric patients concluded that about 75 percent can be effectively treated with medication, 20 percent show little or no improvement, and 5 percent actually become worse. It is inappropriate to dismiss the effectiveness of medication. The mentally ill we usually see on the streets who are not being medicated are powerful examples of what happens when a psychotic person is left without medication.

Unfortunately, overall, only one out of five persons afflicted by mental illnesses seeks treatment. The majority of the population of mentally ill persons is reluctant to take medication. About half of these individuals deny they are sick and may refuse any treatment. This denial is characterized by a daring struggle to maintain self-esteem. Tragically, refusing or discontinuing medication most often results in the disastrous symptoms continuing or returning.

Psychiatric drugs come in four categories: 1) antipsychotics, especially for those who suffer from hallucinations and delusions (most often schizophrenics and schizoaffectives); 2) antidepressants, mainly used to treat serious depression; 3) mood stabilizers, primarily used to reduce mood swings involving mania and depression (most often for those with bipolar disorder/manic depression); and 4) antianxiety drugs, mainly used to reduce the anxiety that can occur with a wide assortment of mental illnesses.

Psychiatrists are often uncertain regarding which symptoms represent which illness and, therefore, which medication is most appropriate. As indicated previously, in all fairness this has most frequently been due to the ambiguities of their main diagnostic manual (*The Diagnostic and Statistical Manual of Mental Disorders*—the *DSM*). Of the four *DSMs* published over the years (beginning in 1952), each has been larger and more detailed than the previous manual. The most comprehensive *DSM-4*, published in 2004, is twice as large as its predecessor and presents the most accurate guide available for psychiatric diagnosis.

The world of psychiatric medicine looks ahead to soon-to-come diagnostic tools that involve descriptions of structural brain changes associated with those with severe mental illness. Instead of the too often lengthy guessing game now required to determine which medications will best benefit the mentally ill, a sophisticated understanding of the function and chemistry of the brain will enable medical experts to define each individual's specific diagnosis and most effective treatment. Also, by identifying specific genes associated with specific mental illnesses, useful gene therapy can be administered to treat the mentally ill.

Currently, atypical or novel antipsychotic drugs are leading the field in treating psychosis (schizophrenia, schizoaffective disorder, and some bipolar disorders). The newer, atypical antipsychotics mainly utilized are clozapine (i.e., commercial title Clozaril), risperidone (Risperdal), quetiapine (Seroquel), and olanzapine (Zyprexa). The "extra-pyramidal side effects" (EPS) on the whole, but not always together, being slowed movement, restless limbs, and nonreversible distorted facial expression—appear much less frequently than in standard antipsychotic medications. Unfortunately they can cost up to ten times more than some of the older antipsychotics, and their long-term effectiveness remains questionable.

A psychiatric drug was first administered to me during my second hospitalization (atypical psychiatric medication was not available at that time). I was in the midst of a serious psychotic breakdown and, upon entering the hospital, the first thing I remember seeing was a nurse holding up a hypodermic needle. Assuming the contents were for me, I asked what the needle contained. I was given the official name (probably Thorazine). Since that meant nothing to me, I asked what the drug would do to me. I was given no answer. It is impossible to express the fear I felt, being injected with a medication I knew nothing about.

The next thing I recall was awakening, restrained to my bed, with a bandage around my head. I was told I had suffered a seizure (most likely a side effect of the medication I had been given) and had damaged my head before I could be tied down. The restraints were for my protection, to keep me from banging around any further. I had been given no choice about taking or not taking the medication and had suffered for my helplessness and cooperation. From that time on, each time I initially took a new medication, I could not be certain it would work on my individual symptoms. I could be most often sure of something else: some agonizing side effects.

Once out of the hospital, I found a pharmaceutical guide with current information, which became an immensely useful purchase. It gave me descriptions of various medications, including their potential side effects. Since I could not depend on the doctors to inform me of these crucial facts, I relied on my own published resource to keep me aware of the good and bad of each medication. A pharmaceutical guide was also helpful in enlightening me about new, potentially superior medications to suggest to the doctor (with hope that the doctor was open-minded). Whatever information this book lacked was provided by a quick phone call to a local pharmacist.

The education required to practice psychiatry is extensive. My various psychiatrists went to school for years to learn how to dispense pills. The good doctors listened, with open minds, to whatever feedback and suggestions I provided. The trick was not only to find the medications that best diminished or eliminated the serious symptoms of the mental illness, but to also dispense as few medications as was necessary to handle my pain. The rationale was very simple: the fewer pills I took, the fewer side effects I likely suffered.

When hospitalization was required and some painful side effects occurred with a medication, I was provided with another medication or a new combination of medications. Occasionally, I was informed no better choice was available. I could refuse any medication. However, this would give the doctor the option to discharge me from the hospital and its vital treatment. Or, if I presented a danger to myself or others, the doctor could hold me over for usually around 72 hours until a court would decide if I should be hospitalized and medicated against my will.

The bottom line held a clearly distressing message: If a certain medication with painful side effects was my best choice, I could either 1) not take the medication and, therefore, suffer the original symptoms of my mental illness or 2) take the prescribed medication and benefit from its advantages but suffer whatever painful side effects occurred. My original symptoms frequently involved hearing voices, seeing what was not there, or falling into bottomless depression; alternatives that left me incapacitated and unknowingly in danger to others and/or myself (not even able to necessarily cross the street safely). Therefore, my only real choice was to try whatever antipsychotic(s) was prescribed and endure grievous side effects each time I took my medication.

Anguish resulting from severe muscle spasms in my neck and upper back were my most distressing side effect. The sources of this pain were any antipsychotic medications from the family of phenothiazines (frequently used for schizophrenia). The higher the dosage of this medication, the more agony from my muscle spasms. During a breakdown and subsequent hospitalization, some phenothiazine was added or increased to eliminate my hallucinations and/or delusions—until the pain was unbearable.

Once out of the hospital, I usually benefited from a gradual reduction in antipsychotic medications to a somewhat more tolerable level, which reduced the muscle spasms. I could only hope that my complex body chemistry would choose to significantly delay cycling me into another breakdown and, again, delay requiring the heavy medication of the hospital. The misery of each medication's side effects varied with the amount of medication dispensed. Some side effects typically remained constant companions in substantially varying degrees in or out of the hospital, especially the muscle spasms.

I endured a pharmaceutical obstacle course as my various doctors pursued which specific pills would work the best. I tripped over hurdles of guesses as these doctors speculated. The search for the most useful combination of medications often required that I sample a battery of pills that made me hurt inside and out but still often kept me outside of the hospital. A good doctor would ask me detailed questions about what I was thinking or feeling and would prescribe medications that research had found reduced my specific painful thoughts and feelings. Studies showed that some medications reduced fear, some reduced anxiety, some reduced depression—and so on. Unfortunately, because my biochemistry was unique from any other, my reaction to each medication I was given was also unique. A pill may have reduced fear in one patient but only caused certain painful side effects for me. Even more unfortunate was whatever medication initially enabled me to exit the hospital would, most often, eventually stop working at a prescribed lower dosage. Then, my symptoms would escalate to such a degree that hospitalization and higher amounts of drugs were again necessary.

With more drugs, new side effects occurred, often so debilitating they created their own set of symptoms. This would then often impair me more than the original psychiatric disorder. Side effects could range from drastic hand tremors to crippling headaches to terrible nausea to slurred speech to memory loss to distressing weight gain to mental confusion to skin rash to seizures to muscle weakness to muscle spasms to blurred vision to thyroid problems to fatigue to constipation to disorientation to temporary hair loss to dry skin to seizures to general body pain to reduced libido (even impotence) to incontinence—ad infinitum.

The most serious side effect resulting from taking certain antipsychotic drugs is tardive dyskinesia. About 15 to 20 percent who have taken antipsychotic drugs for several years develop tardive dyskinesia (presently, about 300,000 people). Symptoms include involuntary blinking, lip-licking, tongue-twitching, or other grotesque facial distortions. Patients who suffer from this side effect become socially crippled. Worst of all, these symptoms are most often irreversible. Newer antipsychotic medications that carry significantly less risk of tardive dyskinesia present a major breakthrough in psychiatric medicine.

The seriously mentally ill typically reject the thought of having to take medication(s) each day. The term for this disagreeable posture is noncompliance. About half of all medicated schizophrenics recovering from a relapse stop medication within one year. The major cause of noncompliance in schizophrenia (as well as with other serious mental illnesses) is probably denial of the illness. Mental illness is immeasurably stigmatizing, and daily medications are regular reminders of being ill. Also, close to intolerable painful side effects frequently lead to noncompliance. Patients feel terribly limited with the side effects that often leave them sedated and mentally sluggish. They complain about not being able to perform as well at work or even simple tasks at home. It may take several involuntary hospitalizations for them to become convinced that it is preferable to accept the limiting side effects rather than to endure what they feel when they refuse medications, become psychotic, and suffer frequent hospitalizations.

For me, side effects often made it impossible to progress toward goals that were important, such as returning to work or to school. A medication may have reduced or even eliminated debilitating depression. However, side effects such as hand tremors (which often made it impossible to take class notes or write a check) or impaired memory and concentration (even worse than without the medication) often made it more difficult to read and study. When I reported that a medication created side effects that were unacceptable, the doctor would usually try another medication, hoping a better alternative could be found. If any medication I was taking was from the family of benzodiazepines, it was extremely difficult to discontinue since these medications are physically addictive. Withdrawal can include anxiety, shakiness, headache, dizziness, sleeplessness, loss of appetite, and even, less often, seizures and psychosis. (Some psychiatrists refuse to prescribe benzodiazepines on a long-term or even short-term basis, though they can be extremely effective at reducing agitation and mania.)

Many doctors I tried had their favorite kinds of pills. Often, rather than go through a thorough interview or even look in my medical file and read what had worked for me in the past, doctors would try their preferred collection of possibilities. If I did not respond well, then they would often respond as if I were consciously doing something to prevent their dream pills from working.

Likewise (in some areas of the US) healthcare systems routinely disallow access to less preferred, newer, more effective antipsychotic medications; until patients initially try and fail to respond successfully to systems less expensive and less effective from older-generation, generic drugs. This risks the delay of patient stabilization and too often creates greater side effects.

When schizophrenia became my first diagnosis (the result of my suffering psychotic symptoms such as hallucinations and delusions), there were only a small handful of antipsychotic drugs available to treat my symptoms. When I was 28 (and ten years into my disability), lithium carbonate (a mood stabilizer) was added to my plate of pills. Unfortunately, to some patients, lithium brought no relief at all. For me, like with 35 to 40 percent who try it, lithium reduced my painful mood swings. (Eventually, other mood stabilizers were approved by the FDA, prescribed to those who did not significantly benefit from lithium; primarily valporic acid (Depakote) and carbamazepine (Tegretol). With lithium, the change in my comfort level was somewhat dramatic. The following was my effort to write down some of my observations and emotions surrounding my newly stabilized moods:

> During the past week, I found relationships more harmonious than ever. I still have weak moments of aggression or lazy moments of non-assertion, but life is advancing in a more rewarding manner than before my past breakdowns. I'm finding it easier to express affection to others and, in fact, I am increasing my capacity for love. Of all the benefits, this is the greatest. And, because it is the greatest benefit, my future fulfillment will best be realized by my continuing to practice and perfect the actions that reveal my love to others.

To my great disappointment, while just taking lithium, I continued to have psychotic breakdowns. This was not unusual since lithium is not an antipsychotic drug. It is a medication that is meant to level off the emotional highs and lows of mood disorders, not stop the escalation of full-blown psychoses that involve the invasion of hallucinations and delusions. Lithium made life less of an endurance test. However, the periodic hallucinations and delusions that persisted, along with a residual depression, landed me in the hospital at least once a year. It was then when I needed an increase in antipsychotics to reduce the psychotic symptoms that remained after the depression and mania were diminished.

Lithium's benefits, however, should not be minimized. It was after two days of lithium that my mood swings were noticeably reduced, and I felt a certain measure of relief I had not felt in years. I remember going to a movie and actually enjoying the event. The quarterly blood tests to check my lithium level were a minor inconvenience, and I soon became accustomed to the needle.

Another ten years went by after I was introduced to lithium; and an abundance of new medications were approved for use in

America, most of them antidepressants. Primarily unfortunate was that the multitude of these drugs could sustain rapid cycling, a terrible, frequent occurrence of mania followed by depression that cycles at least four times in one year. Or, mixed states would occur where the "rapid-cycling" effect would occur in as little as 24 hours. Here the individual's psyche could even experience mania and depression at the same time, causing the person to be hyperactive and angry while also feeling incredibly sad—a terribly painful state. Both these crises states became familiar to me. Rapid cycling put me on an emotional roller coaster, while mixed states created a desperate propensity to feel torn in two.

Finding the right doctor to treat my distinctive symptoms sometimes took months; with some symptoms, even years. My desperate quest required that I discover a doctor able to not only identify medications that worked on my grievous symptoms, but to find those that had side effects I could tolerate. Though new, more effective medications were constantly being discovered, many psychiatrists did not adequately stay current with the new research. As a result, there were often better medications available while my particular available doctor was often unaware of their existence.

Psychiatrists like to call their personalized combination of medications a "soup." This consists of each patient's most appetizing, individualized combination of medications. For patients such as myself, the soup customarily consisted of an antipsychotic or two (which too often caused the painful muscle spasms I found it necessary to live with); possibly a dash of antidepressant (not so much that rapid cycling occurred but enough to reasonably reduce the depression); and a pinch of mood stabilizer (lithium or another mood stabilizer).

My carefully mixed soup of medications helped. However, I was constantly in and out of the hospital. The medications would work for a limited time; then I would suffer a break (breakdown). I knew the danger signals preceding a break and tried to identify them to obtain a medication change before hospitalization was necessary. However, along with whatever doctor I was seeing, I usually just couldn't get it quite right. The nature of psychosis is that it sneaks up on you, making it nearly impossible to catch before it becomes so bad that life becomes unmanageable.

Trial and error, trial and error, trial and error was the typical routine until the best drug or combination of drugs was found. The trial-and-error path to recovery may not be easy, but it is the only alternative with modern psychiatric medicine—and frequently a successful one. And so it was that I was often put up against a series of mental, emotional, and physical barricades, until the chemical answers were found that significantly reduced the enormous hurt created by whatever diagnosis was presented.

My prized antipsychotic medication was introduced to me after everything else failed my seemingly hopeless biochemistry. It was clozapine (Clozaril). Though it required weekly blood tests to make sure my white blood count stayed normal (a diminished white blood count was a possible though unlikely side effect), this medication brought me out of my main brain pain. My mood swings nearly disappeared (with only a small amount of antidepressant necessary to comfortably reduce the depression); and I completely escaped hallucinations and delusions.

After taking Clozaril for about five years, I was able to nearly consistently escape the confinement of the hospital. The two exceptions were brief hospital stays to lift me out of heavy (what had become cyclic) depressions. My doctor had since refined her ability to accommodate my delicate biochemistry and effectively alter my medication when depression occurred, primarily involving a temporary increase in my antidepressant, Effexor (venlafaxine). And, so I was better able to avoid hospitalization. The only distressing side effects I suffered were sedation (I found it harder to get up in the morning and sometimes slept 11 hours or more); I tolerated mildly troublesome muscle spasms when I exercised; and I had become a bed wetter (demeaning incontinence that I found it necessary to accept each night).

Clozaril presented a main disappointment for me: It produced very little improvement in my cognitive skills (thinking ability). I had not responded as well as many other patients when it came to this potential improvement. I was still absentminded and extremely forgetful. I neglected to remember characters and plots of movies or TV shows the day after I viewed them. Often, it was impossible for me to follow the story lines as I watched the screen. I did enjoy movies when I understood where the plot was going. This sometimes required the occasional whisperings of a patient friend to catch me up on what was happening.

Reading was also still difficult. I found it nearly impossible to digest a book for any major amount of time since my concentration was seriously impaired. The newspaper presented itself as one great gray mass of copy, succeeding in eluding me whenever I tried to digest its information.

These are all typical symptoms and/or side effects experienced by patients who suffer serious psychosis. I feel blessed that I can still sit down and write, though it is on a limited basis each day. This is the one skill that has seemed to remain in my limited repertoire of abilities. Social interaction has remained a major chore with Clozaril. I often have such a difficult time concentrating on what people say to me that I fake it by pretending I know just what they are talking about and hazard what is occasionally a meaningless answer. I sometimes chance asking others to please repeat themselves; an option I most often avoid because often asking others to repeat what they say just causes more misunderstanding and embarrassment.

Still a miracle medication for me, Clozaril has made my life easier to endure, despite its limitations. Originally used almost exclusively for schizophrenics and schizoaffectives, it has shown to also be useful for reducing bipolar (manic-depressive) symptoms. For me, it took away about 80 percent of the suffering I had never been able to grow accustomed to. Though it did not give me back the mental agility I took for granted all the years prior to my late teens, and failed to eliminate the four or more episodes of depression I suffered through many years, I cannot ignore how my quality of life has been magically enhanced because of the 275 milligrams of Clozaril I have begun to take each day.

When ziprasidone (Geodon) came along, a limited, local test showed this extremely new antipsychotic proved to be immensely successful. Those schizophrenics and schizoaffectives tested were able to avoid relapses during the five-year study. Some were able to go back to work part-time or full-time. The average cognitive (thinking) ability increased 30 percent. Plus, there were not as many weight gain problems to deal with as was the case with Clozaril.

I was impressed and pleaded with my doctor to put me on this new wonder drug. She finally conceded.

The results were disastrous. The only positive thing that happened was I lost 18 pounds. However, I found myself physically and mentally miserable from considerable stress and chronic anger. I also found it difficult to get my required amount of sleep. I finally ended up in the hospital. After being discharged, I kept on trying Geodon for a few more weeks with no major change. Finally, I knew I needed to return to the comfort of Clozaril. I had wanted to be smarter, skinnier, and more productive. However, changing my medication had been too chancy and the results were too impossible to live with. I was soon back on Clozaril and a psychology I could endure.

With more medications available, the question, "Should I switch?" has been raised by doctors and patients alike. The wisest answer has been, "Don't switch if your present medication(s) is acceptably comfortable." That means that an ideal candidate for switching to one of the newer medications is one who is not doing well. "Well" can best be determined by both the doctor and the patient. One reason for switching has been that a medication(s) has stopped working. Another reason not to switch is if the patient is about to make a major change in life. Switching is a strategic issue. It can take two to three months for side effects to decrease to an acceptable level (assuming the medication works). The byword is caution. It is heartbreaking when a patient on a combination of medications that have kept him or her out of the hospital gets permission from the doctor to switch, and has a relapse requiring considerable hospitalization. It is not unusual for such a patient to fail to respond positively on his or her original medication(s) when he or she tries to go back to it. Therefore, it becomes necessary to start all over with a whole new medication or group of medications.

More money for research is urgent. However, society's commitment to the research of mental illness is low when the societal burden caused by these disorders is considered. Our knowledge of brain disorders is still far behind our knowledge of other health problems; though we have finally become convinced that genetic factors, biochemical imbalances, and brain abnormalities cause the bulk of mental illness. More research is needed for better methods of diagnosis so that better treatment can be administered. Immediately important is a detailed investigation of what easily accessible, affordable network of supportive community services are provided in the various states. Too many states spend the bulk of their funds targeted for the mentally ill on hospital care rather than preventative, outpatient, supportive services.

New and improved psychiatric medications (many with substantially fewer side effects) are introduced each year. While 25 years ago lithium was the only drug 75 percent of patients left hospitals with, today, only 25 percent leave the hospital with just lithium. The rest are discharged with a mix of medications (often involving antipsychotics, antidepressants, and other mood stabilizers), producing 70 to 80 percent who improve significantly. Using lithium with other drugs has shown to still be effective. In fact, it is sometimes the chosen pill at preventing suicide in bipolar disorder.

An abundant assortment of new antipsychotics were approved by the Federal Drug Administration (FDA) in the fairly recent past. In the 1990s, the new antipsychotics thankfully carry with them fewer side effects for many patients (especially a decrease in the onset of debilitating tardive dyskinesia). For many patients, positive results have been spectacular. Serious mental illness is slowed down or stopped by these medications for a significant number of patients. Some antipsychotic medications are not just keeping hallucinations and delusions under control, but are also introducing mood-stabilizing benefits. Doctors' goals have been to treat patients earlier and better and, in the process, reduce or even remove stigma. These goals are becoming realized more and more. Many patients have been able to return to daily household responsibilities and/or school and/or work. The next generation holds great promise for new, innovative drugs. The treatment of severe mental illnesses carries the potential of becoming increasingly as effective as the treatment of other complex medical disorders.

Research for better medication is a priority for me. It is no wonder I am so sold on being treated with chemicals—chemicals have saved my life. Around 10 percent of patients with schizophrenia and 15 percent with manic-depressive illness take their lives by completing suicide. I find it fairly easy to believe that without medication I would have already exited this earth in a premature, gruesome, self-inflicted manner.

However, medications were originally not so dream-come-true solutions for me. During the past 39 years I have experienced the effectiveness—and lack of effectiveness—of almost every available psychiatric medication as it came along.

My first antipsychotics were chlorpromazine (Thorazine) and trifluoperazine (Stelazine). This was during the mid-1970s when the physical pain of mental illness was not much addressed by medical health experts. As a result, though these medications took the hallucinations away (which was, indeed, a great relief), terribly painful muscle spasms in my neck and upper back (textbook side effects) kept me in constant suffering. Other major aching involved my legs, overall back, and even my body in general—an arthritic type of throbbing. These other pain types occurred usually as I was escalating toward breakdowns. The muscle spasms in my neck primarily occurred during my breakdowns themselves, and persisted as I awaited my recovery.

It was not until 1979 that I received my first pain reliever, a limited amount of ibuprofen (Motrin). Muscle relaxants were also dispensed. Both provided limited results. Discussion about the amount of physical pain I endured was only general with my care providers.

However, it was especially during the 1980s, when discomfort from physical pain was recognized as a typical side effect of the numerous antidepressants, that the problem of physical pain was first so strongly, appropriately addressed. Unfortunately, it usually took four to six weeks to discover if a certain antidepressant would be successful. After I tried all of them (and it seemed about eight) one last one finally worked: venlafaxine (Effexor). It was a long time to remain in pain.

In the 1990s, with new, atypical antipsychotic medications with significantly fewer side effects, patients suffered with considerably less pain than former and older-generation antipsychotic medications. As mentioned above, only Clozaril (but thankfully Clozaril) worked for me.

Today, many psychiatrists and clinicians include in their treatment questions that include, "On a scale of one to ten, how would you rate your level of pain, level ten being the greatest level?" If necessary, the patient is treated with large doses of acetaminophen (Tylenol) and ibuprofen (Motrin). Benzodiazepines in low doses (since they have potential for dependency) such as clonazepam (Klonopin) are also effective for muscle spasms and general nerve pain. With the physical pain wonderfully diminished, the mental anguish can be more successfully addressed, and the patient can lead a more functional and productive life.

So the research goes on. There have been many studies with DNA that have produced abundant evidence that serious mental illness is transmitted genetically in families. This research shows serious mental illnesses are "complex" genetic disorders very much like other major medical illnesses (heart disease, diabetes, and cancer). The possibilities exist of correcting the wiring of the brain by stimulating new neurons or new neuronal connections at a genetic level. There is ample evidence that viruses and bacterial agents can play major parts in causing serious mental illness to emerge, especially if a person is predisposed genetically to acquiring substantial psychiatric problems. The ultimate goal is to intervene before the illness develops, therefore making mental illness as preventable as polio.

Dramatic new discoveries have emerged where doctors will soon be able to identify even more than current parts of the brain that cause specific symptoms through brain imaging. With this valuable information, prescribing effective medications will become less of a guessing game. Doctors will be able to move from engaging in random drug trials on patients to identifying which predictors in the brain respond best to specific drugs.

Just a note concerning street drugs and alcohol. The combination of mental illness and substance abuse or dependence is called dual diagnosis. This combination often results in increased symptoms from whatever mental disorder is present. Research, especially a study involving 20,000 people, showed that having a psychiatric illness at least doubles the chance of developing a substance abuse disorder. More specifically, the research indicated that the lifetime prevalence of any substance abuse disorder in schizophrenics is 47 percent; in those with bipolar disorders it is 56.1 percent; and in those with major depression it is 27.2 percent. Those with mental illnesses reported that they engaged in substance abuse to improve unpleasant moods (anxiety and depression), to increase their comfort level around other people, and to increase the amount of general pleasure they feel.

Substance abuse is a problem with as many as 50 percent of persons having severe mental illnesses (in general), and is the most common co-occurring disorder among the mentally ill. People with a dual diagnosis experience other extremely negative consequences: homelessness, victimization, HIV infection, hospitalization, and incarceration. Those serious mentally ill who experience dual diagnosis and recover from substance abuse, also greatly improve their quality of life. They benefit from reduced noncompliance, reduced hospitalization, reduced homelessness, and increased positive socialization.

Despite current success with the use of medication to treat the seriously mentally ill, this selection of drugs is presently, sadly limited. The future holds hope for a better time. While we wait, serious mental illness is a problem encountered by those who continue to choose the best assortment of medication they can manage. While we wait, mental illness has also become a mental/emotional monster for friends and families. And, while we wait, it creates nationwide financial loss while, in the process, generating the devastation of so many promising lives.

Chapter 8
PRISONS AND ASYLUMS — CONFLICTING CONFINEMENT

The most utilized (and most dubious) criteria for hospitalization—that the potential patient must be a danger to him/herself or others—began to be employed in the mid-1950s when (in 1955) chlorpromazine (Thorazine), a new antipsychotic drug, emerged as the first effective medication for serious mental illness. Indeed, this drug did stop many patients from hallucinating and helped them to initially, once out of the hospital, live independently and safely. Hospitals that had just "warehoused" the mentally ill were now able to empty their psychiatric wards of all patients who responded to medication. Hence, the term deinstitutionalization became familiar in the psychiatric community.

By the 1970s, every state had elevated the standard for commitment from being ill and needing treatment to being dangerous to themselves or others. In the 1980s (from 1980 to 1988) the numbers of homeless persons increased 300 percent, while the total population increased only 7.6 percent. Approximately 75 percent of the homeless were mentally ill (including those with drug and alcohol problems), while 35 percent of the total population were mentally ill using this criteria.

In 1994, about 92 percent of those who would have been living in public psychiatric hospitals in 1955 were living somewhere else (a multitude on the streets or in prisons). A count of those treated and discharged showed 50 to 60 percent suffered from schizophrenia and 10 to 15 percent from manic depression. Where did these patients end up? In a 1983 study, 27 percent discharged from state mental hospitals became homeless within six months. In a 1995 study, 38 percent of those discharged had no known address within six months. Today, one-third of the nation's homeless persons (600,000 individuals) have a treatable, severe mental illness.

Besides dwelling on the streets, more than 10 percent of the 1.5 million individuals in jails have severe mental illness on any given day (250,000 people). There is evidence, especially among juveniles, that this number is growing. A person with a severe mental illness can more easily get arrested than get treatment. Almost one-third of all US jails incarcerate people with serious mental illnesses who have no charges against them, or carry on their records minor misdemeanors (trespassing, disorderly conduct, etc.). Some prisons provide some medical treatment to those in need. However, these mentally ill are basically waiting for available hospital beds via transportation to a mental hospital. Such incarcerations are done under state laws allowing emergency detentions of those suspected of suffering mental illness. The Los Angeles county jail is the largest psychiatric institution in the US. Over 3,000 seriously mentally ill (out of 21,000 inmates) require psychiatric services on a daily basis. More than 10 percent of all US inmates, 250,000 persons, suffer serious mental illness. Jail has become the last resort when there is no other place available for the mentally ill.

US jails confine the innocent, guilty of nothing more than suffering from a treatable disease. Contrary to public opinion, once they receive the appropriate medication, very few of the mentally ill fill the violent stereotype the general public creates for them. And, even before arrested and medicated, most of the imprisoned mentally ill have only committed minor nonviolent crimes, while a major percentage of other prison inmates have been convicted of violent crimes (e.g., robbery, sexual assault, and murder).

One study of college students showed that 52 percent of those polled believed that "aggression, hostility, or violence" were common among the mentally ill. The plain truth is that three factors predict violent behavior among the mentally ill: 1) their history of past violence, 2) the extent of their abuse of drugs and/or alcohol, and 3) their compliance in taking prescribed medications. This leaves only a minority of the mentally ill who can be defined as violent.

Frequently, no attempt is made to keep potentially violent, mentally ill persons who leave prisons on medications that will prevent them from harming someone. Fewer than 50 percent of prison personnel who release seriously mentally ill individuals are aware if those persons receive any outpatient psychiatric care once they leave. Those who say they do know report 36 percent receive follow-up treatment. In California, 40 to 50 percent of mentally ill persons convicted under an insanity plea of serious crimes of violence and eventually discharged from prison, left their prison environment without provision for follow-up treatment.

More mentally ill defendants are sent to prison in states where they have a fixed sentence, as opposed to being admitted to a hospital where they are released upon recovery. Some states have established "Mental Health Courts" to meet the needs of the mentally ill and to secure "therapeutic justice" and not just criminal justice. Here, the capable mentally ill are able to circumvent prison stays and get the medical treatment they need. Still, over 20 percent of prisons provide no access to in-house psychiatric resources. In 84 percent of jails in the US, police obtained no training or fewer than three hours of training on problems of individuals with mental illness. It is no wonder that treatment of the incarcerated mentally ill is excessively harsh and does not acknowledge the involuntary nature of crimes committed by the mentally ill.

Deinstitutionalization without appropriate placement resources has been a failure. The severely ill have been forced back into their family's care, into jails, or onto the streets. Hundreds of thousands of mentally ill Americans are barely existing on city streets or underground in subway tunnels. Parents are put into care-giving roles for which they have been untrained and are unprepared to fill. Renowned spokesman for the National Alliance for the Mentally Ill, Dr. E. Fuller Torrey, MD, describes the barbaric reality of deinstitutionalization as follows:

> While between 5 and 10 percent of those 3.5 million individuals who suffer from schizophrenia and manic-depressive illness need long-term hospitalization, this need is not being met due to the United States losing 93 percent of state psychiatric hospital beds since the mid 1850s, when mental patients were discharged and psychiatric facilities shut down.
>
> There are as many individuals with schizophrenia, homeless and living on the streets, as there are in all hospitals. Approximately one-third of all the nation's 600,000 homeless persons suffer from severe mental illness.
>
> People with mental illness utilize more hospital beds than heart disease, cancer, and lung ailments combined.
>
> There are as many individuals with schizophrenia in jails or prisons as there are in all hospitals.
>
> There are more people with serious mental illness in prisons in America than there are in state mental institutions.
>
> Two times as many individuals with serious mental illnesses live in shelters and on the street as there are those committed by individuals with schizophrenia who are not being treated.
>
> There are increasing episodes of violence committed against individuals with schizophrenia.
>
> Housing for many with schizophrenia is often abysmal.
>
> Half the individuals with schizophrenia are receiving no treatment at any given time.
>
> Of all health insurance policies in America, only 37 percent have inpatient coverage for mental illness and only 6 percent have comparable outpatient coverage.

To add to Dr. Torrey's bleak list of atrocities, the precise number of state psychiatric hospitals that have reduced in number are as follows: In 1970, there were 277 state hospitals, while today there are 223. During the last three years, 21 hospitals were closed by 14 different states; it is not only the quantity but the quality of state psychiatric care that is of major concern by those who have been victims of poor treatment in state hospitals. Unnecessary use of restraints and seclusion contribute to lasting trauma along with physical and/or sexual abuse.

Broader standards for providing involuntary commitment (than being a danger to self or others) have been adopted in some states. But, they are too few and often not broad enough. The National Alliance for the Mentally Ill suggests the following criteria for hospital admission:

> The individual is gravely disabled. This means the person is significantly unable (except for lack of funds) to secure basic needs (food, clothing, shelter, health or safety).

> If not provided with timely treatment, the individual is likely to significantly deteriorate.

> The individual lacks the judgment to make an informed decision regarding medical needs.

When "proof of danger to self or others" is exclusive and current standards as in some states, there are too often disastrous results. The individuals deteriorate needlessly outside of the hospital. There, danger to self is often not determined before safer involuntary commitment and/or court-ordered treatment can be secured. When I became incapable of preparing meals or sleeping or safely crossing the street—or just generally taking care of my basic needs—I was deemed a danger to myself and hospitalized. Only two hospitalizations used attempts at suicide as criteria for admission. Studies conclude that postponing necessary treatment until a person is "a danger to themselves or others" results in significant harm including increased resistance to treatment, more painful symptoms, and more frequent and longer hospitalizations.

The presence of some psychiatric disorder is the number one reason for hospital admissions nationwide. Mental illness is suffered by 12 to 14 million Americans. No wonder about 21 percent of hospital beds are filled by mental patients at any given moment. Once my psychotic momentum began generating a breakdown, it was necessary to take dramatic steps to suspend the process as quickly as possible. However, the cruel nature of psychosis is a loss of the awareness that hospitalization is imperative. During the early stages of my brain disorder, I sometimes resisted being hospitalized (though passively, not violently). However, each hospitalization would start me on a road to recovery that I would continue when I left that medicinal environment. Leaving the hospital did not mean leaving doctors. They were everywhere and their environment was called outpatient services.

Every hospital had its own style of care. However, the reason for hospitalization remained the same: to provide sheltered, low-stress rest, and medical observation; and to adjust medications as needed. I once heard of a psychiatrist who was bipolar and checked into a psychiatric ward once a year, on schedule, for a restful getaway. However, it was really not a vacation: He could have chosen Paris.

State mental hospitals present the most available help for the mentally ill without military records, primarily since it is free. The quality and style of care varies along with patients' rights, sometimes drastically, from state to state. You may consider relocating to another state that presents more generous services for the mentally ill. Before engaging in this major option, you need to closely examine the services available in the various states. A good place to start is to contact the NAMI (National Alliance for the Mentally Ill) in your specific state or call national NAMI at 1(800)950-NAMI (6264). NAMI will provide you with an idea of the states that provide strong mental health programs. Then, with the possibilities narrowed down, you can investigate those states that most effectively treat the mentally ill.

Various questions that need to be asked before a major relocation occurs are:

  - Should there be a crisis, which service programs are

available to work with the doctors and hospitals in the community to monitor medications?

- Is transportation available to those in crisis?
- What housing is available for the mentally ill, the cost of such housing, the application process, and what supervision is available in this kind of housing?
- Is training and support available to assist the mentally ill in obtaining employment, and what kinds and how many jobs are available in the target communities?
- What personal and social needs are addressed such as help with housekeeping and recreational activities?
- Are there service programs to help with managing money?
- Are education programs available for those with mental illnesses?
- In what states are there quality PACTs (Programs of Assertive Community Treatment) established and operating well?

(PACT teams provide 24-hour-a-day, seven-day-a-week attention to those mentally ill they are assigned. Treatment, rehabilitation, and support services are provided for the mentally ill in their homes, at work, and in the community.)

Whatever state you investigate, you will find it difficult to escape stigma and discrimination, the leading barriers to effective treatment for the mentally ill. The voters' lack of empathy for the mentally ill reflects a society where the permanent label of "crazy" plants fear in the hearts of even the most compassionate.

The stigma created by my mental illness dramatically caused disgrace to my life during my first hospitalization (which occurred while I was still in the military). At age 23, I became tarnished and would remain so forevermore by that first stay in a mental hospital. That hospital was available to those who warranted it. However, it brought a blemish that would never be removed. Every subsequent hospitalization reinforced that stigma. To those future acquaintances who learned that I spent any amount of time in a mental hospital I would be labeled crazy, basically meaning I was seriously flawed and best to avoid.

Chambers was the gruesome pseudonym selected for my first hospital. It was built exclusively for army personnel. I was serving my last six months in the military, and my first mental breakdown required that I place my faith in the treatment that awaited me inside those heavy, grim walls. The bizarre behavior demonstrated by the patients, combined with the reality of being in a mental hospital, was initially terrifying. Some patients talked incessantly into the air, while others stared blankly into their own empty spaces. Their personal hygiene was generally poor, often resulting in producing frightening appearances. However, I soon found the patients more confused and lethargic than threatening. The medication seemed to successfully eliminate any real danger that might have existed.

Joining in a perpetual game of volleyball on the patio, continuous pacing, and lying in bed were my main activities during that first hospital stay. The pacing produced an anxiety of its own by the monotony it created. This continuous movement and the volleyball satisfied many craving for mobility since side effects from the medications often caused a restlessness that demanded motion. The patients' athletic abilities were usually considerably limited. Their body coordination was typically hampered by their medication. The medications (as well as their symptoms) also sometimes brought some physical pain that desperately needed a diversion. Therefore, volleyball was a feeble vehicle for filling the time with distracting activity.

About half of the patients remained in bed most of the day and usually progressed more slowly than any of the others. These patients especially suffered a high degree of boredom that resulted in a prolonged hospital stay. When they were awakened for group sessions, they were the ones who most frequently reported hallucinations and/or deep unhappiness. I remember one of these patients, during group therapy, reporting he saw a demon in the corner of the room.

The monotony of this place built for healing fostered its own kind of madness. Hallucinations and depression were reduced or even eliminated by the medications. However, many of the medications' side effects accentuated the original symptoms or brought on new symptoms that were sometimes more severe. The patients who shrewdly managed to see the psychiatrist in charge most often were the patients who were able to negotiate a change in medications.

Most of my hospitalizations were in Veterans Administrations (VA) hospitals. There are presently about 170 VA hospitals in the US, hiring about 190,000 people in the health care system, and providing about 15,000 psychiatric beds. The VA medical system works with a $17 billion budget. There are 386,000 mentally ill in this system. However, it is estimated that a total of 500,000 veterans suffer with serious mental illness. Of the 386,000 veterans treated annually for severe mental illnesses, 125,000 are hospitalized. The VA is the second largest federal bureaucracy in the United States (the largest being the Department of Defense).

There is at least one VA hospital in nearly every state. They range from huge, high-tech teaching hospitals allied with universities, where medical students are provided learning environments for them to complete their internships and residencies, to small rural hospitals.

Most VA psychiatric facilities have both inpatient and outpatient programs. The VA considers outpatient monitoring as very important for maintaining quality in the care of veterans with mental illness. (Indeed, studies have shown that access to outpatient services strongly reduces the need for re-hospitalization.) Presently, no medical system in the world has the range and quality of services that the VA has.

The VA treats only veterans. There are two categories: high priority and low priority. High priority covers either those with disabilities that were obtained or significantly escalated in the service. All medications and most services are free to high-priority veterans. All other veterans are low priority and are required to contribute an extremely low co-payment for VA services.

In the past, the VA system was highly decentralized. Each hospital was autonomous to such a degree that even patient records failed to be transferred from one hospital to another. The result was inefficient and time-consuming care, where new, vital information on each psychiatric patient's history was accumulated during each new stay, and expensive tests were duplicated. In the recent past, the establishment of a Computerized Patient Record System (CPRS) has remarkably improved the handling of information.

I have been a psychiatric patient in five VA hospitals. Also, I resided in three civilian hospitals while, each time, waiting to be transferred to an empty bed in an available VA hospital. The quality of care varied. NAMI has recognized the need for higher quality care in the VA medical system and has initiated consumer councils to act as watchdogs over the system. Extremely poor care was provided by two of the civilian hospitals where I received treatment while awaiting a vacant VA hospital bed. Callous staff and, again, cruel monotony was dispensed along with the variety of prescribed medications. Also, one VA hospital in which I was hospitalized was sadly understaffed and the patients suffered poorly from the resulting neglect. Again, boredom was served as a steady reminder of the misery each patient endured when left to themselves. In this way, these hospitals often enhanced the suffering they were meant to alleviate.

Four other hospitals I temporarily called home (one civilian and four VA) gave the patients considerably more options about how to spend the day. The civilian hospital had walls that were more colorful and doctors who were more accessible. Otherwise, there was little difference between the typical VA and typical civilian care I received in these hospitals. There was exercise equipment (two with swimming pools), occupational therapy (crafts), group therapy, comfortable patios to lounge on, outings— and always television.

Television was viewed frequently by most patients, except for those whose tender psyches could not endure the impact of sound and picture. For these patients, it was the nature of their psychosis that prevented them from enduring too much external stimulation. Noises were amplified and visual images vexing to their raw senses. I shared these symptoms with patients in several hospitals. As we began recovering, we were gradually able to watch TV without feeling assaulted by the picture and the sound.

My psychiatric wards were usually locked wards, simply

because that was all that was available. Understandably, some patients required consistent limitations on their freedom. As others progressed with their recovery, these wards most often allowed them to leave for a limited time and explore the hospital and the grounds and buy merchandise from the hospital shop. Even on open wards, I was always required to have special permission to leave (if just for a short time). Having had occasion to experience both locked and open wards, I much prefer the relative freedom of open wards to being held captive by my healers. And, open wards accommodated profoundly healthier patients whose mental conditions were substantially more comfortable and less ominous. They could be trusted not to leave the hospital.

Locked wards housed together patients with a variety of serious mental problems: some who looked and acted fairly normal, and others who exhibited a wide range of grotesque appearances and behavior. On my locked wards, the more serious schizophrenics and some schizoaffectives were fairly easy to identify since they seemed to find relief in perpetually muttering to themselves and making little sense. In addition, their external lack of sanitation was difficult to endure inside a radius of three feet. Their hair ranged from closely cut in a ragged manner, to long, wild, and frightening. Many of these patients had come right off the streets. Often angry souls when they arrived, unmedicated, they exercised harsh, frequently vulgar speech. I was regularly audience to horrifying cries coming from locked and padded rooms where new, uncontrollable patients were isolated. Once the medications began to take their formidable effects, these patients calmed down and joined the contrasting collection of pacing patients in the halls and meeting rooms.

Less serious patients, who often had no choice but to share the territory of more serious patients, were understandably fearful. I especially recall an older woman, probably younger than she looked, who was seriously disheveled. She truly resembled a witch. Her particular psychotic style was to shout out confusing and crude obscenities.

Contrary to popular belief, there is a significant population of schizophrenics who are able to function with medication successfully outside of hospitals. However, the ones I most likely encountered in the hospitals were in the process of rehabilitation and generally provided conversation that was nearly impossible to comprehend. Their perplexing, often angry garbling turned me around in deranged circles. I was unaware, as were most other more lucid, psychiatric patients, of the reassuring research that concluded schizophrenics who were taking medication were seldom violent. The result of this lack of information made occupying a mental ward exceptionally frightening to less serious, more rational patients such as myself.

The bottom line, however, was that anger inside locked wards seldom presented danger. During my 25 plus hospitalizations, I saw only four or five incidents in which a pacing patient became uncontrollable and needed to be restrained. Admittedly, there were the locked rooms, full of fury, which prevented the possibility of violent behavior toward unprotected, nonviolent patients.

Once released from the hospital, safely medicated patients often discontinue their medication and, therefore, discontinue interfacing with the world. Many of them present menacing images that society finds safest to avoid. It is the ones on the streets who discontinue medication who are more inclined to deliver acts of violence. Noted, there are those living on the streets who faithfully pick up from a state pharmacy and consume in a timely manner their weekly supply of medications.

The mental hospital's traditional image as a perverse prison has undergone major changes in many communities. More patients are able to leave their wards during established times during the day, walk around the premises, go to hospital jobs assigned to them, or even go to carefully scheduled jobs out in the community. The doors on such wards are only locked at night. Patients must acquire these freedoms from their doctors. Still, more and more patients are also allowed to be involved in making rules that govern their hospital environments and are, more and more, treated by the staff with warmth and respect.

Two hospitals I stayed in had open wards. The patients had less severe mental disorders and could come and go for predetermined periods of time. Most of these patients were probably severely depressed, manic-depressive, or mildly schizoaffective or schizophrenic. Though many of them were bitter and angry, occasionally they displayed a sense of humor. I initially found this characteristic strange. Suffering with the stigma and loss of self-esteem that accompanied the internal and external pain of mental illness, I just could not see what was so funny. Early in my disability, I failed to realize that such patients were most likely in a creative, manic, even euphoric phase. With my most frequent phase manifesting itself as a deep depression, I gravitated to these manic patients, hungry for the lift their often elevated, creative moods provided. These semi-caged comedians were not able to remain in their euphoric mania for long. Then came the depression when my former friends would turn into strangers, dispensing verbal attacks and angry outbursts. Doubly bad for me—even my own mania was seldom euphoric. Instead of being humorous, I could become bossy and demanding.

Once psychologically sick, I was at the mercy of the psychiatrist. This kind of raw power had not entered my life prior to needing psychiatric care. Regardless of the hospital I entered or how sick I was or how well I became, my recovery and my exiting the hospital, either on a short-term or long-term basis, was still in the hands of the doctor. Herein lay my chances for recovery and freedom or continued misery and confinement. It was the psychiatrist who decided if I needed the hospital, the psychiatrist who determined my care while I was in the hospital, and the psychiatrist who determined when I was ready for freedom. This power permeated the entire nursing staff. It was the nursing staff's rotated daily observations of the patients that the psychiatrist relied on while determining my treatment. How caring the nurses actually were was as crucial to recovery as were medications. Typical of serious mental illness is "high-expressed emotion" where patients are super-sensitive to criticism or disapproval. Tender brain receptors create tender egos that leave patients susceptible to excessive shame. It often only took a negative glance or an unkind tone from a staff member to destroy a whole day's worth of recovery. The hospitals where I was most comfortable and in which I recovered most rapidly were those where the staff exhibited an abundance of compassion.

Therefore, while the nursing staff seemed to take on the role of surrogate mother, there were always some whose parental attention I did not welcome. This was from nurses who noticeably disliked the patients and their job as healers. Fortunately, such staffing mistakes usually kept themselves as distant as possible from the patients, almost as if they feared catching "the disease." I often suspected they already suffered from many of the health problems they treated. Fortunately, the mental health practitioners of the 1990s began to realize the importance of caring hospital staffs. Patients began to be cared for by staffs who were significantly kinder.

The network of power that characterized my mental wards was initially terrifying. However, after two or three agonizing breakdowns, it became easier to welcome instead of dread medical help. The first few days of hospital visits were difficult. However, as I struggled with the wicked symptoms of a full-blown breakdown, my original fears subsided; and the gruesome presence of some of the more menacing patients became more acceptable. Hospital care became less loathsome and brought more relief. I began to be more aware that it was the hospital that took away the voices and terrifying images that made my life nonfunctional. It was the hospital that kept me off the streets and made sure I took the right medications and ate three meals a day. Despite its flaws, it was the hospital that saved me from myself.

My typical hospitalization lasted about two weeks. The first week, as I initially endured the pain of psychosis, the doctors tried out an assortment of medications to relieve me of a brain made raw with persistent, psychotic pounding.

Occasional negative interpersonal interactions with the staff were also painful. In addition, sporadic mistakes made with medications made a patient even sicker. One unusually agonizing example was when I was accidentally given a double injection of Prolixin (chlorpromazine), where one injection was meant to last three weeks. This medication is an antipsychotic drug that has some hideous side effects, among which are dizziness, weakness, extreme restlessness (where I can't sit in one place for very long), and muscle spasms of the face, jaw, neck, back, and extremities. When a double dose was accidentally administered, hideous turned to tortuous. Upon leaving the hospital, I suffered Prolixin's side effects, doubly, for about three weeks until the medication finally, mercifully, completely left my system. My outpatient doctor immediately recognized that I had been overmedicated. I eventually wrote a letter to the hospital administration governing the psychiatric unit I had occupied. I related the details regarding the incident and the excruciating consequences on my mind and body. However, I never even received a reply and was too sick to pursue the matter.

Though it was inconvenient (if not psychologically impossible) for me to write while I was in the hospital, my 14th hospital stay (when I was admitted to the VA hospital in San Diego) was a pleasant exception. When I entered this facility, a desk was made available to me in my room. I found writing at my own personal desk a glorious luxury. It brought me great comfort. Though my intentions were honorable, some days were so rough I could not manage to create a line.

It was while in this VA hospital that Clozaril (generic name, clozapine) was introduced to my treatment agenda. Clozaril had seemed to perform magic for manic-depressive, schizophrenic, and schizoaffective patients. My diagnosis had become schizoaffective disorder, a psychosis somewhere between the seriousness of manic depression and schizophrenia (commonly misdiagnosed). There was a trial period with this new medication and an assortment of immediate and permanent side effects to hazard. However, the risk was worth the taking.

Following are excerpts from some of the simplistic letters I wrote while having Clozaril introduced to my difficult biochemistry during the two and a half months I was in this hospital. The positive results of the Clozaril made it possible for me to correspond more than during any former hospital stay:

A Thursday —

As I write you this letter today, I am very drowsy. The sedation of the Clozaril has begun to set in. I'm also hungrier than usual, and I almost blacked out in the shower this morning. I just sat on the shower floor and turned on the cold water. That resuscitated me. The doctor later told me to avoid hot showers as the Clozaril could initially cause fainting in a hot environment.

I have to move more slowly right now and be careful about standing up too fast—there is the risk of blacking out.

I'm already experiencing more clarity. The ongoing pain and pressure in the side of my head has already begun to diminish. I'm feeling very optimistic.

New news. I found out more about Clozaril today. Any side effects will continue at least until they level off at a therapeutic dose. It is then that they will start diminishing. That will be in about three weeks. Also, the benefits of Clozaril can continue to increase for a full year after I first start this medication.

A Wednesday —

The doctor gave me a little booklet on Clozaril today. Here are some interesting facts:

- The drowsiness will usually go away in time.
- Only one to two out of one hundred have diminished white blood cell count that causes them to discontinue the medication.
- The higher the daily dosage, the greater chance of seizures. However, after I am on a higher dose for several weeks without seizures, I should be able to drive.

Pretty interesting stuff.

I get my blood pressure taken two times a day, each time lying down and then standing up. I have blood taken to check my white blood count once a week.

A Friday —

The Clozaril is definitely working! I'm feeling more mental clarity, and I'm taking lukewarm to cold showers to stay on the safe side. Slight nausea hits me now and then, but just a hint. I also seem to want to sleep in. I didn't even hear the alarm this a.m.

A Tuesday —

This morning they increased my daily dose of Clozaril—from 37.5 mg. per day to 50 mg. per day.

After my vigorous daily walk, I felt pretty good.

The janitor is finished with my room and it looks and smells better. Considering my former roommate's obsession over sanitation, how the floors got so neglected is a mystery. She really was a fanatic. But, like me, she is sick.

Due to the great decrease in hospitalization of the seriously mentally ill, a booming growth of outpatient treatment has resulted—a place patients can go to get verbal therapy and medications to keep them out of the hospitals and out of jail. Every new medication that has accompanied me as I left a hospital has also accompanied me to outpatient treatment, which usually has involved visiting a psychiatrist every two to four weeks who dispenses a variety of medications, and visiting a therapist (social worker) every other week.

During the 1970s, outpatient care was just beginning to be truly useful to patients leaving the hospital environment. Much of the money that had been previously allocated to the hospitals was being transferred to care for patients outside of the hospitals. Research showed that good outpatient care made overall care less costly than when just hospital care (too often involving revolving-door visitations) was provided.

One sophisticated outpatient program I became engaged in during the early 1970s involved a small weekly stipend for rent, earned by working a limited number of hours per week at a low-stress job in a local live theater. I qualified financially for food stamps. However, I had no immediate financial resources for a telephone. Rent would make it possible for me to advertise for and acquire a roommate. A roommate was essential since she would provide half the rent and, so, provide me enough funds at the end of each week. I turned to my church for help and they provided me with this critical instrument that made it possible to secure a roommate. It was a hard time. I legitimately bore the oppressive brand of poverty along with the stigma of mental illness. However, it was a beginning to managing my mental illness.

The wonderful reality for me is I have been on Clozaril over six years (with a brief interruption while I tried another medication, ziprasidone), requiring only two or three stays in the hospital where my medication was even more thoroughly fine-tuned to reduce some surfacing depression. Because of my diminished pain, accompanied with a longer track record living outside heavy hospital walls, inpatient hospital treatment has been less imminent.

Today, my present positive performance is the direct result of quality outpatient care. Too many state mental health systems ignore the importance of providing the mental patient with the outpatient time and attention necessary for that patient to avoid hospitalization. One patient in New York reported her life was renewed when she left the hospital and began outpatient treatment. "In the institution (hospital), you can't do anything. Just eat and sleep," she lamented. "Now (in an outpatient program) I'm going to day programs. I'm learning to cook and to handle money. The institution is just not for me."

The outpatient experience may not only require therapy but also housing. Here, individuals requiring ongoing psychiatric care may reside with other patients in a group home monitored by a mental health professional. They share household duties while supervised by a professional who makes sure doctor's appointments are met and medications are taken. There is pervasive discrimination regarding this kind of housing for the mentally ill throughout the US: No one wants "crazy" people in their neighborhoods. The most effective tool available to fight this discrimination is the federal Fair Housing Amendments Act of 1988. Every HUD office has a discrimination officer to assist in preventing damaging bias regarding housing for the seriously mentally ill.

Daytime clubhouses are also becoming more available where

the mentally ill can socialize and share duties (cooking, housecleaning, yard care, and producing a newsletter as well as other PR). Job search training and assistance is often available, as well as other valuable training (often regarding computer skills). Fountain House in New York City has provided a model for clubhouses across the country.

Nevertheless, too many of the mentally ill who leave the protective hospital are expected to go it nearly on their own. These neglected souls often lead lives of quiet desperation. Their homes are isolated, single-room-occupancy hotels, or cheap boarding houses paid for with modest stipends. Their futile search for work is often the result of rejection due to their past hospitalizations. Sixty-two percent of schizophrenics who leave the hospital must return at some time.

Instead of pushing fragile people out into isolation and poverty, making sure former patients are provided with food, shelter, counseling, and job training results in fewer relapses that require repeated hospitalizations. However, due to lack of funds, few adequate community and residential treatment mental health facilities exist. The ones that do are often sorely limited. A ten-minute appointment once a month is too often the treatment provided by state outpatient programs and insurance coverage. This standard repeatedly just does not work. It is then that less expensive outpatients too soon become exceedingly expensive inpatients.

Just a note regarding managed care for the outpatient. It is conclusive that improvements are vital should this system work effectively in the public sector. A different mind-set, putting service ahead of profit, is crucial. The business owner asks, "Who are my customers, and what do they want?" The doctor asks, "Who are my patients, and what do they need?" Key areas needing attention are:

- Sufficient funding for the managed care program
- Coordinated funding that meets both medical and support needs of the mentally ill
- An allocation process that involves consumers and family

members on a selection committee
- A selective process that involves the company best able to provide quality care rather than the lowest bidder
- Retaining the best of the current system
- Reinvesting money spent to close down hospitals or saving money used within the system to pay for community treatment and support services (including housing)

Right now, Clozaril, my antipsychotic of choice, is keeping me out of major brain pain and most frequently out of the hospital. However, there are trade-offs. Some negative side effects Clozaril carries are greater than with any other antipsychotic. With Clozaril, the inner mechanism that controls my appetite has gone haywire and I have gained 55 pounds since I started on it 13 years ago (regardless of desperate struggles on numerous diets). In addition, my cognitive abilities have diminished to an uncomfortable level, with a weakened short-term memory that has left me considerably absentminded. Finally, Clozaril creates an extreme sedative effect that causes a need to sleep 11, 12, sometimes even 13 hours per night. This side effect has caused tremendous conflict as I have struggled with a background abundant with strong work ethic.

Nevertheless (under the generous VA umbrella), I am provided with a half-hour doctor's appointment every two weeks, along with a weekly hour of therapy from a social worker and some group therapy. Combined, these create ample and appreciated interruptions from my regular daily routines. With Clozaril for now, other, better, new antipsychotic medications exist right around the corner. The hope prevails that such future treatment will permanently spare me from such frequent visits to VA clinics and more permanent visits to hospitals.

Chapter 9
THERAPISTS —
DIMINISHERS OF DEMONS

Psychotherapists exist to help ease the pain of serious mental illness. Good, private, one-on-one outpatient therapy is crucial to the success of my overall treatment. Regular time (30 minutes to an hour at least every other week) spent with a good therapist is often necessary to resolve some deep and persistent issues.

Populating the troubled climates of therapeutic offices, typical psychotherapists (social workers, psychiatric nurses, psychologists, and psychiatrists) often appear to have their own roots from troubled homes. They enter and graduate from colleges, work in hospitals, and often evolve into private practitioners. They manage to do it all while sometimes unraveling their own neuroses or even psychoses.

Their offices all seem to have a common decor. The lighting is soft but strong enough to clearly illuminate the soul. The floor is carpeted in a pastel. There is often a desk. There is almost always at least one couch and one or two comfortable chairs that coordinate nicely with the carpet. On the walls are a couple of pictures, usually well-foliaged, placid outdoor scenes. Also displayed are framed college and seminar diplomas celebrating the competence of their owners. The walls themselves are painted a beige or a light pastel—solid, serene backgrounds designed to create as much tranquility as can possibly benefit the customary occupancy of troubled minds.

A profile of a therapist could perhaps begin in this manner. However, my therapists were too complex to be summarized in such few words. Possibly, their complexities were best reflected by their various, personalized brands of therapy. Some were warm and caring, and some detached and clinical. Some were eager to offer suggestions to promote sane interaction, while others quietly listened away the pain. Some made suggestions that were comfortably followed, while others recommended behavior most anyone else would censor. (A former patient once told me a psychiatrist recommended he see a prostitute to relieve the lack of sexual satisfaction in his married life.)

Specific types of verbal therapy vary from therapist to therapist, some approaches more successful than others. Classic Freudian psychotherapy has been used for years and has not only been primarily unsuccessful but in some cases harmful. Dramatic success has been experienced with more recent therapies, especially cognitive-behavioral therapy. This approach focuses on the patient's role in managing symptoms by managing his/her thoughts. Treatment is brief, taking from 10 to 36 weeks. Sessions are weekly or biweekly. Patients find that delusions, hallucinations, and other negative symptoms are reduced or even eliminated. Therefore, often medications are even reduced.

Therapists who articulated an exchange of healing language for me have seldom been psychiatrists. As a veteran with what was termed a service-connected nervous disorder (more specifically first schizophrenic, then manic-depressive, and finally schizoaffective), I mainly received treatment with chemicals from psychiatrists who were hired by the VA. Their style typically involved 15 to 30 minutes of attention. This was just enough time to ask a couple of pointed questions about current mood variations and possible hallucinations, and to make any necessary adjustments in current medications (write out an order for refills of present medications and/or prescriptions for new medications).

There was little time for verbal therapy. This was left to the assigned VA social workers, psychiatric nurses, or psychologists. Only three VA therapists left a positive mark on my heart. They were psychiatric nurses, Wendy, Susan, and Annie.

Shy for a psychiatric nurse, Wendy provided a sensitivity to our sessions that made it apparent some event(s) during her 40-some years on this earth enabled her to understand my grief. Her voice seldom rose above a moderate whisper, but I quickly learned it was worth listening to what she said. Her style carried with it an empathy that led me to believe she was aware of a deep, personal pain. She never shared her own anguish but was free in giving an abundance of encouragement, much needed by my frail ego. "You look good today," Wendy might begin. "How are you feeling?"

Just hearing that I "looked good" was enough for me to begin to divulge the chaos inside of me. "I'm on the brink of a scary depression. My life is worthless. I don't know what would make living worthwhile."

"Do you have any hobbies, or something you enjoy each day?" Wendy might question.

"Nothing. I don't remember what fun was all about."

"That is what clinical depression does to us, Two," Wendy would disclose. "You carry around a biochemistry that creates for you a terrible despair. It is not your fault. You are a quality person and have much to offer. Serious depression is getting in the way. Could anything be specifically going on that could be encouraging this trauma?"

"I can't seem to attach this depression to a particular happening." I was initially baffled. "Wait! I had a frustrating conversation with my mother yesterday. But, would this cause such a grievous state of mind for me?"

"It is possible that your conflict with your mother is the event that triggered your breakable biochemistry to flair up. It would be best if you came to an understanding over this disagreement. Do you think you can call her and do that? Think of it as a stress-reducing action that will help you through this crisis."

Eager to feel some sense of recovery, I could not help but acknowledge, "Yes. I need to do that, in case that is contributing to this torment. I will not hesitate to call her when I go home today."

Wendy was sometimes not just satisfied with verbal therapy. Though she knew how troublesome side effects could be, she also appreciated the potential of many medications in keeping patients out of the hospital. So, if the time was right, she would declare, "In the meantime you need an immediate chemical remedy. I will go see if the doctor is available for me to talk with concerning your symptoms. A new prescription might be advisable if you feel comfortable with that. Or, a more critical change in meds might be necessary. I would like to hear what the doctor says. Does that sound okay with you?"

Her concern with how I felt about introducing my delicate body chemistry to a different medication or combination of medications was always appreciated. "Yes, Wendy" was my usual reply. "Anything to help drive this gloom (or this mania, or this agitation, etc.) from my body."

Dialogue with Wendy was before Clozaril, the future medication that would miraculously keep me stabilized and more frequently out of the hospital. However, whatever medication Wendy and the doctor recommended, which I ordered and I consumed, usually resulted in a psychiatric lift that I preferred regardless of whatever uncomfortable side effects occurred.

When Wendy quit the VA to teach at a local university, I was sorry to see her go. But I am sure a multitude of students benefited greatly from her profound knowledge of what mental illness is all about.

Susan was as unconventional as her patients. Another VA psychiatric nurse, her complex intelligence combined with an offbeat wit were, initially, her most conspicuous characteristics. Soon, I found these traits supported by a sturdy foundation of kindness. Susan was middle-aged. Her variety of therapy was open and revealing. Her keen understanding of the endurance that came with being seriously mentally ill manifested itself in her treating me with an abundance of trust and respect. The result was a considerable elevation in my ego. To Susan, I was always her equal. Her trusting style of therapy created a rare bond between us. Consequently, I soon became comfortable disclosing my deepest thoughts and feelings during our sessions. Therapy with Susan was occasionally predictable, but never boring.

"Hello," Susan might start. "It is good to see you."

"Hello, Susan," I would reply and maybe add, "What you see may be good; however, what you don't see is very bad."

Susan would sit back in an analytical posture and inquire, "Tell me what you mean?"

My voice would be full of desperation as I reported, "I can't seem to conquer this constant agitation. It causes me to want to just give up and try to sleep all the time. I try my best to fight it by keeping as busy as I can. This helps. However, the agitation is pretty persistent in tearing away my ability to overcome its damage. It even manifests itself in physical problems: I have recurring headaches and backaches. It all just wears me down and I'm exhausted at the end of the day."

During sessions, it was typical for Susan to disclose personal issues relevant to what was being discussed. To my great gratitude, she contributed information to me about her mentally ill daughter that resulted in my starting a new medication, which proved to significantly lessen my frequent agitation. Susan just one day proclaimed, "I believe I deeply understand how you are feeling. My daughter recently began suffering from similar symptoms. Her doctor tried a new medication on her, and the results were very positive. It can possibly remove or at least reduce your agitation. Do you think you would like to try it?"

Medication changes always made me wary. Such suggestions prompted me to sometimes ask, "Will any of my other medication be taken away?"

Susan understood and offered reassurance. "Likely not. This new medication is often used with other medications, often like the ones you are already taking. And, the antipsychotic drug you are now taking will not likely be affected."

I was encouraged. "It sounds like this medication is worth a try. If your daughter benefited, I may, too."

"I'll go see right now if I can catch the doctor between patients," Susan declared. "She can usually be found wandering through the halls. I sometimes find it difficult distinguishing her from the patients."

Excellent decision-making abilities combined with a valuable sense of humor enabled Susan to provide a quantity of recovery that few therapists furnished me. And, the medication did create a reduction in my agitation for a substantial time. However, like many prescribed medications, it did eventually lose its effectiveness.

Annie has been my psychiatric nurse for about four rewarding years. From conservative Boston kin, she still calls me Ms. Lenz. However, though professional, the distance is not cold and not at all uncomfortable. Instead, it is totally competent, and I always prefer competence over closeness in my therapists.

Annie and I started therapy with a cognitive approach and completed an entire year-long workbook on the subject. It was a major accomplishment, and David Burns (editor and pioneer of cognitive therapy) would have been proud.

Next, we addressed my social phobia by simply reading, at my request, from Dale Carnegie's *How to Win Friends and Influence People*. This has proven to be entertaining and comfortably challenging as I practice Carnegie's ideas in the real world.

Between these formal activities have been times when I just had to talk about something immediately pressing my mind, and have been grateful Annie was available to provide comfort and useful therapy.

Of all my therapists, Annie has provided the most practical approaches to recovery. Fortunately, she has been able to remain my therapist longer than any other.

Quality therapy was rare inside the VA. Therefore, I did occasionally seek more stable help from therapists outside this system. Two private therapists are especially worth describing. They were social workers and were employed through nonprofit systems that allowed fees to be paid on sliding scales. Despite their modest offices, both had a passion for their work and instilled in me a passion for recovery.

Jenny was the most animated of the two. Her wiry body housed an energy that fortified my fragile psyche. This electric intensity transmitted the sensitivity of someone who cared enough to feel along with me. She assisted in dealing with issues like early separation from my mother and persistent shame, which I bore like cruel crosses. Before Jenny, no therapist had ever probed as deeply into the chasms of my mind. She helped maximize my sanity and, therefore, preserve my dignity during times when I needed to project a sound personality in the workplace. When there were the inevitable times that I could no longer endure the stress of a job, she found a way for me to discreetly obtain hospitalization. She would do this in a way that I felt least threatened. Her style preserved my pride, while obtaining the crucial medical assistance I required.

I especially remember a specific occasion that characterized Jenny's brand of therapy when hospitalization was needed.

"Two," began Jenny. "You are escalating (snowballing) into a psychotic state. (At times like this, it was usually mania.) I want to call your VA doctor right now and have you admitted into the hospital. Do you feel okay about that?"

Not eager to be confined again, I responded, "Is it that necessary that I go in the hospital?"

"Yes, Two. I am sure of it."

"Wait. Don't call. I'm not sure…" I responded.

Jenny respected my hesitancy. "I understand, and I do want your approval that I do this. I want you to feel comfortable about going to the hospital. You are in dangerous territory right now and you need the hospital."

"Okay. Go ahead and call, though it's hard for me to realize I'm that bad."

"I know, Two. Not being aware of how sick you are is what serious mental illness is all about."

Jenny was not surprised at my agreement. She had worked hard to establish a foundation of trust between us.

"I am glad you chose to trust me, Two, that you agree you need the hospital for a little while."

Picking up the phone, Jenny called the appropriate doctor, all while I was right there in the room. She let the doctor know of the seriousness of my condition and declared it was her opinion I would benefit significantly from short-term hospitalization.

A major measure of dignity was provided by Jenny's approach to hospitalization. She always allowed the decision to be mine and, therein, I felt a semblance of control. She drew an appealing picture of being in a mental hospital, describing it as a valuable place to rest and experience some recovery. Because of Jenny, though the hospital wards' doors were likely locked to outsiders, my mind was made open to the hope of better days.

Through Jenny's professional zeal was hardship I noticed nearly from the beginning. I could not detect from where the hardship originated, but her chronic compassion convinced me something was wrong. Ignored too frequently are the intuitive skills manifested by the mentally ill. Often, while the therapist is treating the patient, the patient is analyzing the therapist; and frequently, the sensitivities of those suffering in therapists' offices are remarkably accurate. Governed by my instincts was the following poem I wrote about Jenny:

Intentions for a Happier Day

> While torment drew me to your door, I knew from the
>   first
> You had a hardship, too.
> First, I guessed, "It must be her work."
> But, your shining satisfaction
> Halted my questioning
> The rewards of a counselor.
> Then, "It must be her health.
> Maybe it is in her fragile frame.
> She seems so breakable."
> But, your daily walk
> Reflected a sturdiness
> My first impressions ignored.
> "Perhaps her child
> Has abused her generous heart."
> No, three children, all
> Had grown up strongly, goodly true.
> There was no detecting

What tears your will in two
And keeps you apart
From a lighter, freer you.

Mysterious as Jenny's pain seemed, it was revealed one day during an otherwise typical session. She disclosed that her husband had crippling arthritis that needed serious attention and kept him in constant pain. Our mutual pain then enabled me to finish my poem:

Then, the answer.
Your home, too,
Was cloaked with a sickness
To create a darkness
In an enlightened life
That so generously shared all the answers,
Cruelly teaching that
Sometimes there are no answers.

While torment drew me to your door,
There I learned lessons on recovery
Are often inspired
By a teacher's own brand of pain.
While torment drew me to your door,
A hope within me emerges
That my continual recovery
May carry away the heaviness
That loads your shoulders
With a weight just one of you manages to lift.

While torment drew me to your door,
A possibility arises
That your persistent, healing gestures
May express away all suffering
And gradually indicate a happier day
For you as well as for me.

I stopped seeing Jenny when she moved to Texas. She left her job as my therapist, but her wisdom and kindness illuminated me through many difficult situations.

My memorable non-VA social worker, Barbara, began to tame away my demons soon after Jenny left. Though with a comfortable graduate degree, she was younger than I and fairly new to the profession of healing minds. Initially, it was difficult to imagine that someone as young and attractive as Barbara was able to understand the severe, even horrendous pain I harbored. The steady happiness conveyed by her consistent smile was distracting, at first. But, soon I found she commanded a maturity that insisted a meaningful amount of happiness was possible for me. Her quick mind allowed her a membership into Mensa (an organization that only allows participants with genius IQs). She was unusually skilled at clearly comprehending the torment my mental illness created.

While treating me one day, Barbara confided that she was a mild manic-depressive. Her smile had concealed an inner affliction that set her apart from her fellow professionals. She told me that she had always felt different and it was only after joining Mensa, when she found the opportunity to relate to a good number of eccentric people, that she enjoyed a major measure of mutual understanding. (Mensa members typically exhibit bizarre personalities, sometimes reflecting varieties of mental illnesses.) Barbara's own psychological state prepared her to treat the mentally ill with the kind of understanding no college degree could provide. Barbara was a singular brand of therapist who understood the deep, inner dungeons of others that had kept her many feelings prisoner for years.

During the nine years I saw Barbara, she became more and more adept at identifying what was important to say during a session. She had an uncanny way of absorbing feelings I tried to explain, then contributing a depth of understanding that reflected wisdom far beyond her years.

Not often, I might begin, "I can't think of anything much to say today."

A dead-end for many therapists, Barbara's response would likely be, "I have found that, when that happens, it is the time you need to talk the most."

"I wish I could think of myself as a success"—a reply that would confirm Barbara's prediction of my need for therapy.

"Two. What makes you think of yourself as other than a success?"

"I can't stay on a job long enough to get a promotion, I don't know how to talk to people, I don't own anything of real value—and so on and so on."

Indeed, I had the need to talk.

"What about the other side of the ledger?" Barbara might ask when I revealed my frail pride. "You have earned a master's degree that you paid for yourself, not common for a woman; you have a peace-loving personality that presents itself in a nonthreatening, appealing way; you have a significant level of intelligence; you are attractive—and so on and so on. Just because you never made it as the first female president of the United States does not mean you are a failure."

"Funny you should say that since that was some people's expectations of me when I graduated from high school. That assumption came with my being voted 'Most Outstanding Senior Girl.' Look at me now. I'm lucky to manage to stay out of a mental hospital during a whole calendar year."

Providing deeper insight, Barbara might rapidly stop my pitiful discourse with an intensity rare among therapists.

"Wait. Now you are talking about your health. Your health is not a reflection of your success or worthiness as a person, unless you recklessly ignore taking care of your body. I think we can accurately say you do not fit that category. You eat right, you exercise, and your personal hygiene is excellent. In fact, you are more conscientious about taking care of your health than anybody I know. With you, Two, your health is not a moral issue since you do all you can to stay well. You are well or you are not well. It is as simple as that."

"Then why do I feel so guilty when I have a breakdown?" I might whimper.

"Because that is the nature of your disability. There is no right or wrong, but your disabled ego insists you have made a mistake."

"That may be true, Barbara, but when I start getting sick I lose track of that bit of wisdom. What can I do to not feel so much shame when my mental illness overpowers me?"

Stretching me as far as she felt was safe, Barbara might add, "Think of your guilt as an external feeling, not really a part of what you are. Then, as you contemplate the guilt outside of yourself, you can more objectively view it as a foreign feeling, ready to be exported to some distant country."

Keeping up with current research helped Barbara to frequently provided new information that was relevant to the therapeutic moment. She developed a competence that led her to appearances on national talk shows as the guest expert. Besides her tremendous proficiency as a therapist, she had a strong sense of ethics. During the early years of our visits when she worked for a nonprofit government organization, I paid just $20 a visit. When the day came for her to join with other therapists and start a private counseling firm, she offered me the option to remain her client at my original sliding-scale rate. She strongly felt it was unethical to just drop me because I could not pay her for her private therapy rate, which was five times more than I was accustomed to paying ($100 per session). Over the nine years I benefited from Barbara's skills, I was only able to gradually double the meager $20 fee Barbara asked of me. Therefore, I was still privileged to observe Barbara grow in her field while Barbara observed me grow in my capacity to carry the weight of the anger and sorrow that plagued me.

One-on-one therapy with a professional whose judgment I decided to trust was often frightening as my emotional nucleus was scrutinized. There were few times in my life that I was as vulnerable as I was in this kind of interaction. For about an hour at a time, it was necessary for me to rely on another person's ability to handle my hidden thoughts and deepest passions. Perhaps it was when I fell in love or perhaps it was when I prayed that my heart was as open as when I disclosed my most hidden self to a therapist.

Chapter 10

GROUPS — INVESTING
IN THE KINDNESS OF OTHERS

W hile one-on-one therapy (relying on one trained professional) most often created an immediate bond, trusting a group of often seriously psychotic individuals with my deepest secrets was something I was more hesitant to do. Disclosing my soul to one therapist had its challenges and its rewards. However, disclosing my soul to a group of strangers who disclosed right back began as an especially traumatic experience for me.

Regardless, most of my group therapy experiences developed into valuable events, worth the time and emotion invested. At the very least, my groups provided support and useful information about my disability. (Due to serious problems with concentration, I had difficulty reading and learning on my own.) Built on foundations of both love and confidentiality, my groups evolved into places where I was able to reveal to what first were strangers secrets I declined to share with my family or friends. However, these strangers turned into allies, new families of friends who battled as we struggled mutually to find sane solutions to our grief. They helped me break loose of denial of my disability as I shared stories of similar symptoms with people who knew my pain. I was given direct proof that, despite their various diagnoses, others were surviving. My groups taught me it was vital to learn that I needed to take substantial responsibility for my own recovery each day; and emphasized valuable keys to ongoing recovery such as exercise, proper diet, good communication with my doctor, etc.

Typical support groups that are usually easily accessible in most major cities are obtained through the National Alliance for the Mentally Ill (NAMI, designed to assist families of mentally ill persons as well as their mentally ill loved ones); Emotions Anonymous (EA, a 12-step program for those who find anxiety and stress major adversaries); and The National Depressive and Manic-Depressive Association (NDMDA, comprised of and exclusively for those who suffer these specific forms of serious mental illness). Other support groups are often available, especially in large cities, and can usually be located by referring to the newspaper. Or, you can start a support group of your own, either as a local affiliate of one of the above national organizations or as a completely independent pioneer. It usually just takes a place to meet (churches, etc.) and a way to advertise (in a regular, free self-help column in the daily paper; on posters in strategic places; in notices in appropriate newsletters, etc).

My first group was a test-anxiety-reduction group, which I joined during my first successful undergraduate semester of college. I knew many believed that group therapy was a product of quacks who just wanted to profit from others' emotional vulnerability. But, I was desperate to crush the fear that seized me each time I confronted an exam. There were about seven of us, and we each had braved the horror of exams in our own terrible way. When I joined this group, I joined with the intent to succeed in the terrible task of test-taking. Soon, I became witness to the dramatic effectiveness of group therapy.

I especially remember Candice, mainly because she displayed such extreme behavior when exam time came. I recall her describing how she would aggressively grab her exam when it was handed to her and literally clutch it frantically as she first gazed at the dreadful challenge that faced her. She described her corresponding desperate mental state so vividly I was able to easily connect with her struggle.

After one semester of attending this weekly test anxiety group, I never suffered from debilitating test anxiety again.

My most intense group interactions took place among individuals with a variety of serious mental problems. Members were former, current, or future official mental patients. Each group was led by a trained therapist, an educated mental health expert who provided a back-wall from which anguished group members bounced their feelings. Some members were hospitalized or just out of the hospital. The group members paid a sliding-scale fee, or their fee was covered totally by the state, the local government, or some charitable organization. I was, initially, fairly quiet in these types of groups since paranoia was a dominant symptom for me when I was sick enough to be in such a group. I watched as every kind of negative emotion (anger, fear, hatred, despair, etc.) was exchanged. Positive emotions (trust, hope, comfort, peace, etc.) were shared as well. Therein, minds were healed.

A good example of this kind of group was one run by Joyce, a VA social worker in her late thirties or early forties. A customary group session was composed of seven or eight members bearing personalities typical of the medicated seriously mentally ill. The group varied in its interaction, but it managed to establish a basic pattern. It usually began with 30 seconds of what seemed like endless silence. Following is a typical session described using fictional characters.

It was the therapist who first spoke. "How is everyone doing?"

Perhaps it was Mike who was the first to answer. Mike was 30 years old, blond, handsome—and schizophrenic. Recently released from the hospital, he lived with his parents. He had never lived on his own. Though he tried working at simple jobs, he always ended up hospitalized after a few months. This made it necessary to endure a recovery period that was required before he could even look for new employment. He had become greatly discouraged since he had not worked for about two years. Mike was engaged, but concerned about being able to maintain a quality marriage.

"My mother says she is about to kick me out of the house," Mike began. He definitely had a need to talk.

"Why is that, Mike?" the therapist began her gentle inquiry.

"I don't know, except maybe she thinks I should be doing something."

"What do you think, Mike?" The therapist wisely gave Mike the responsibility of making a decision.

"I don't know. I think if I try working again, I will just end up in the hospital like with my last job."

"What happened with your last job?"

"I went manic while at work, and my boss called my mother to come and pick me up to take me to the hospital. I lost my job and haven't gone back to work since then."

"It must have been pretty painful," the therapist responded.

Mike's reply was simple while equally relevant. "I sure don't want it to happen again."

"Does your mother know how you feel, Mike?" Inquiring about the support of significant others was crucial to this exchange.

"I don't think she would understand. She doesn't really think I am sick now that I am out of the hospital."

"Do you think you are sick?" Again, the therapist handed over some decision-making to Mike.

"I was in a mental hospital, wasn't I?" Mike's answer carried with it a measure of aggravation.

"Yes, but you are living at home now." The therapist was not easily intimidated.

"I guess I am just afraid to try work again. What will people think of me if go manic again?"

It was at this point that the therapist typically addressed the group. "Does anyone have any answers for Mike?"

Kyle was a chronically depressed 25-year-old who had been in and out of the hospital two or three times a year for the past five years. He was tall, with a menacing countenance. His hair was usually as disheveled as his clothing. When he became depressed, he was nonfunctional, even unable to feed or dress himself. He lived with his parents, who provided necessary financial support. Kyle emerged from his depression, taking the time to suggest, "Maybe you should try a different kind of work, Mike."

Randy was the next to contribute. At age 40 he had

schizoaffective disorder. Like Kyle, he also was seldom acceptably groomed. Presently on medication that seemed to handle only some of his symptoms, he usually displayed an abundant measure of unhappiness. He was prone to fits of mania that frequently escalated into hallucinations and delusions. Randy was regularly in and out of the hospital and unable to work. He lived alone, able to maintain financial independence on VA disability checks, social security payments, and any other aid he could manage. Both his parents chose to avoid him, ignoring his need for serious emotional support.

Managing a meaningful measure of mania, Randy was able to respond to Mike's distress. "Or maybe you should just go on social security disability, food stamps, and live in state-funded housing."

Paul spoke next. In his mid-thirties, he was prone to extreme fits of anger. Diagnosed as bipolar (manic-depressive), his bulldog body and menacing expressions presented the likeness of a vicious animal. He had been picked up by the police numerous times for threatening and illegal behavior, ranging from assault to petty theft to indecent exposure. Paul's stays in prison varied in length. When he stopped his medication, he was eventually identified as having serious mental problems. It was then he was transferred out of prison to a psychiatric ward and put back on medication. Once stabilized out of the hospital he resisted taking his prescribed pills, preferring to self-medicate on alcohol and street drugs. He mainly lived on the streets and sold illegal drugs to support his habit. He continued to be periodically jailed, then hospitalized.

Paul's hostility revealed itself as he ventured an answer in a tone filled with anger. "Yeah, and be a leech, living off of the government."

Randy persisted. "Hey. If you can't work, you can't work. I've been on the streets. It's no picnic."

Kyle, though still preoccupied with his deep depression, managed another suggestion, "Yeah, but Mike should be able to do something, part-time work or something."

"What work?" asked Mike, with more annoyance in his voice. "My doctor says I can't tolerate working in a competitive setting. Everyone seems out to get me and I just get afraid."

Kyle maintained a remarkable courage as he again surfaced from his depression long enough to help. "How about working at home, by yourself, where no one is around to hassle you?"

Still annoyed, Mike inquired, "Doing what?"

"Do you have a computer?" asked Kyle.

"No," Mike curtly answered, "and I can't even imagine affording one."

Kyle was becoming frustrated, which solidly complemented his chronic depression. "I don't know. But a cheap paperback book on home businesses could help you get some ideas."

Fairly well balanced on medication, Randy skillfully managed his schizoaffective disorder as he replied, "But, if nothing works, what is left for him to turn to? Don't reject getting government money. It has been the only answer for me."

It was time for the therapist to intervene. "Well, maybe we can look a little closer at the cause of Mike's problem. Mike is prone to mood swings, which especially become a problem when he is under stress. Kyle has suggested the possibility of Mike working. However, Mike has a history of failure when it comes to keeping a job. Still, there are some possible tools he can use to try again to handle employment. He can identify warning signs that precede a breakdown and list them on paper. When any of these signs appear, Mike can ask his boss for permission to take the rest of the day off. Then, Mike can immediately contact his doctor for a medication adjustment and, if necessary, he may want to take a couple of days off to rest. Stress can build up in any job, and stress is Mike's biggest enemy. Who can give Mike some warning signs he might look for before a breakdown occurs?"

Sara was a 29-year-old manic-depressive who had been hospitalized five times in the past seven years, mainly for mania. She had started living with her parents seven years ago when her symptoms first appeared. She managed to make a little money cleaning houses. However, she found it difficult to keep steady clients. The hospital loomed as a persistent obstruction preventing her from being able to work every time she was needed.

Chronically manic, Sara found this a good time to speak in the typically rapid manner of a manic-depressive. "I find myself getting less and less sleep before I get so manic I have to go to the hospital. Once I actually didn't sleep for a week. The trick with mania is to catch the problem after two or three bad nights. Otherwise, you lose the ability to see there is a problem at all."

Sally was the next to contribute, a divorced 35-year-old with schizoaffective disorder and three children. Her unembellished appearance masked an enormously compassionate personality, molded from the sensitivity that often evolves from years of suffering. Sally was able to stay out of state hospitals, barely living on government benefits. The courts allowed her to keep her children as long as she stayed reasonably stabilized on medication, primarily Clozaril: the new and very effective antipsychotic drug, paid for by the state. Suggesting another symptom to watch for as a warning of a breakdown, Sally contributed, "I find it really hard to sit still when I get manic, and I talk, talk, talk a lot."

Then Richard spoke. He was a frail yet earnest 21-year-old who underwent ongoing care for manic depression (consisting of verbal therapy and medication). He was finishing up his fourth year of college. His talent in writing had earned him a full scholarship, which lured him to pursue a degree in journalism. He looked forward to graduating in one more semester and had been able to manage a 3.4 grade-point average. This academic success had required that he study an extreme amount of time to compensate for his limited ability to concentrate on assigned reading. He was anxious about getting and keeping a job after graduation. He knew a college degree would help land a job in journalism. However, he was unsure how he would be able to handle the stress of deadlines.

"I find it difficult to concentrate on even simple reading material, especially when I get close to a break (breakdown)," said Richard. "When this happens, I read in one-hour sessions and take ten- to fifteen-minute breaks in between."

"Do you find Richard's information helpful to you, Mike?" The therapist knew, though Mike was mentally ill, his residual ability to judge was what was most important in finding a comfortable answer to living with a serious disability.

"How can it be helpful?" Mike replied. "I can't take ten

minutes off every hour at work. That just would not be allowed."

"It sounds like working at home is most feasible for you," said the therapist.

Mike was visibly frustrated. "I guess. I'll try to concentrate on reading a book on working at home. But, I don't know how I'll do since I have a hard time concentrating on reading anything."

Randy maintained his belief in government assistance. "Sounds to me like you have a legitimate serious disability. You paid your taxes for a good number of years. Now, let the government pay you."

Despite his disability, Mike had managed to maintain a substantial degree of autonomy. "Mooching off the government is just so humiliating. My fiancée is in love with a man, not a leech living off government benefits."

Seldom were there easy answers in groups where members were chronically in and out of hospitals. Progress was often painfully slow, as with Mike. Most of the time, group members were somewhat confused, unable to find suitable ways to manage their lives in a satisfactory manner. The angry ones were sometimes subdued by the therapist's gentle support, or encouraged to express their anger. If too disruptive, they were asked to leave and come another week. If thought dangerous by the therapist, the potentially violent patients were referred to a doctor for a medication adjustment or hospitalization.

Frank, tall and imposing and proud and passionate, was married with three children and suffered from manic depression. He was angry. It was an anger that could not be overlooked. It shrouded the groups he joined like a massive mantle and dominated every therapeutic discussion. It insisted on being addressed.

"You look like you have something on your mind, Frank," observed the therapist.

"I'm sick of being sick," raged Frank. "I have forgotten what it feels like to be happy. I can't work. I can't go to school. I get angry with my family all the time. I wish I was dead or I might hurt someone."

"Have you been taking your medication?" asked the therapist.

It was medication that kept anger like Frank's under control and Frank out of jails and hospitals. However, Frank typically resented taking the prescribed medications. "I miss now and then, when the side effects become too much. I get tired of the tremors, the mental confusion, and the impotence."

The necessary strategy was clear, and the therapist showed no hesitation with this patient. "I'll set up an appointment for you to see your doctor this week. You might need a medication change to reduce those side effects. Meanwhile, some private therapy (one-on-one sessions) can also be arranged."

Such group members were usually taken very seriously. Untreated, borderline violent anger that targeted inward or outward was potentially hazardous to the patient or to others and required prompt attention. Angry clients often got help from the therapist and from others in the group. However, sometimes a medication change or hospitalization were the only answers.

Members who were united by their common brand of anguish formed a self-help support group. Such a group was not led by a therapist, so required no fee. The members were usually pretty highly functioning (not usually immediately out of a hospital) and were guided by members who took turns as group facilitators. All expedited the process of self-help. Their bond was mutual understanding. Their interaction was an amazing thing to behold.

Members did not come to meetings to judge one another. They sometimes disagreed, which was fine. However, arguing was not acceptable. Support-group members provided each other with a feeling of value and positive identity. They learned how to deal with each other's problems and needs—and became friends.

During the period I was diagnosed as bipolar (manic-depressive), I found a place to meet and started a bipolar support group. This type of group was especially rewarding since those with bipolar disorder are typically more intelligent and talented than the population in general (see *Touched with Fire*, Jamison, 1994). Initially, I facilitated the meetings with my best effort at leading. The group's size typically ranged from four to nine members. Eventually, however, the group became so large (usually varying from 15 to 25 members), we had to accommodate with a different group structure by separating into several smaller groups.

Meetings would begin with someone reading a brief introduction explaining about the group (especially for the benefit of new members). Then the main group typically subdivided into smaller groups of six to eight. Each small group selected its own facilitator and its own format for discussion. Sometimes a specific subject was addressed, or sometimes each member took some time to discuss how their week went. Occasionally, a guest speaker (usually a mental health specialist) would come in and spend about half the group session speaking and answering questions. Now and then an appropriate video was shown and discussed. However, group interaction was paramount and always a significant part of each meeting. The members' basis for meeting at all was to provide each other with crucial support.

The following are the theoretical identities and interactions of those in this bipolar support group. A typical self-help group, it created enchanted evenings of substantial relief and so reduced the suffering of courageous people. Here, the profile of each group member was a composite cluster of personalities that were typically encountered. Interaction between these members of one regular self-help support group routinely convinced such members that others also suffered, that others also functioned, and that others also cared.

Bill was hurting. He was in a depressed phase disguised by a handsome, confident appearance. An underlying depression usually creates an unattractive countenance. Bill just did not look depressed. However, his despair created an immense desire to isolate himself. How he managed to escape through his apartment door, into his car, and to the support meeting was truly a wonder. He just wanted his disease to go away. He insisted alcohol and drugs worked the best. He was present to find out what else he could do to make the miracle of good health occur.

Bill often was the first to speak. "How I got here tonight, I don't know. The depression is unbearable. If it weren't for the alcohol and cocaine, I would choose suicide."

Ben was Bill's individual small group facilitator. As he listened to Bill, he knew there were never easy answers. Ben had preserved his pride by earning a college degree and a middle management position. Usually dressed for business at group meetings, he presented an imposing appearance. He did his work well and was shaping a career. He was remarkably sensible about maintaining his sanity. Sometimes, he found himself hearing voices or getting the glimpse of a hallucination on the job. Most of the time they disappeared after a few minutes. If they did not, he went home subtly declaring himself sick and saw his psychiatrist for a medication adjustment.

Ben was careful about not discussing his disability with his employer or coworkers. He knew the dangerous stigma that the words bipolar or, especially, manic depression carried. However, he had a couple of friends who were impressed with his financial success. He confided to them about his tarnished health. They soon knew the warning signs that preceded Ben experiencing a manic state. They visited him regularly and, in the process of enjoying his friendship, thereby maintained an outside check on his behavior. When these valuable friends noticed behaviors such as talking obsessively, pacing nervously, or exhibiting any number of familiar and specific symptoms, they warned him that a breakdown might be eminent. Then, he visited his doctor for necessary professional observation and a change in medications, if warranted.

Ben's exceedingly responsible approach to mental health was sometimes irritating to the group. However, his prudent attention to his illness turned a seriously disabled man into a productive worker who could afford suits and ties and a new car. He provided feedback to Bill's depression.

"It is alcohol and drugs that will destroy you, Bill," said Ben. "The highs may be nice, but they end up disappearing and you end up where you are now. I don't have to tell you about the depression and mental confusion that alcohol creates. And the mood swings and insomnia as well as suicidal tendencies created by dependence on cocaine are no secret. Plus your dependence on marijuana is creating mental dullness as well as aggravating your mental illness. Check yourself into a hospital with treatment for dual diagnoses (serious mental illness plus alcohol and drug abuse) and get a new start."

Jake intervened. Physically powerful but mentally fragile, Jake mainly lived on meager social security checks. He was well into his forties, but his parents still provided supplements to his income and dinner once a week. It had taken years for Jake to accept having to still depend on his family for financial support. But, unable to tolerate the stress of a job, he knew he would be out on the streets were it not for the extra help. Jake lifted weights daily to remind himself he was still a man.

Lately his masculinity had been additionally challenged by a nasty fall from a roof. "These crutches for my crushed ankle are such a hassle. Falling off of a roof was pretty stupid. And the bizarre thing about it is my family is giving me more sympathy and attention than they have ever given me for my manic depression. What they don't understand is the ankle surgery is causing less pain than the manic depression. I would rather fall off a dozen roofs than live with my mental illness."

"Hey, buddy," said Jake to Bill. "I've been where you are and it is no fun. My divorce sobered me up and it's a good thing. Get help, man. Get help."

Cathy was courageous enough to attend a support group that compelled her to address her childhood and adult demons. She was middle-aged before she discovered she was bipolar. Continuous ups and downs had mysteriously plagued her life. Despite her suffering, she had maintained a marriage, raised a family, and contributed in a useful way to the community—often involved in volunteer work or church activities. An early history of sexual abuse compounded her pain. She was an imposing woman and gave to her husband, her children, and her community. Medication barely managed to keep her out of the hospital. Nothing seemed to free her of the emotional torment life had delivered to her. She continued to give as she interacted with the group, too often neglecting her own needs.

When Cathy spoke, she never sounded accusing. "I guess I'm lucky I agreed to try a variety of prescribed medication. The side effects have been difficult, but there have been some real benefits for me."

Sam came to group meetings consistently. His wife always

accompanied him. They appeared to be an engaging but desperate team. He had courageously battled his internal wars for five years, surviving reoccurring suicide attempts. With a wife and eight children to support, he found self-employment the only alternative. Frequent mood swings and occasional hallucinations made it impossible for Sam to function in a competitive work environment under the stressful surveillance of a boss. So, he managed to support his family while self-employed as a landscape designer and gardener.

Initially, the doctors tried electroconvulsive therapy (shock therapy) for Sam's deep depression. At first, besides causing temporary memory loss, the shock therapy substantially diminished the depression. However, in a short time, the bottomless sadness returned; there was another suicide attempt, and Sam was back in the hospital. Doctors observed that Sam also had manic episodes, and the diagnosis of bipolar disorder seemed the most appropriate. After several more suicide attempts, Sam found the support group. His hunger for some element of happiness created an immense appetite for knowledge. He read volumes of medical information, becoming the most medically informed member of the group.

Like Cathy, Sam also provided consistently sensible input. "All you have to do is go to the library and read about the harmful effects alcohol and drugs have on your body, especially if you are also taking medication. When you learn what you're dealing with, you may sober up and get real help."

Connie possessed a professional air that was intimidating. She remembered owning and running a small factory of 150 workers— and she remembered losing it all. Her life featured nearly continuous mania, accented with occasional depression. The mania kept her on top of a competitive market, and depression carried her to the bottom more than once. She entered the group on lithium, with a craving to understand her yo-yo life. In the group, she met others who also tried and failed and tried and failed. Soon, she was ready to again try making a meaningful living, juggling her doctor and lithium with company phone calls and appointments.

Connie had fidgeted in her chair all evening. Finally she

admitted, "I'm having a hard time. I've been manic all day. I can't stay still and concentrate on the group and am afraid to drive myself home."

"No problem, Connie," said Sam. "Would you like to go home now? My wife and I can drive you."

Connie was visibly relieved. "Oh, thank you, Sam. I think that would be a good idea. Then I'll call my doctor tomorrow and pick up my car."

(Sam, his wife, and Connie left the meeting, and the group discussion continued.)

Ben restarted the group momentum. "I have felt particularly lonely lately. I can't seem to shake the despair."

Cathy responded in her typical compassionate manner. "I know it is so horrible not to be in charge of your feelings with no one to understand, even when you describe how you feel. If you ever just want to talk during the week, Ben, just give me a call."

"Thank you, Cathy," Ben gratefully responded. "But you have your own set of problems that you seldom talk about. How is your family lately?"

"Oh, I guess they are okay. I make sure they are clothed and fed, as long as my husband manages to bring home a paycheck. I don't know what else I can do, but it never seems enough."

Facilitating in his own personal, supportive style, Ben declared, "You need to watch out for yourself, Cathy. Overwhelming yourself with your family will just result in misery and maybe even the hospital. You have told the group about the incest you had as a child. Maybe you should talk more about that. To carry around all the guilt it has caused you would be too much for anyone. It was not your fault. You were an innocent child. Maybe the shame you feel over the incest causes you to feel this persistent obligation to cater to your family." (Years of therapy had made Ben a fairly good amateur at figuring out other people's pain.)

Ben's comments left Cathy in tears. "What you are saying makes sense. My past is so full of garbage and guilt I don't know how to take care of myself anymore. I think I need to have a frank talk with my family. They need to understand my pain and let me have more room to recover—not just from my past, but from the present. That much healing may not be possible, but I think I deserve trying." (Over the years, Cathy had also developed her share of skills as a psychiatric client.)

Janice was well acquainted with mental hospitals, having revolved in and out of them for 15 years. As the product of a rough, lower-class neighborhood, she had been arrested and hospitalized twice for assault. Her aggressive style of speech and shabby dress revealed a resident of the streets. From the beginning, the group was cautious of her verbal hostility. One week Janice became offended with another group member's teasing.

A slight, friendly shove was enough to provoke Janice into a physical attack. The scuffle was broken up before it became a definite fight, and Janice left the meeting. Three days later she was willingly hospitalized and, once out of the hospital, returned to the group two or three more times with the group's cautious permission. Thereafter, she was gone—somewhere.

The last evening Janice was present, she abruptly emerged from behind her wall of pain. "Well, I'm out of the hospital again. I just can't help physically hurting people. Someone triggers my anger and I explode. I don't want to be this way. The medication helps. But, I am left feeling like a zombie, not able to think clearly. If it weren't for social security disability I would be out on the streets again, getting into fights and getting raped."

Do self-help support groups work? As a member of several of these types of groups, I have witnessed miracles. There, I have learned I am not isolated, that others also suffer.

Since it has been found that so many of the mentally ill successfully commit suicide, there is no doubt in my mind that this simple collection of caring people saves lives. Wherein, I have learned there is hope that others go on. The process has caused me to marvel at what wonders can occur from the caring exchange among suffering people.

PART III:

MAINTENANCE AND MIRACLES

Chapter 11
A SOCIAL LIFE —
PRESCRIBED AND APPLIED

Early in my mental illness (by the time I had experienced a second breakdown and an extended hospitalization and before I had 28 hospitalizations under my belt), an outpatient group therapist advised me to organize a collection of compassionate people that I could depend on to meet the specific needs created by my disability. In other words, I was advised to make some friends (ideally, besides those inside my therapeutic group experiences).

This therapist was right on the mark. The abundance of research on the effects of love and support indicates love promotes survival. If you ask the question, "Who loves you?" and the answer is, "No one," you can anticipate five times higher risk of premature death and diseases of all kinds.

An active social life was never a problem until I graduated from high school. I played the guitar and so was in demand at parties. In high school I was elected to every student body office I aspired to hold. In my senior year, those who knew me (and everybody seemed to) thought I would likely make some kind of important contribution during my life. Graduating 19th in my high school class of about 350 convinced me I could handle most academic challenges. I had no idea that the challenges that lay ahead were more formidable than anything academic. Being voted as Most Outstanding Senior Girl sealed a promising future, bursting with success. Perhaps I would be a successful business person or, perhaps, an important politician. Optimistic speculations concerning my future were numerous.

However, as my mental illness became more and more serious, purging my life from nearly all close acquaintances eventually ruined my social life. The stigma of mental illness left me with a label I was afraid to reveal to anyone; and the closer I became to someone, the greater the danger that they would realize my secret: I was a deranged deviant. Mental illness is one of the loneliest of diseases. My best high school friend, Sandy, moved away. I had not corresponded with her for a substantial amount of time. I was ashamed of my illness. I had found myself unable to love. It seemed all-encompassing, not just part of who I was but absolutely who I was.

It has always been vital that I have a select support system of friends who appreciate me for my qualities and whose dependable presence keeps me out of the hospital as much as possible. However, time has taught me that caution is vital in selecting which significant others should become aware of my disease. Rejection, as a result of the stigma my illness had created, was perhaps a liability second only to the disease itself; rejection being the most terrifying nightmare I could experience, whether asleep or awake.

One day, in the 1970s, I found myself in the middle of delivering a church talk on interpersonal communication, something I was rapidly becoming ineffective at exercising. I knew my growing seclusion was not healthy. My words reflected my concern. It was as follows:

> Silence is an important thing. We need reverence during church meetings, we need silence when we study, and something close to silence when we pray. But, how important is talk?
> Henry David Thoreau, the famed author and not as famed

recluse, recognized (even in his solitude with the beauties of nature) a need for conversation. Said Thoreau, "I had three chairs in my house; one for solitude, two for friendship, three for society. When visitors came in larger and unexpected numbers there was but the third chair for them all. However, they generally economized the room by standing up."

Robinson Crusoe, another well-known recluse (though not by choice), discovered his need for talk the hard way. Not until he became isolated on an obscure island did he begin to desperately cherish talk. Even language was a minor barrier when at last he found the companion, Friday. He eventually taught Friday enough English to engage in conversation. To talk with another was such joy. Through their comradeship they discovered happiness.

Today, we have our televisions and our radios and our busy schedules and almost every kind of noise imaginable. And, somewhere, there is the sad hush in place of the sound of talk. Where once conversation was casual and frequent—even an art—it has become for too many an unwelcome strain, an uncomfortable obligation. Its real value has been forgotten, removed by modern-day diversions. Are too many of us becoming contemporary recluses, retiring too often to our own Walden Ponds and remote islands?

In March 1977, I finished a third or fourth hospitalization and joined an assertiveness training class. My insecurities surrounding talking with others had reached the point of chronic self-doubt. I thought an assertiveness training class would provide for me the skills and courage necessary to speak with others.

The premise to this class was that there were three basic approaches to communication: 1) aggression, where the communicator encroaches on others' rights, often expressing themselves in a hostile manner; 2) non-assertiveness, where the communicator fails to claim their rights in a direct manner, most often being a victim; and 3) assertiveness, where the communicator claims the right to express themselves in a direct, straightforward manner. Naturally, assertiveness was the preferred approach to quality communication.

I began by recognizing how poor my eye contact was. I had failed to engage in good eye contact since I was a child. The importance of this behavior while pursuing quality conversation was emphasized by the instructor. As I attempted to develop this skill, I accented my effort with my own untitled poem:

> They say the eye reflects
> Intentions of the heart.
> But, to meet another's gaze
> Can tear my soul apart.
>
> Perhaps I fear the eye
> Will tell me all too much.
> It might be I fear the truth,
> So cower from its clutch.
>
> So, by avoiding other's eyes
> I know no pain or joy,
> But only stoic images
> I'm certain won't destroy.
>
> But, if behind the eye
> There dwells a hallowed chain
> Of nerves and cells and tissue
> Which lead us to the brain,
>
> Perhaps we can perceive
> Just where the mind has been
> By kindly searching others' eyes
> When words won't let us in.
>
> But I can only challenge,
> The threat's so hard to bear,
> That knowledge of the mind or heart,
> Should cause me to beware.

They say the Savior's eyes
Could discern the soul,
As he looked back lovingly
With such divine control.

Oh, to see men's virtues
With the hardship they've endured.
Oh, to share compassion.
My caution would be cured.

My futile fears will vanish,
My prisoned life set free,
As I learn to meet men's gaze
With perfect charity.

During the class, I frequently apologized for tiny mistakes I made, as if they were a terrible burden to others. Though my eye contact was slowly improving, I found myself taking on the main burden of others' sensitivities. The instructor's gentle guidance helped me realize that I need not feel a huge responsibility to make others happy. Another untitled poem reflected my thoughts on this matter. It follows:

Why do I suffer others' pain?
Why does it torment so?
Oh, how I long to quench or drain
The anguish and the woe.

Or to extinguish others' hurts
With one supreme embrace.
But my longing only flirts;
I cower at pain's face.

I cringe to think men suffer,
So, when pain appears,
I try to stand as buffer,
But crumble at men's tears.

Someday I'll learn the words
To make the world rejoice,
And men will soar with birds;
Such bliss, a welcome choice.

But, now I mutely wait
Until I can endure
The agony of hate;
And know the words that cure.

As the class progressed, the importance of compromise was emphasized. Conversational conflict was something that could easily be avoided by compromising interaction. Again, following is a poem inspired by this valuable class—this time, specifically on the subject of conflict:

Is it wise to compromise,
Or such a sin to win?
With truth at stake,
There's much less ache
At tamely giving in.

Yes, truth can be preserved
Above a common ground.
With some degree of harmony,
Soon hungry minds come round.

But those who shun the feast
Cannot be forced to dine.
It's hard to bear, when friends won't share
A bounty so divine.

So, always there is suffering
When others won't agree.
How hard to know, some prefer woe
To blessed harmony.

Class graduation finally came around, and I was included. I celebrated. The challenge had been so great, I could only give credit to God for my success. I ultimately knew I deserved to pass the class when I succeeded in avoiding an argument with my stepfather. My optimum efforts provided an important degree of peace as I balanced what would have been troublesome conflict into sweet equilibrium. Though my fragile emotional makeup left me exhausted by my successful encounter, celebrating was accomplished by the following final, untitled poem:

> How frail I feel tonight;
> How drained I have become;
> For now I see it's not from me
> Comes equilibrium.
>
> It's granted as a gift,
> A blessing from on high,
> To make life less intense duress
> From dying at each try.
>
> It's given out of love
> As I learn to obey,
> And come to see humility
> Can balance pain away.
>
> In my feeble state
> How grateful I've become;
> From harsh defeat, how grand to greet
> Sweet equilibrium.

Despite the valuable tools I learned in my assertiveness training class, consistently applying them was another thing. The courage and concentration required to always assert myself as I suffered a serious mental illness crushed my initial efforts to such a degree that I soon sabotaged myself and forgot nearly all I had learned.

By 1984, 14 years had passed since I had seen my high school friend Sandy. I had flown with my family to New York City to attend a birthday party for my elderly grandmother. I decided to visit Sandy in her small apartment in Greenwich Village. She was working as a waitress. I knew that, since Sandy had dropped out of college and moved to New York, she had suffered her own pain involving some radical relationships and drastic changes—including her name. She now identified herself as Nevada. She seemed comfortable in her tiny apartment with a legion of locks on the door. She suggested we dine together just down the street at an East Indian restaurant. During the hour-long meal there were long, awkward spaces of silence. Longing for her refreshing humor, I was, instead, primarily audience to cynicism. Later, when I arrived home, I finally wrote to Nevada. As so often before, my communication was in the form of poetry. I made a feeble attempt to express the burden my disability created and how much I had relied on her for some form of temporary recovery. These verses are as follows:

It's Been Too Long, Nevada

It's been too long, Nevada
Since you've been around.
Remember how we laughed?
How I miss that sound.

Livin' in the city
Must be right for you.
But, I can't believe, Nevada;
The laughter now is through.

Once we both were children
In a crazy way;
Givin' teachers trouble.
Livin' every day.

Though that's all behind us,
Let's not let time destroy

All we shared together.
There's still much to enjoy.

I recall the day you left.
Our lives were both confused.
I was goin' nowhere.
You were bein' used.

Distance seemed to matter.
You had to get away.
The moments that we tried to talk
There wasn't much to say.

The years have passed so quickly.
It hasn't been all fun.
We've both learned to accept pain
And learned to love someone.

I guess that we've been growin'
While knowin' all the while
There was a time when we both found
It easier to smile.

I do not remember getting an answer from Nevada and, as time progressed, we became strangers to each other. However, I had no way of knowing how she suffered serious depression in her adult life (probably inherited from her father). Through the years, I spoke to her two or three times on the phone. Finally, her family called to give me the terrible news of her suicide. Nevada shot herself while in her apartment.

During many of those years that Sandy (Nevada) was alive, I was alone, allowing myself to confide only to therapists. Sandy had become a distant acquaintance. Making new friends would mean starting over. However, desperate not to experience the agony of another breakdown, I was prepared to go to any extreme. If making friends mattered so much (like my therapists so frequently and vividly announced), I would make friends. I set out to systematically meet people.

Church functions seemed like a good place to start. However, though the structure of an established religious organization provided a likely vehicle for social contact, this did not mean new friends rushed to my side. Subduing my fears enough to attend church functions while mingling enough to engage in sustained conversation created an ordeal I had not fully anticipated. It felt all wrong. People seemed distant, possibly even offended by my presence. Perhaps I acted peculiar. Perhaps I was boring. Perhaps I tried too hard. The whole effort just seemed to create another dilemma in my life: getting people to like me. My efforts did not fail completely; I did cultivate some temporary relationships. Unfortunately, they did not seem to meet the original requirements of a personal support group; that is, a collection of people who knew I was mentally ill and still accepted and supported me in my struggle. Granted, this was not primarily their fault since I consistently lost my courage and failed to tell anybody I was a revolving-door psychiatric patient.

Those fleeting friendships I developed could best be described as peculiar. It seemed that no sooner would I establish the beginnings of a relationship than I would find that the new, potential friend exhibited some bizarre characteristics. It was not so peculiar that I attracted unusual personalities. Being mentally ill had left me with some eccentricities of my own and the inclination to attract the unorthodox and, most frequently, unstable. However, I needed stability in my new support system, not others in desperate need of support. Unfortunately, I seemed to attract the bizarre, often the emotionally crippled. The association would last through a few phone calls and maybe even survive a lunch or two. Then, whatever friendly conversations I managed to generate evaporated into an atmosphere of alienation. I would be left emotionally exhausted and somewhat humiliated for letting any of my afflicted feelings out for even brief examination.

I tried a few roommates, thinking that I could make a resident friend while hiding my psychiatric peculiarities. This lasted until I found it intolerable dwelling very long with another person with human frailties. Then a breakdown would occur. Though I was never violent, my behavior was certainly distractive when I became ready for the hospital. My rapid roaming around the apartment, nonstop talking, and eventual hospitalization discouraged and often frightened even the most accepting soul. Roommates eventually fled to more stable, less fearful households.

Romantic relationships were also brief and always strained. It quickly became awkward talking about love while pondering the unlikelihood of a stable future. Most of the time it never got that far. I would go out on a date or two and then feel threatened by the attention. So much fondness too soon did not constitute support for me, only suffocation.

While I developed a total of six serious suitors, three of these relationships eventually prompted me to make significant emotional investments. These men had characteristics that initially attracted me. I was persuaded to accept proposals of marriage.

My first two engagements took place while I was still in the military. Kevin was a handsome, vibrant man who loved life. His passion for living was contagious; and I was frequently prompted into episodes of intense amusement and affection. Kevin was remarkably generous to me, allowing me to drive his little sports car and use his expensive camera equipment. How we became engaged is curious. One of Kevin's friends congratulated us one day on our engagement (though neither Kevin nor I had discussed marriage). After that, it was just assumed by others that we were going to get married fairly soon. When soon became nearly immediately, I had to break Kevin's heart with the dismal news that I was not in enough love with him. Kevin was considerate about the break and kindly retreated into his own world of pain as he adjusted to rejection.

Kyle was a former monk and became a conscientious objector in the military service. His powerful frame, the product of a background in football, provided an alluring contrast to his gentle personality. When he expressed his love for me, even eventually proposing marriage, I was astounded. Though he caught me off guard, I knew from his accounts of past damaging romances, (this time) my answer had to be immediate and honest. I again chose "no" and again left for my barracks with the grim awareness I had deeply hurt another human being.

It was not until I was well out of the military, in undergraduate school, that my last attempt at a stable romance occurred: Tod entered my life. He was a mathematical genius who loved writing children's poetry. Not unusually handsome, his childlike manner was appealing—communicating innocence unusual for a 35-year-old. He, too, was generous in our relationship, allowing me to use his car when it was needed. His simple sense of humor was entertaining. He also had been a victim to mental illness. While his psychiatric problems were not as serious as mine, he was familiar with the regimen of taking psychiatric medications. Though some might think our mutual brand of pain would provide a strong unity, instead, I felt it difficult to tolerate his moody disposition. Even today, I would not recommend that two mentally ill people live together. The stress could likely be incomprehensible.

Once wedding plans were called off (again by me), Tod was furious. He dumped me in front of my apartment and drove off in a rage. I felt too guilty to fault him. After all, like usual, I had agreed to commitments that I inwardly knew would be impossible. In the process, I had caused several persons considerable pain.

Though a bond somewhat akin to love was created with these three men, the inevitable time always arrived when I disassociated myself (usually when concrete wedding plans became imminent). I was not prepared to reveal to anyone the complications of living with a seriously mentally ill person, much less endorse it under the questionable canopy of marriage. A damaged psyche was always my outcome when any romantic relationship terminated, the result of investing so much of my heart.

Undergraduate work came and went, and so did a meager collection of fleeting friends (male and female). I continued to obtain occasional roommates along with temporary support from individuals I met at church functions. Otherwise, I lived a close to isolated existence, interrupted now and then by a friendly cashier or lowly janitor. This pattern continued when I moved back to my hometown to attend graduate school. It was then that I moved into a studio apartment by myself while I shared a central kitchen with three other persons. Again, I continued to be paranoid that someone would find about my secret.

It would have continued that way had it not been for Jessie.

At first she was just another church contact. After a few preliminary conversations that made me feel unusually comfortable, a friendship was established. It seemed uncanny how safe I felt with Jessie. She loved to talk without being overbearing. I had become awkward at conversation, not knowing how to fill in the pauses. With Jessie, pauses just gave her the opportunity to contribute some interesting new idea or fact that amused her active mind (she read voraciously). She was physically smaller than I, but carried an inner strength that provided a valuable anchor for me. Could it be? Had I at last found someone I could depend on being stable?

It was not long after we met that I took the terrible chance of telling Jessie I was mentally ill. Jessie was interested, but her casual "Okay" indicated she was not at all well informed about the enormous dilemma my medical problem presented. I think I even mentioned having to stay in the hospital but do not remember getting much more of a reaction from Jessie. I was not sure if she was being polite or if she just genuinely liked me. Both possibilities were acceptable. Therefore, a precarious new friendship had a dubious beginning.

However, nearly from the start, Jessie showed a unique brand of understanding of my distressing mental disorder—an affliction that had, in spite of my efforts, previously left me socially crippled and alone. She simply did not allow me to retreat into myself when depression arrived. She would usually insist that we go out to dinner, to a movie, or just go out. It was remarkable how quick a remedy was created by the diversion of Jessie's carefree personality. Combined with her capacity for fun was also a capacity for caring. When she seemed to run out of her collection of compassionate resources, we were both rescued by her sense of humor.

These qualities succeeded in changing the pattern of my unhappy life. I began to capture glimpses of gladness, then moments, then full hours. It was momentous when I actually declared I had a pretty good day.

The occasions finally came when Jessie became witness to the harsher cruelties of my disease. Several times, she helplessly observed me suffer mania that prevented me from sleeping for days and days. And, she became no stranger to my hallucinations, which resulted in my describing foreign images and responding to their promptings by roaming around the house or talking to the air. It was during these breaks from reality that I would each time become desperate enough to let Jessie drive me to the hospital.

I learned to count on frequent visits from Jessie during hospital stays. She would come bearing small gifts and valuable extra supplies. I had seldom had visitors during former hospitalizations. Jessie's attention brought a whole new dimension to recovery.

For me it remains unmistakable that, from roommates to romances, my feeble efforts at acquiring a quality supportive relationship were a fiasco until Jessie made herself graciously invaluable. What about my family? I believe they were in denial over the seriousness of my illness for many years. During that time, they just did not seem there for me. Things have improved. My brother has visited me in the hospital more than once, and his family provides an open invitation for Sunday dinners. Since my stepfather died, my only living parent is my mother. Eventually she was able to reach a better understanding of mental illness and treat me accordingly. And, I've always known she loves me. Today, I also know that my brother and his family are there for me whenever I need them. They just needed to come around to their own brand of understanding.

After living with Jessie for 14 years, my diagnosis was changed from manic-depressive (formerly changed from schizophrenic) to schizoaffective. The new diagnostic criteria for psychiatrists was updated in 1994, with my major mental illness more correctively identified.

Nevertheless, Jessie occupies the center of my social life. She has become educated in the complexities of mental illness and loves me enough to make that knowledge important. Therefore, Jessie and I have remained roommates, sharing a common roof where she weathers my eccentricities while keeping a cautious eye on my always-present symptoms, aware of any serious warning signs that could land me in the hospital if not treated early with medication. This task has become a considerably smaller burden for Jessie since I started taking Clozaril.

Jessie's gregarious personality has been somewhat contagious: I have developed more of a propensity for social contact than in the past. I have, therefore, acquired a select (though small) family of friends, some who know my diagnosis and still find value in my acquaintance. This family has included some comfortable relationships with church members.

Loneliness no longer consumes me, which creates a frame of reference considerably superior to where I was 28 years ago. I do still, too often, feel inclined to fall back into seclusion. I daily find myself often preferring the isolation of my home office, where I can read sporadically, make routine phone calls (where I am not required to meet another, eye to eye), and manage what is sometimes drudgery but most often the reward of writing (between everyday house chores). Jessie does the grocery shopping. There is hardly anything that produces more anxiety for me than the weekly task of mingling down the aisles with other shoppers and managing the crucial chore of accurately paying the cashier in whatever manner is appropriate.

Despite my lingering social paranoia, Jessie's acceptance continues and convinces me I can make a difference to others. Jessie rescues me from whatever residual denial remains part of my awareness. Since high school and the onset of my initial psychosis, I have not experienced such total acceptance. I remain certain more than ever of the importance of social activity. Today, with Jessie's support, I usually successfully avoid the symptoms of solitude.

Now, Jessie has learned the cruelties of my disease and seen my pain. Not only has Jessie's staying power been unique, but her reasons for staying have made her exceptional. She has identified a collection of qualities in me that she maintains makes my friendship worth whatever extra effort she may make. Jessie has been able to see kindness, intelligence, justice, endurance, and strength of character in me where I thought for years I was just crazy.

Chapter 12
ATTEMPTING ACADEMIA

W hile a somewhat more than satisfactory life was the standard for me during my high school years, I was not prepared for the terrorist that engaged into full attack when I graduated from high school and started college.

Preparing financially for college required that I spend the preceding summer earning tuition. I got a job that paid well. However, recurring headaches plagued me throughout those three industrious months following high school graduation. It did not occur to me that my entire biochemistry was advancing toward chaos.

A biological brain disease became more visible when college began—with a whole new set of stresses. First, there was the problem of reading. I could not concentrate on my texts. Every word was a struggle, and phrases were nearly impossible. In a panic, I labored to take more notes during lectures. However, the legibility and relevance of these strained efforts were dangerously poor.

My professors appeared as threatening figures, ready to fail me at a whim. Then other students became frightening as I struggled to pass to and from classes. It was especially during those times that I barely managed to suppress the urge to run, not understanding how my inner body contained so much energy. How could I have been aware that mania was beginning to escalate inside my genetically vulnerable form?

Midterm exams arrived. I was way behind and in a panic. In desperation, I dropped out of all my classes. Too humiliated to face my friends, I retreated to my bedroom and hid there for the rest of the semester.

Great courage was essential to start school again in January, knowing I was a semester behind my high school classmates. For my second try, I attended school only part time and selected different classes. I had become horrified at the more difficult curriculum that had eluded me the previous semester. Again, midterm exams arrived and, again, I dropped out before allowing myself to accept the challenge of tests.

I had failed a whole year of college. However, giving up completely was unacceptable. A product of a family that revered higher education, I refused to even imagine myself without a college degree. I tried school again the following fall, again the next semester, again the next semester, again the next semester, and again the next semester. Sitting for an hour attempting to absorb a lecture produced unbearable stress for a nervous system that had begun to prohibit me from even a reasonable amount of tension. In three years, I passed three classes while withdrawing from the rest—not able to face the professors with a required proper drop card. In so doing, I "earned," with great humiliation, failing grades.

Mental retardation is often confused with mental illness. This confusion is understandable since the high stress of mental illness often creates great difficulty engaging in organized thought and, so, in effective academic endeavors. However, there is a definite distinction between mental retardation and mental illness. Mental retardation is seen as experienced from birth where there is decreased intellectual capability (IQ below 70). Exceptions occur with those who suffer with Savant Syndrome, who exhibit amazing skills in specific areas such as math or music. However, mental illness is a brain disorder that most researchers agree is genetically based (and can be environmentally influenced) without IQ below 70 (usually well above), which typically appears full force in late adolescence or in the early twenties. Cognitive (thinking) problems may appear when other symptoms appear, such as poor concentration, poor memory, depression, hallucinations, and others. These distractions could disrupt a person's life realities so that there is serious neglect in correction of everyday situations and responsibilities. A good number of high achievers have suffered from severe mental illness: Abraham Lincoln, Isaac Newton, Tennessee Williams, Beethoven, Winston Churchill, Teddy Roosevelt, and many more.

I subsequently entered the armed forces, and two years passed by before I accumulated more college credits. While in the service, I again tried and failed while attending a few classes on local college campuses. I then discovered the military would give me the free opportunity to earn two years of basic college credits through testing while I was still enlisted. Conditioned at avoiding tests, I cautiously approached these new indicators of my academic competency. Surprisingly, the questions merely presented a fairly challenging review of what I had thoroughly learned during my more astute years in high school. If I had not excelled in high school, I probably would have done poorly on these tests. In a few hours, I had completed and passed every exam.

After leaving the military, I was left with more than I had knowingly enlisted for: I not only had money for college (the GI Bill) but also a good supply of credits obtained through testing.

I knew it was time to succeed outside of the army at higher education. My immediate choice of schools was a small church school almost 800 miles from home. However, I carried a major problem on my shoulders: I had accelerated to seriously psychotic.

Hallucinations (both visual and auditory) and delusions characterized my state of mind. However, my interior chaos was not easily discernable and I was able to quietly secure a room with a small family, the Conners, soon after I arrived in my new college town. The mother was a nervous woman who taught piano for extra money and was devoted to her three children. The children were well-behaved and friendly.

I soon settled into my modest rental room. After attending a few classes, I decided it was my responsibility to improve the college. I began by informing the faculty of their errors. I wrote a letter to reach this goal. I do not remember how or if I distributed it to all the faculty members. However, I am fairly sure it was sent to the administration. This letter shouted out arrogance, which would have easily been diagnosed by a mental health expert as delusions of grandeur. The single typewritten page was filled with religious references, most of which were distorted descriptions of religious concepts. I earnestly sought to raise the quality of the school's theological education. My effort read as follows:

Dear faculty member,

As a sincere church member, I'm attending your college to be intellectually and spiritually edified. During my first week of classes, I have had harsh disappointment on both counts.

Consequently, I would respectfully suggest the following to you, since you are entrusted to shaping my mind for higher learning:

1) Fast and pray more that your eye may be single to the glory of God; divine intelligence, which specifically involves the truth you happen to specialize in.

2) Follow rules set by the administration as you would have your students follow. This involves not bicycling on campus walks, referring to fellow instructors as "Brother" or "Dr." instead of on a first name basis on campus; and enforcing attendance and any other class policy the administration has initiated. I've had at least two instructors verbally refute school policy in the classroom.

3) Clearly explain an assignment once, preferably writing it on the board. Ask if there are any questions on the assignment, then carry on with the class. Any questions not asked can be clarified between students, and need not take valuable class time. This procedure would encourage students to listen more carefully when instructions are first given.

4) Utilize every moment of class time with valuable instruction. This would involve fewer elementary analogies unless specific questions are asked that warrant them and would include reducing ludicrous remarks. Too much class

comedy breaks the trend of serious productive thought. Laughter is enjoyable in friendly conversation; but, humbly, I remind you the greatest joy requires no laughter. I admonish you to encourage from students an inner quiet delight with what they learn, what they discover, and what they create.

Devotedly,
An eager student

I followed this letter with bizarre behavior on campus. In the middle of a class lecture, I walked up to the front of the class, stood next to the instructor, and glared at the students. A short time later, I ran down a school corridor shouting that students must repent before it was too late. As my psychotic symptoms escalated, I locked myself in my room, reading the Bible and praying for answers to a collection of religious questions. I emerged from my portion of the house mainly for meals.

Tracked down by school administrators after about a month as a student in their college, I was transported to a nearby community hospital. My psychiatric hospitalization lasted two weeks. I was then discharged. My next step was to pick up my belongings from the Conners'[1] home and fly home. This proved to be an easy task since Mrs. Conner had packed all my things and placed them in a convenient spot in the front yard. It was apparent she was eager to see me go. The humiliation I felt as I found my suitcases on her lawn (clearly informing me it was appropriate to leave) was beyond words.

A college degree was, nevertheless, still on my agenda. I was not finished with the prospect of completing school. It would be another year (which included yet another hospitalization) before I seriously attempted college life again. With so many academic failures behind me, I finally decided to be more scrupulous in choosing a major. I had previously chosen classes in math and science, subjects for which I did not possess strong aptitudes. It was time for me to select classes for which I was most likely to succeed rather than perpetuate academic defeat after defeat.

After honestly evaluating my academic strengths to identify a subject in which I felt confident, writing emerged as a top contender. I enrolled with a major in journalism at a new and much larger campus 500 miles away from home, a comfortable distance from my initial humiliation at my former college, and just across the street from a VA hospital. I moved into a boarding house with 14 other young women and an elderly lady who was a live-in house director. This director was on the grouchy side but the other, substantially younger occupants united to raise the morale of the house. I was fond of what resembled a newfound family. I shared one of the nine bedrooms with a talented, attractive language student. She had previously been a dance major until she suffered a back injury. Emotional and affectionate, she found herself uncomfortable with the distance I maintained. Eventually, she moved down the hall into another room with a close friend. Most of my other fellow boarders were carefree dance students and respected my appetite for solitude.

I cautiously stayed to myself, afraid my diagnosis might be suspected or, even worse, detected. I believe it was just assumed I was quiet and a little eccentric, nothing unusual on a college campus.

This university accepted all the credits I tested for in the military plus the very few I had earned in my academic struggles prior to entering the armed services. After just a semester, I was a junior, with the GI Bill continuing to pay my way. I was ecstatic, finally feeling like an established student of higher education.

I made college work well for me during the following four years. Due to having my mental disability identified as "service connected," I became qualified for Vocational Rehabilitation from the VA, which more generously assisted in undergraduate school costs than did the GI Bill. This aid not only covered tuition, but even paid for books and supplies, and provided a monthly stipend. This enabled me to put aside my GI Bill for other education that might become important.

I began my first semester with a weekly support group designed to overcome test anxiety, which it successfully did by the end of the semester. With test anxiety behind me and with my military-tested credits I was optimistic, hoping I could complete a degree in two years. However, my denial caused me to ignore that I still had a serious mental illness. Therefore, I had to tolerate short annual hospital stays, which required that I miss an entire semester annually.

Soon, wanting more privacy, I moved out of the boarding house and into my own tiny apartment. This nook consisted of two rooms (a main room and a bathroom) and a small kitchen area. I slept on a sofa bed and managed to prepare acceptable meals in the tiny kitchen section. I wanted the seclusion, a bad sign with other symptoms that soon landed me in the hospital. After about a year had passed, I moved to a larger space across the street: a four-room, basement apartment that only cost a few dollars more each month.

Hallucinations plagued me annually, during January and February, or sometimes into March. It was then I would cross the wide street from the college campus to admit myself into the VA hospital. I would make up some classes during the summer. The cycle was pretty predictable. I would not have been surprised if the VA hospital staff put me on their yearly calendar.

My study habits were tailor-made to compensate for a troubled brain. I took all my class notes in a question-and-answer format, which made it convenient to quiz myself when preparing for an exam. I also fed these notes into a tape recorder each day. With this accomplished, I was prepared before each exam to test myself by playing back the recorded material. To avoid last-minute stressful crunches I began preparing for exams (quizzing myself with my written and recorded notes) at least two weeks before the exams occurred. Whatever special assignments (term papers, etc.) were required were sometimes completed well before they were due, again preventing debilitating stress. This study pattern was custom-made for a chronic mental patient. By minimizing last-minute pressures, I was able to maximize my academic performance and earn a somewhat comfortable 3.4 grade-point average. I presented my learning system to the director of the University Learning Center, and he enthusiastically requested a manuscript describing my system. I eagerly complied. It was my hope that others who also found college a major challenge would also benefit from my study method.

Transcendental Meditation, morning and evening, helped keep me as focused as was possible and gave me the emotional endurance to fight off a lot of depression. Therefore, I was able to awaken on time every morning and remarkably arrive at each class on time. My most comfortable memories of college center on the early mornings and late afternoons when I took 20 minutes to quietly meditate and rejuvenate my heart and mind with a meditation mantra.

Study habits that required lengthy sessions at the tape recorder, fixing daily meals, two meditation sessions per day, regular exercise that helped me to reduce clinically chronic depression, and miscellaneous errands left me with less time than most other students to develop a social life. These routines, however, provided a valuable structure to my chaotic inner world. I gladly chose to stay away from sorority parties and campus clubs. These scheduled social activities seemed frivolous. Then, there was the potential danger that I would become too trusting and confide to someone about my illness. The safe alternative was to remain solitary: I was most comfortable not allowing myself to engage in close relationships.

A typical school week involved closely scheduling my activities on paper. I found I was lost with no daily direction if I did not create a written schedule to guide me through each waking hour. I programmed my study time in detail, always a week ahead to prevent last-minute stress. Every day I knew upon awakening what I would be studying and when I would study it.

Nearly every morning I awakened at 6:00 a.m., showered, dressed, and meditated. Then there were three to four classes to attend. Lunch broke up the day around noon, providing a therapeutic distraction from the intensity of note-taking through lectures. Swimming provided some relief from depression, and I included it in every day that I could manage (about three times a week). However, just walking to class with a heavy backpack of books provided a wealth of daily exercise. At the end of the last daily class or after homework in the library, I was prompted to cook my dinner and fit in some evening studying. I was usually in bed by 9:00 p.m. enabling myself an ample nine hours of sleep each night. I found if I did not get this much sleep, I was not alert enough to take quality class notes the following day. This was due to an exhausting inner emotional fury that insisted on accompanying me during my waking hours.

My tight timetable of scheduled classes included weekends of treating myself to sleeping in, a meal out and/or a movie, a trip to the nearest shopping centers for groceries, clothes, miscellaneous items, and church. Since I had no car, I needed to use the bus and stay close to home. This was a comfortable arrangement for me since I did not trust my driving ability and so preferred the protection a bus provided.

I spent my weekends alone.

Breaks occurred each school quarter, usually lasting two weeks. I never left town during these periods of potential amusement. Again, I reveled in being alone—the best way I could find to recharge my mental/emotional batteries.

Since hospitalizations caused me to miss about a semester a year, I did my best to make up for the lost time by always attending summer school. Though these hospitalizations often occurred during mid-winter, I could not count on absolute consistency. Certainly, I would have preferred predicting just when these interruptions would arrive, but was obstructed by a psychotic barricade that insisted on being unforeseeable.

An inner persistent anger created by my impaired mind caused my inner mind to frequently repeat obscene words as I trudged from class to library to class to boarding house. Where this profanity came from completely eluded me. It was not my way to swear. The only viable answer that made any sense to me was that my mind was a victim of overexposure to previous, rough army language. This, and my inescapable anger with the army, left me essentially unapproachable. I do not think I was offensive, just hard to pin down and enjoy.

Notoriety came my way following a request from the school newspaper to write my own editorial. I called the column "Two's Views." Eventually, I was given the editorship of a campus magazine. But the glory only lasted two issues. I then resigned.

The stress was overwhelming to a psychotic who desperately decided she could not handle the intense anxiety that could again prevent her from failing to earn a college degree.

I attempted suicide twice during undergraduate school. Both times I reached a horrendous point where everyday life seemed impossible to endure. It was no wonder. It did not require a great deal of courage to try to end my life. Mental and physical biochemical pain plagued my days to such an extent I could not attend classes. Death was the only effective solution I could think of to remove my misery. I recall feeling glad anticipation during my first suicide attempt as I located the 25 aspirin and predicted the abundant relief as I washed them down. I then lay quietly in bed in eager expectation, grateful for the only remedy that made sense.

Though I failed to end my life, I did get extremely sick from the aspirin and ended up in the hospital (fitting the psychiatric criteria of being a danger to myself). In about another year, I made another attempt at suicide, this time using twice as many aspirin, and getting twice as sick. My new and inept doctor did not choose to admit me into the hospital, even snickering at my feeble, ignorant attempt at killing myself. It was not long after my second attempt that, after considerable reading and reflection, I became convinced suicide was wrong. I identified it as an immoral, selfish act that left loved ones in unfair despair. I remain grateful that I twice failed to die from my own unsuccessful efforts.

Graduation came, and I found myself with a satisfying grade-point average. My undergraduate school had only counted my grades during my junior and senior years. They ignored my earlier disgraceful grade-point average that resulted from my previous pattern of carelessly discontinuing classes without dropping out properly. Therefore, I was also elected into the National Journalism Society. Another academic reward I achieved was when I won honors in a national writing contest, competing with professional writers. This achievement was an important beginning to acquiring additional reassurance that I could write.

I became blindly confident that I could stay out of the hospital after a few semesters of unusually comfortable recovery. During this time I either lived with a roommate or roommates. These arrangements resulted in my worst nightmares. I ultimately suffered breakdowns, displaying what later became humiliating (though textbook) symptoms. Then, as always, with my roommate's insistence, I ended up in the hospital; and no permanent place to go when I was discharged. I do not recall what my living accommodations were each time I was disposed of by whatever roommates I happened to have during each breakdown. However, I know I was never homeless and on the streets. A benevolent God always put a roof over my head.

With the military's GI Bill money unused (VA Vocational Rehabilitation monies had been nicely utilized for my undergraduate work), it made the best sense to continue on to graduate school. I moved back home and selected my original hometown college to attempt earning a Master of Arts degree. By this time, I had become an accomplished student, not so intimidated by whatever curriculum came my way.

Sociology seemed a good choice as a major, simply because I enjoyed studying people as an objective observer. My adult life had left me frightened by the times I had dared to view others from too close a position. Now, sociology provided an intellectual discipline that allowed me to examine humanity from a safe distance.

Graduate school passed quickly. During those two years, I was awarded a graduate teaching assistantship, which provided extra funds to live on, and my own private office. The final semester was noteworthy because I completed a thesis and passed a comprehensive graduate exam. Both were made endurable by extra medication. However, fogged by the pills as well as the classic symptoms of my mental disability (especially poor concentration and confusion), I was concerned about my mental acuity. I invested in an IQ test before taking my graduate school comprehensives. The results showed an IQ about seven points lower than it had been in junior high, when I had taken my only previously recorded IQ test. This especially concerned me since IQ does not normally fluctuate more than five points during a lifetime. However, I attempted and managed to get through graduate school, exams and all, being awarded another graduate teaching assistantship for a PhD program in a sociology program at another university several states away.

My PhD curriculum involved tackling mounds of books and reports, more reading than my master's program ever required. After two months in this program, I was convinced it was not worth the mental misery. I found myself suffering from a dangerous abundance of stress and, again, rapidly accelerating into a psychosis. In addition, the Sociology Department had a history of internal friction with students pitted against students, faculty against faculty, students against faculty, and faculty against students. This additional unwelcome stress provided extra impetus for me to exit from the PhD program and its interdepartmental anger and anxiety.

Jessie rescued me from my dilemma. She agreed with my decision that it was best to transport me home. The trip would be formidable (about 1,200 miles), but Jessie made it tolerable by meeting me and my car at a nearby airport. From there, she drove me back to the security of our mutual home.

I was out of college money and scholastic ladders to climb. Life suddenly became awkward. It seemed that for years my life's goals had been centered around college. I had somewhat mastered the skill of being a student. With that skill I had earned two degrees, though I could never declare it had been effortless. My brain and heart had worked hard. I had maximized all mental and emotional resources available to me. I had managed mental illness in a way that could accommodate a considerable amount of higher learning. Like a multitude who came before me, I had proven wrong the misconception that if you are smart, you can't be crazy (again, a result of the common confusion between mental illness and mental retardation).

Immediately, it seemed I had proven myself in a way that would never fail. It was time to choose new goals, dream new dreams. I rationalized that if I could squeeze substantial scholarly success out of my limited package of potential, surely I could make the rest of my life work for me.

Soon, as I would attempt a dubious career, I would learn that school was an achievement that stood alone. Rather than a guarantee of future success, it was a proving ground that could command distinction without the necessity of further merit. Though my college degrees may not have guaranteed accomplishment in my life, they were accomplishments in themselves, and brought an element of dignity to whatever future efforts (or failures) my life held.

Chapter 13
WORK — AN UNKIND DECLINE IN PRODUCTION

In or out of college, paying my own way was always important, and I nearly always did until I had sustained a mental disorder for a few years. Raised with a strong work ethic, I was praised and paid for numerous chores around the house. In my early teens I worked at miscellaneous jobs and was exalted by my employers. It was important to do the job well, even when I stopped being well enough to do the job. Then, unaware how often research results were against me (10 to 15 percent are fully employed), I started a career.

Initial signs of my exhibiting incompetence on the job occurred during my first summer after high school graduation when I found it necessary to save money for college and acquired a job as a lifeguard. However, I soon suspected something was going wrong. I began suffering from headaches and found it difficult to concentrate on the swimmers. My attention was easily distracted by sunbathers, by other lifeguards, and by nearly anything but swimmers. I should have felt a comradeship with my fellow workers: I mainly felt fear. I suspected they were collaborating against me and stayed my distance. If I had visited a psychiatrist at that time, I would have learned that intense fear of rejection and criticism were textbook symptoms of severe mental illness.

I still managed to accept myself as a lifeguard. This luxury lasted until a boy and his little sister nearly drowned in an area that I should have been concentrating on. Another lifeguard rescued them while I watched from my lifeguard chair. After that, I became an outcast. I was reassigned to an inferior pool, and the humiliation soon sent me away to another job. After an unsuccessful semester as a full-time student, trying college on a part-time basis allowed me the time to attempt a job as a cashier. It was then I became extremely frightened about my ability to work effectively. No matter how patient my supervisor was, I failed to learn how to operate a cash register in a reasonable amount of time. I lasted about two weeks. There was only one honorable answer to my incompetence: I agreed to resign.

I considered working full time while continuing to attend school on a part-time basis. What made that package so appealing was a new job proposal: I was offered work as a photo-lab technician, a skill I learned while in high school. The salary was good. I began with ample confidence while maintaining a limited class schedule. However, again incompetence quickly began to show. The photos I processed were regularly flawed, again and again. I could not consistently produce in a manner that made my employer and myself happy with the paycheck I earned. Again I had to adjust to the unfamiliar status of incompetence. The shame lasted nearly a year. Why I wasn't fired eludes me. Finally, exhausted from my futile efforts and at the brink of termination—I quit.

Needing psychiatric attention and still living at home, I knew I would be unable to pay for a doctor. The thought of my parents attempting to buy my sanity as they were barraged with bills from psychiatrists was loathsome to me. I was determined to handle my own bills or decline to seek treatment.

Enlisting into the military was an idea that made its way into my darkroom via an upstairs secretary who had decided to enlist. It seemed a good way to escape from present financial burdens and my failures as a university student. And, I was told the armed forces provided financial assistance for college, my primary future goal. Why was college so important? Job security and better self-esteem seemed like two defensible answers.

Managing to pass the elementary military entrance tests and getting through the elementary classes in basic training, I was transferred to another state to begin Advanced Individual Training (AIT) in a medical lab. However, my unsound mind could not absorb the more sophisticated curriculum of AIT as I struggled to learn the complexities of blood. I was finally assigned a scheduling clerk's position in a small office. Again, my brain could not focus. I was continually frustrated. During most of my younger life, I had been accustomed to possessing a measure of intelligence that enabled me to comprehend most any kind of work required of me. Now, I just could not link one fact to the next. Doomsday eventually arrived. I had forgotten to schedule in a regular news show the commander watched diligently. When the commander discovered I was at fault, he had me transferred (the same as "fired"). I was sent to the personnel office to be placed in some unknown job that I could master.

Fate was more than kind: I was given a lifeguarding job at one of several swimming pools. My sergeant was not aware of my former poor performance as a lifeguard. All he knew was that I was a certified lifeguard and swim instructor, something he needed.

My pools were mainly workout pools for enlisted officers, retired personnel, and the swim team. This time, concentrating on my work was not a major required skill. Nearly everyone who swam at my pools competently completed daily laps. The biggest danger was the possibility of an elderly retired soldier having a heart attack. Fortunately, elderly retired soldiers rarely visited my pools. The ones who did maintained an abundance of endurance from years of plentiful exercise.

Teaching GIs lifesaving techniques was my most challenging assignment. Though I was initially somewhat disorientated, the repetition each class presented turned me into a competent swim instructor. I developed considerable affection for my students, who seemed so sincere at acquiring my approval. The rest of my time was mainly spent on vacuuming the pool and hosing down the decks, low-stress responsibilities I was able to perform with a major measure of proficiency.

Six months before leaving the military, I had myself transferred to another desk job. I had remained at the same city during my three-year tour in the armed forces with no plans to transfer since I had purchased a small house. The confidence I had acquired from lifeguarding and teaching, and owning my own home convinced me that attempting a desk job would work this time. I felt more adequately prepared to tackle the perilous academic world that lay before me but decided to have myself transferred to a desk job to accommodate the transition into college outside of the military.

This decision was a disastrous one. I was assigned a job in a health physics office. Again, it was impossible to perform my duties competently. Keeping track of simple daily paperwork was an overwhelming challenge. Besides my basic routine tasks, this job required that I work alongside a vulgar and verbally abusive sergeant. The military in the early 1970s was a stranger to acknowledging sexual harassment. This job led me to my first nervous breakdown.

The post mental facility, Chambers, was my home for two weeks. Then, not quite sure of what to do with me, personnel decided the most practical job to give me was behind an insignificant desk, located in an obscure corner of the personnel office, with about a 30-minute daily workload. I felt fortunate to be utilized in such a limited manner as I had developed distressing hallucinations since leaving the hospital. These aberrations would have interfered with a real job. However, with my activities so limited, my serious symptoms (typical of critical mental illnesses) were not detectable by the rest of the office. I remained placid as I endured each day, attempting to read the minutes away. Perhaps if I had been given greater responsibilities causing my disastrous mental health to be more easily detectable, I would have obtained proper treatment.

After the army and a couple more hospitalizations, I found myself an outpatient, tackling a new job. I was assigned by the Veteran's Administration to work in a psychiatric rehabilitation program. The VA organized the responsibility of my showing up for limited daily work by securing rewarding employment at a small, live theater. For this, I was given a meager stipend to pay the bills. Food stamps kept me fed, and my church supplied me with a telephone, which enabled me to secure a roommate (who shared the rent). Saturated with antipsychotic medications I could be found each morning shuffling down the street, again and again, attempting to walk the eight blocks to work.

Staff, actors, stagehands, and other creative personalities frequented the theater. They all accepted me as just another bizarre personality. Indeed, the three owners of this small theater had, no doubt, been acquainted with their share of eccentrics. Actors and set designers came and went each day, blasé about my curious deportment. No doubt my slurred speech and unsure stride would have alienated me in almost any other workplace. At this little theater and with its crew, I fit in. I cleaned out the prop room, passed out programs, and assisted with building sets all while I was given encouragement. I was even given the title of Assistant Director for a play I still don't understand. The director generously worked around me, and gave me menial tasks I could easily complete. When a staff party came along I was invited. Though my responsibilities were limited, the elevation in my self-esteem was dramatic. The kindness that was shown to me there will never be forgotten.

An additional outpatient program to reduce my medications was followed by my choice of work or school. I found myself ready to again attempt what seemed the most promising challenge—school. For extra cash I spent half of one summer as a clerk in a university financial aid office. Though my duties were minimal, I found myself frequently terrified I would make a mistake. I made plenty. A benevolent staff secretary quietly ignored my incompetence and showed me nothing but patience, never allowing her voice to deviate from a cheerful tone.

Graduate school in sociology accommodated a part-time job with a travel agency that provided a comfortable salary. There, I managed to properly greet tour groups at the airport but often became confused when orchestrating transportation of people and baggage to hotels. Somehow, probably due to a tolerant supervisor,

I kept the job for a year before resigning. This employment was followed by a prestigious part-time position as a graduate assistant due to my academic success. This job provided free tuition and a modest but satisfactory salary plus my own office. I was given limited responsibilities and only asked to lecture in a few classes. Mainly, I corrected test papers. These responsibilities only required about ten hours a week. My academic and other limited employment efforts ended with my earning a Master of Arts degree.

The real-life challenges of daily, full-time employment lay before me as I began contemplating a bona fide career. However, after completion of graduate school, the rest of my work experience would not be quite so agreeable.

Working full-time seemed foreign. The pragmatic activity necessary to finally earn a full paycheck did seem to make the most sense. Unfortunately, undertaking a career would be followed by many cruel moments of severe regret. It would not be long until I would join the 70 to 90 percent of persons with severe and persistent mental illness who are unemployed, and the 70 percent of that population who still want to work.

A state employment office was my first serious workplace, where I began the standard eight hours a day on the job. My immediate supervisor was more than benevolent. The only major disadvantage to working for him (and so beside him) was enduring a persistent cloud resulting from his stifling smoking habit. Otherwise, this work presented few major challenges, allowing me to excel enough to earn a state-wide award. Plus, during the year and a half of this employment, my salary nearly doubled. I would have continued with this job and probably enjoyed rewarding advancements. However, psychotic symptoms emerged as I started believing two office women had formed a wicked conspiracy against me. I tearfully confided my fears to the office director, who seemed genuinely baffled. The following day found me checking into a local psychiatric hospital. Two weeks later I left the hospital, having quit my job but possessing hope that better opportunities lay ahead.

However, the future would hold just more of the same

disappointment that initial state job brought. Paranoia would characterize the work history that lay before me. It would be typical for me to feel threatened by coworkers and managers, resulting in escalated stress. Tense relationships sometimes ballooned into major conflicts. These conflicts became usually quiet, highlighted by a strained silence. This made all days subsequent to the initial conflict additionally miserable.

Job security along with potential future income were real issues. There was always the chance that I would be fired. The stress would become impossible for me to endure. I would ultimately quit my job in terror and even become hospitalized. Sometimes I would just take a few days off to rest. However, I typically landed back into the hospital. It was initially the toxic (anxiously competitive) relationships with my coworkers that made it impossible for me to usually function in a job for more than a year. Later, as my disability worsened, a poor memory and chronic confusion were added to my list of liabilities.

I painstakingly studied the art of job interviewing to compensate for my frequent job turnover. I had myself videotaped and critiqued by a vocational counselor. We studied each gesture and phrase and appraised carefully what I wore during each job-interview experience. I finally felt pretty confident of my interview skills. I became so skilled that I found myself most often after job interviews declared as a top contender at worst and getting the job at best. By deciding it prudent not to mention my psychiatric disability, I gave an imposing first impression. Occasionally, the question of my health was raised. Somehow, I always had an honest answer that adequately sidestepped the reason I might not be hired—my mental illness. After all, the main issue was if I thought I could do the job right. And I always thought I could.

A variety of jobs were attempted: financial planner, volunteer bureau director, real estate appraiser, and right-of-way agent.

As a financial planner, I was required to pass four tests: two that allowed me to sell securities, and two that allowed me to sell insurance. I barely got through this assortment of exams. Then, tested but not yet tried, I took the hard road by soliciting door-to-door. I was confident that using this strategy would enable me to acquire the sales necessary to earn a generous living. I probably worked harder than anyone in the office. However, though I rehearsed and rehearsed my pitch, my mechanical, detached manner alienated most potential customers.

Equally distressing was my inability to adequately understand the complexities of insurance, the main money earner. So, I stayed away from insurance, focusing on mutual funds as I provided each customer with a free, computer-generated financial plan. However, the results of earning the title "financial planner" was financial disaster for me. Even after transferring to another company, I found it impossible to sell sufficient financial vehicles to transport me to enough income that would even begin to allow me the comfortable living my supervisors cheerfully predicted.

During my year as a volunteer bureau director, my performance was somewhat strenuous, considerably rewarding, and poorly paid. I had started doing just basic volunteer work for the office, and soon found myself hired to head a county-wide clearinghouse where volunteers were matched with jobs they found appealing. The Volunteer Bureau was situated a comfortable distance away from the main offices, allowing me to avoid much stressful interaction with the other employees. However, with the multitude of daily tasks substantially overwhelming, I burned out in a year.

Real-estate appraising had piqued my interest as an appealing profession during my last few weeks with the Volunteer Bureau. It appeared to be custom-made for a person who disliked the typical office milieu. I could do the bulk of my work at home, and just four appraisals a week would equal what I had earned as a Volunteer Bureau director. I took the necessary class, barely passed the required test, and found myself submerged in a quagmire of demanding lenders who never offered a comfortable amount of time for me to do the job well. The stress was unbearable. I had typically and tragically selected a painful profession that refused to accommodate my mental disability. After one year as a trainee with one employer and a second year as a licensed appraiser with another employer, I saw the light and abandoned this profession to those made of sterner stuff.

The insight this failure provided illuminated me for about a month. I was beginning to understand employment as dangerously stressful. However, it became easy to back into denial after a surprise call from the State Department of Transportation. They reminded me of an application I had submitted a year before. The job was right-of-way agent and the salary higher than I had ever earned. I could not resist a job interview.

My matchless interviewing skills secured the disaster of another job I found impossible to perform in a competent manner. It was incomprehensible for me to absorb the legal guidelines that were necessary to proficiently perform the job. The profusion of paperwork left me hopelessly confused. Tragically, I refused to identify the predictors of psychosis and actually had a breakdown on the job.

My coworkers became aware that there was something seriously wrong with me when one day I pestered everyone with intense and persistent manic conversation. The verdict became complete when I decided to confide to everyone in the office that I was a former mental patient. Reactions ranged from fear to compassion. Having a breakdown on the job was a dilemma I had always dreaded.

After three weeks off the job (involving hospitalization and rest at home), I was back at work. In about two more months I was fired, allowing just enough time for my supervisor to document in a lengthy list every possible detectable blunder that characterized and so permanently tarnished my job performance.

The pattern was becoming predictable. All my jobs involved sincere, sometimes even effective initial efforts before lethal stress built up and sent me out the door. It was after about a year, with job stress compounding daily, that I found myself leaving each workplace. I typically lingered too long, stubbornly attempting to make jobs work. Most of the time, I persisted until a complete mental collapse occurred, fortunately almost always away from the workplace.

Disappointed at my lack of job success, I thought it might be useful to reveal my mental disorder during the initial job interview. Perhaps then I would not feel so threatened and would cease worrying that the boss would find out. Perhaps, too, my supervisor would happily accommodate me by keeping work stress as low as the job would allow.

This strategy never allowed me to find out how it might feel on the job if my superior knew my secret. From the beginning, my new tactic never permitted me to get further than each initial job interview. What I had always feared was again confirmed: the stigma of mental illness created a hopelessly pitiful impression. It appeared that even the most well-meaning employer harbored a dark side of prejudice and bigotry.

These job interviews would begin with my presenting a matchless first impression of my ability to do the job well. With pressed business suit, plush leather briefcase, and brisk, positive charisma, I could see in the face of my interviewer a million "yeses." I had practiced and was prepared to answer every possible question effectively as competence permeated from every pore.

When the interview was over, and the job secured, I would release the pivotal information: "I suffer from manic depression (the diagnosis I had during most of my struggle for a career). However, this problem does not interfere with my quality of work in a significant way."

Though, legally, what was important was my disability would not seriously flaw the quality of work I was applying for, the term manic depression typically created an immediate change in the interviewer's manner. Perhaps there was a new forced courtesy or a subtle increase in the interviewer's voice volume. However, I always was politely escorted out of the office with promise of a phone call soon. The phone call usually never came and, when it did, someone else had the job.

No doubt, a large assortment of distinct questions were raised in the minds of my employment interviewers as they politely listened to my confession of mental illness. What employer would risk hiring an individual who might go off the deep end at the least provocation? What employer would pay for the extra time it took to train a worker who required some extra attention? What employer would put his/her staff in danger, when you never knew what a mentally ill person might do next? The answer was consistent—no employer.

For about ten years I labored, only to find a career crumbling around me. I became desperate for a profession that would provide me with adequate income and self-esteem. As I continued to search, I found myself becoming more aware of how frightening this world could be for the mentally ill. Not only do they deal with imaginary fears, but also with a whole category of paranoia created by a world of true-to-life, brutal skeptics. This included employers who doubted if people who had inhabited psychiatric wards could ever contribute in a positive way to a predominantly sane society.

I searched my heart for an acceptable answer to it all and emerged with ambivalence. Would I ever be able to supply society with something valuable? Granted, like other disabled workers, I needed some accommodations. Though I did not need items as obvious as a wheelchair or guide dog, I still needed initial patience from my employer as my psyche adjusted to a new work environment. Once I started on the medication Clozaril, there were the weekly visits to the patient lab for blood tests and to the doctor for evaluation of those tests. My medical history also indicated I needed occasional (possibly yearly) two-week hospitalizations, and one or two additional weeks off to transition out of the hospital.

Was I unethical if I did not let my future employer know what I believed were surmountable limitations? I am not sure. Granted, the competence I displayed at those job interviews was most often significantly reduced once I got the job. However, a little more patience in training for the job; occasional time off for medical appointments; possible yearly hospitalizations; some extra attention for necessary training; and a fair paycheck—all for a devoted worker. Was that an unfair arrangement?

However, the alternative, being willing to confess to being a slow starter and having trouble handling details, was not out of the question for me. In addition, I was also eager to offer eventual devotion to duty that few other workers brought to the workplace. Knowing that my employer was on my side, accepting me for my qualities as a worker, willing to give me a little extra time up front to prove myself, and a little extra time off (acceptably, without pay) was what I needed to realize the simple ambitions this dreamer dreamed.

When work becomes impossible, some kind of supplemental income is necessary. It may come from family and/or from the government. Almost 50 percent of those with severe mental illnesses obtain either Social Security Disability Insurance (SSDI) or Supplemental Security Income (SSI). This provides an average monthly SSDI benefit of mid $700 and SSI benefit of around $500. This puts those with these disorders among the lowest income households in the country. Indeed, the average income of an individual on SSI is 24 percent of the average American living on one income.

The Americans with Disabilities Act (ADA) originated in 1990 and guarantees equal rights regarding employment to disabled Americans. It does not exclude mental illness. It is crucial that employers, the mentally ill, and their significant others become familiar with this act. It is especially vital that they become aware where potential discrimination is blatant.

Parity (equality) in mental health insurance benefits is one area where employers can assist the mentally ill without victimizing themselves. The basic goal with parity is to provide insurance coverage for the mentally ill that is equal to coverage of those with other health-related problems. It has been the concern of employers and insurance companies that providing coverage for the mentally ill is not cost effective. Research shows that this is not the case and that serious mental illness is about as much of a physical problem (a brain disorder creating a biochemical imbalance) as are diabetes, heart problems, or other physical concerns that are typically provided greater coverage by the insurance companies. Treating the mentally ill is incredibly cost effective to society in general. The cost of not treating severe mental illnesses in the US is $67 billion lost in productivity, including $11 billion in SSDI benefits; and $11 billion in SSI benefits. Approximately $12 billion is the cost of lost productivity, and $6 billion is the cost of incarcerating 250,000 persons with a mental illness in jails and prisons.

Though the studies are exhaustive in their support of parity (or congruity) in providing health insurance care for the mentally ill, currently, the norm is a lack of congruence, where too many insurance companies provide seriously inferior coverage for the mentally ill or no coverage at all. In addition, the lack of continued health insurance coverage is the major policy barrier to gaining meaningful employment for those who live on SSDI or SSI. About 50 percent of those with severe mental illnesses receive either SSDI or SSI. And 85 percent to 90 percent of unemployment exists with individuals with severe mental illnesses.

The National Advisory Mental Health Council of the National Institute of Mental Health (NIMH), under the direction of the United States Senate, has studied parity in mental health care benefits in the US. An important finding dramatizes the need for parity. In work environments not using managed care, introducing parity with managed care results in a 30 percent to 50 percent reduction in overall costs of mental healthcare. In addition, as the overall number of mentally ill employees using managed care increases, the cost of parity for the mentally ill declines.

Another critical area where employers can contribute to providing assistance to the mentally ill without peril to themselves is in utilizing "less restrictive" employee-benefit plans. Here, employees have more access to outpatient mental health services. Research indicates that such employers experience psychiatric disability claim rates about four times lower than other employers.

Typically, state mental health experts find it difficult to acquire the necessary funding to accommodate the mentally ill in a quality manner. Mental illness is not a popular issue and politicians find it most advantageous to accommodate a constituency that supports legislation other than that which subsidizes programs for the mentally ill. One exception has been Maryland, a state that has entertained rigorous pursuit of employment of the seriously mentally ill. Here, administrators and mental health experts pursue an imposing vocational program called The Way Station. This program emphasizes job search, not job placement. The individual's work background and areas of interest are given focus in determining the skills and support required for a "train-place-train" model. In the "train" phase, major emphasis is placed on quality task performance along with improved social and behavioral skills. The "place" phase looks at past work history, both successes and failures. When the individual finds the right job, the final phase, on-the-job training, becomes relevant. Here, making job accommodations and making environmental adaptations are combined with working on the transfer of previous skills.

Despite these efforts, Maryland's successes have been limited. Of those clients Way Station serves, 30 percent are employed and 68 percent of these employed have held their jobs for six months or more. Indeed, between 85 and 95 percent of persons with treatable serious mental illness are unemployed.

As for me—I do not know. However, I am certain I suffered greatly as I struggled to do each job well. And, the regret I felt when I was forced to realize it was time to leave each work environment I had initially entered with hope and high motivation left me guilt-ridden and devoid of self-esteem. Some people with brain disorders can hold jobs and contribute to society with the proper medical treatment. It is often, without doubt, stigma and discrimination that prevent many of the mentally ill from gaining and keeping employment. I tried and tried and tried for nearly ten years to succeed in some career that promised me some sense of value. My disability has been one that resulted in failure to succeed in a competitive workplace.

Today, I am left with a monthly VA disability check and Social Security check that pays the bills without the honor of functioning in a standard workplace. I manage through my days completing required errands (while I don't drive) and attempting to find some serious but cautiously limited time to write. It is writing that gives me a sense of accomplishment. However, it is writing that results in the greatest daily stress.

I turn the restricted minutes or hours I can persevere creating a page or two or three into golden intervals of quality time. It is writing that makes me whole, integrating my impaired biochemistry into a functional amalgamation that combines brawn and brain into a daily endurance test.

Chapter 14
DOMESTIC DENIAL

Before a career ever became a painfully futile fiasco, my parents held great expectations for me, denying I could ever fail. Ours was a moderately comfortable middle-class home. My grades were nearly always above average, and I do not remember my mother and father ever finding it necessary to lecture me about my academic performance. When, soon after acquiring the symptoms of mental illness, I failed to perform well in college, my parents were understandably baffled and rather concerned. What kind of career lay ahead for me? Little did any of us know that we were becoming the one in every 25 families affected by severe mental illness.

Though my biological father and mother divorced when I was three years old, and though my real father maintained residence in the town where I was raised, I never saw him. Occasionally I would ask Mother about him. Always, I received kind answers that painted a portrait of an intelligent (Ivy League educated) but disturbed man who still loved his daughter.

Severe mental illness has less to do with poor parenting or a shortage of willpower. It can strike any "good" family with the appropriate genetic makeup. The genes responsible for my mental illness were most likely passed down to me by my biological father. Though I did not closely resemble him physically, mood swings were characteristic of both my father and myself. Father was a "hyper" sort of man who was the life of the party when he was manic and drank heavily when he was depressed. He was also prone to violent episodes.

My biological father died when I was 22. I had never known him, though he chose to stay in my hometown. He just stayed away. Because I was 2,000 miles away in the military and held distant feelings for him when he was alive, I was absent from his funeral. I was informed of his death by a letter from my mother:

Dearest Two,

We haven't talked about your real father too much, as there wasn't much to say. He chose to not interfere with your life. I'm sure you thought about him more than you said as it would be normal to wonder about one's father.

Your father passed away this week, Two, and it was sad. He died of cancer and, although very ill, did take sufficient pills to stay out of pain. He lived on social security in low income apartment housing for senior citizens and had very little financially.

I talked to the people he was close to these past five years, and was told he made life quite happy for himself and others around him. These elderly people all said they would miss his sense of humor and the fun cooking sessions they all would enjoy together in a recreation area they all shared.

I have saved a suitcase full of pictures, his dental license, a picture of the University of Pennsylvania Dental School, and a few small items I felt you would like. I'm enclosing $165, which was all the money he had in his possession. His surviving brothers wanted you to have it.

Much love,
Mother

Years later, I learned my father had kept in his apartment a news story of some academic achievement I earned. That, along with my mother telling me his favorite name for me was "princess," has created in me an honest fondness for my real father.

208

Ultimately, I prefer to believe my mother's forgiving portrait of a sadly disturbed man who maintained an exceptional place in his heart for his little girl. Perhaps this can be called my own variety of denial. I will never know about his.

My real father's exit was soon followed by the entrance of my stepfather. Shortly thereafter my brother, Kenny, was born. Then there were four of us: my mother, my stepfather, my half-brother, and myself. Members of my little family were most often independent from each other. We held individual idiosyncrasies that frequently alienated us from one another's lives.

My stepfather was a recluse. A bad back created in him a slow gait that left him isolated from a faster world. He discouraged having any non-family members in the house, preferring to read or watch TV in circumstances as solitary as possible. He especially enjoyed game shows where he was able to answer countless questions each show presented. He was always around in the evenings after work, more interested in watching TV and reading than governing a family. This unfortunate man who had abundant intellectual capability and overall talent (musical, writing, etc.) was also a compulsive gambler, which proved to be a sad distraction to his even beginning to fulfill his potential. After I moved away, whenever I called home it was Mother who answered the phone. After a brief chat, she called my father to the phone to say "hi." His comments were polite and always brief. His shabby effort to communicate seemed more out of obligation than sincere interest: his own exercise in denial.

Mother was blind to my stepfather's gambling problem. She eventually found herself easily influenced by his antisocial inclinations. Mother was, by nature, a social person and became frustrated by our relatively unfriendly home. However, she found herself giving in to my stepfather's desire for privacy and found herself staying at home and compulsively often working self-employed there, alone.

With the inclination toward blinding herself to tragedy, Mother's initial approach to my mental illness was denial. This is a posture many families and friends take when confronted with the reality of serious mental illness of friends or loved ones. For an extensive time, my mother was convinced that I was capable of living a successful life. It was not until she began reading and learning about serious mental illness that she began to understand what "psychiatric disability" meant. Though denial has definite disadvantages (the family member fails to meet the special needs of the mentally ill family member), it also has advantages. In my mother's case, by insisting that I could accomplish something important (college education, successful career, etc.), Mother convinced me she was right. So I tried. I did not always succeed, but I did not immediately give up just because mental health professionals said I was not capable of achieving (and at least one social worker discouraged me from attempting college).

My stepbrother, Kenny, was three years my junior. He preferred silencing himself when it came to my mental illness, and silence can be one of the most distressing forms of interaction to a mentally ill family member. It presents itself as indifference, and produces more pain than even hate. Kenny also alienated himself in other ways, initially choosing to stay away from my designated mental hospitals and preferring not to write letters.

The family first began to exercise especially distant interrelationships when Mother opened a finishing school and model agency (about the time I was ten years old). A former model, Mother began to gain some new exposure to mankind. She was also a gifted teacher and was soon a celebrity in the community. Her imposing elegant appearance provided a role model for a multitude of her students. While her new business venture helped my mother unite with the public, it eventually succeeded in alienating her from her family. As the years progressed, she became more and more involved with her business and less and less involved with our lives. Still, she was nearly always the dominant member of the family. Ruling with a strong personality, my mother made most of the family decisions.

My family members were so independent that not having much of my mother around during junior high and high school (due to her intense business activities) was less of an ordeal than most families would have suffered. During high school, I occupied myself with extracurricular activities and two close friendships;

while my mother was not there to conduct my life. However, Kenny and I were seldom any trouble. Our obedience was most likely a result of our church's influence. My mother had astutely exposed us to the concept of "good works" from our early childhoods. This resulted in a couple of good kids who shared their own dutiful brand of sovereignty, and two parents with a minimum of responsibilities raising them.

My parents were not financially unselfish with their children. They bought me a fairly new car when I was old enough to drive and other teenage necessities, which, for me, were usually clothes. But, I eventually found myself resenting their gifts, suspecting they were attempting to buy my love to compensate for their lack of attention. It would take a good number of years for me to learn the similarities between sacrifice and love.

When my serious symptoms of mental illness began to emerge during my late teens, it was about the time I graduated from high school and started attending a local college. I preferred to isolate myself in my bedroom while not attending college classes. I have a picture in my mind of my mother and father sitting in their recliners in the living room, glaring at me with evil-looking eyes. I now know this was truly a distorted view of my parents. I would have been, at best, labeled paranoid by a psychiatrist. What I was really viewing was their indifference. My parents did not seem to exhibit a useful measure of worry warranted by my curious behavior, especially my isolation. Their denial of my escalating mental problems had begun. I was becoming seriously mentally ill. However, during those early years of brain pain, I do not believe that I was difficult for my parents to live with. I was not initially outwardly angry, hostile, or offensive. The difficulty I was experiencing was inside, not exterior to myself. It was easy for my parents to wait out what they probably perceived as curious behavior and see if I would get better.

Attempting and failing at college and work, over and over, lasted a couple of years until I decided I could not endure living at home any longer. It felt humiliating to continue to depend on my parents for so much (mainly food, shelter, and money). And there was the paranoia. I became more and more convinced they felt burdened with my occupying a whole room in the household, as they continued to separate themselves from my troubled mind.

I left home at age 20 while Kenny was a junior in high school. My symptoms were beginning to become more pronounced, and I began to feel more angry and threatened by my parents' indifference.

My first home away from home was a shed in back of a trailer court. It was furnished with a small stove, tiny refrigerator, and minuscule sink. I hung my clothes on a rack I bought for this new home. My bed was situated just to the side of this rack. Cold morning showers required me to leave my shed and utilize a wooden stall around the back, especially distressful in the winter. I was secured inside by only a small padlock on the front door. Though my mother viewed my new habitat one day, she did not express any disapproval. Again denial of the unacceptability of this even hazardous home permeated her personality. After almost three months, I was desperate to move out of my shack and in a house with a family who shared with me an extra bedroom.

I was terrorized by this family's two children. They frequently raided my room, stealing away with favorite jewelry and other prized possessions. Even though I put a padlock on my bedroom door, they seemed to slip in at any opportune moment. I soon left this devastating dwelling.

My next home was with a woman who happened to be a secretary for a living and a fanatic housekeeper the rest of the time. She continually berated me for not wiping the kitchen counter thoroughly enough, not keeping the fringe bordering the living room rug evenly positioned, and on and on. I soon learned her extreme housekeeping was instrumental in destroying a previous marriage. Years later I shared a room in a psychiatric ward with a similar personality.

After graduating from high school, half-brother Kenny proceeded to attend college locally and work while still living at home. I had moved away from home by then. Kenny organized a band and played for high school and church dances. He presented an imposing figure, six foot four, and uncommonly handsome. He began to demonstrate a drive for achievement that had seldom characterized his childhood years. He would eventually own two major businesses and raise a family. How he managed to do it all with such a poor role model of a father is a mystery to me. In contrast to his absentee father, Kenny deserves credit for being there for the family he produced.

Unfortunately, Kenny neglected his extended family. Once he left home, he seldom visited his parents. He, also, sorely neglected my persistent medical problems. He felt inclined to visit me a total of three times (at my request) while I was hospitalized, out of over 25 hospitalizations. Whenever I visited home, it was hard to feel accepted (especially during the Christmas holidays). My brother did drive me to the state crisis center a couple of times to treat panic attacks. However, his uncomfortable silence when he was with me created a troublesome atmosphere in which to breathe. It is likely my brother was not a bad person; just preoccupied and, there is that word again, "independent."

Kenny does deserve credit for a marked measure of patience. As my mental illness progressed, I know I made it difficult for my brother to be around me. I angered easily and was highly judgmental. But, despite my caustic manner, Kenny was never overtly unkind. I admire Kenny for his great capacity for peace, and his good-natured, non-vindictive manner. And he was most generous with his limited time when I occasionally requested his help. However, for many years, his personality developed a gap that was filled (at best) with his indifference. His denial of my mental illness left an empty place where love would have fit nicely. It would take better medications treating my illness, causing many of my negative symptoms to disappear, to convince Kenny to come around and show the love I missed when less approachable.

I felt especially alienated from my brother's family during my thirties and forties. It seemed typical of them to choose to believe just what made them comfortable. Therefore, they most often chose to ignore my mental illness and, therefore, ignore me. Along with the alienation, I also harbored phobias whenever I was around them. I ask myself, "What does my brother's family think of me since I am deranged? Do his children know and, if so, what do they think? Why doesn't anybody ask me how I am? Why doesn't anybody ask me anything?" Granted, it remains a mystery whether my fears were justified.

These derogatory feelings were eventually modified, and the reason for my change of heart was the superior medication, Clozaril, which I am sure left me more comfortable to be around. However, even before Clozaril, one early effort at reconciliation with my family was manifested by a song I wrote to Kenny's family when they had their first child. At age 30, I was touched by the reality of being an aunt. This was combined with the awareness that I could never be a mother since that would require stopping my medication during pregnancy, and ultimately sending me into a painful breakdown. I wrote the following lyrics to a Christmas song for the new baby soon after she was born during the holidays:

First Christmas Lullaby

It's your first Christmas, baby.
The stars are shining bright.
Santa flies his sleigh through skies
This merry, magic night.

You sleep without a murmur,
While laughter fills the air.
The joy you bring as voices sing
Is more than we can bear.

(Chorus.)
So, baby, by,
Don't you cry.
It's your first Christmas
Lullaby.

Baby, as you slumber,
Still not far from your birth,
People without number
Pray for peace on earth.

And just like baby Jesus,
Who gave so much away,
You'll grow up to share love
With hearts and lives some day.

(Chorus.)

Everywhere trees flicker
With lights on every bough.
They glow so we'll remember
The time to give is now.

Underneath are packages,
More than just a few.
As girls and boys unwrap these toys
We'll share the gift of you.

(Chorus.)

While college and early attempts at a career thoroughly occupied my time, my mother remained absorbed with her business and was seemingly oblivious to my disability. (This was my perception.) I am not sure if it was her preoccupation with earning a living, her lack of understanding of what mental anguish I was experiencing, or her belief that I was an adult—no, a super adult—and should be able to handle just about any challenge that came my way. Whatever the case, Mother maintained a sincere belief that I would succeed in life. I guess my past successes had so earned the right to be on my own and prompted her indifference. However, "independence" remained the household byword and Mother just seemed to be carrying on with what had been the family style for many years. My continued belief is it was denial of the seriousness of my mental disability that prompted my mother to neglect me during the early years of my psychosis in a way that injured me most, emotionally.

I admittedly displayed a bad temperament to my mother, especially during my early years of mental illness. I recall her fixing Thanksgiving dinner, then my not attending this traditional family affair. It was her first family Thanksgiving unattended by me while I still lived in the same city, and my absence accomplished my goal: It hurt my mother deeply.

My anger was undoubtedly an indication of my mental illness just beginning to exhibit more serious symptoms. However, it did not make it easy for my family to exercise compassion, and they maintained a consistent state of denial during most of my disabled years.

After my first few years of persistent anger, I began to feel sorrow over my behavior, especially with my mother. It must have been especially difficult for a mother who had such high aspirations for a daughter who was a former high-achiever—both academically and socially—to subsequently watch her steadily falling apart. She wrote to me once that whatever work I endeavored in life I should be the best. So it was that she was always there to encourage me to succeed in whatever ambitions I engaged in. Unfortunately, there were too many different jobs in which I bordered at the worst.

During my early years of severe symptoms and regular attempts at undergraduate school, I was in a state away from home. Mother did keep track of my hospitalizations and efforts in school, while she submerged (or, rather, drowned) herself in business. She corresponded with me regularly with stationery and cassettes, and never hesitated to offer money should I have the need. Fortunately, I never had the need since the VA money was always satisfactory. Mother continued to encourage me to achieve, despite my mental illness. Unlike many mothers, she never pressured me to get married. Her preoccupation was with my sense of self-worth, and she knew a college degree and a successful career would provide for me with vital self-esteem.

After I completed undergraduate school, I moved back home and lived with my parents for a short time. It took about a year to transition into what I was not sure came next. A great deal of the time I was on muscle relaxants, which mainly caused me to sleep away persistent back pain, psychotic pain, and depression.

I never accepted money from Mother while I was in school.

Later, when I left school to start a career, I found it necessary to humbly ask Mother for financial help. She provided an abundance of encouragement to financially launch me off into several different professions. The wealth was combined with gratitude and always with my eventual poor performances. I was provided emotional and financial motivation to keep at it by Mother's steady encouragement to try earning a living. Nevertheless, the workplace always proved to be a disaster.

Jessie, roommate and dear friend, was initially responsible for awakening my mother to the seriousness of my disability. Accustomed to teaching school, she was not a stranger to enlightening the unaware. Her sturdy build supported a powerful personality, durable enough to become my roommate when I was at the pivotal age of 30. We found we shared common ground in our dissatisfaction with our common church and, together, found a more comfortable faith to follow. She was the product of a close southern family that was always there for each other when a need arose. Like her mother, she was devoted to her family. Like her father, she was not afraid to confront injustice whenever it surfaced.

I first appeared peculiar to Jessie's family, and they initially maintained a distinct distance. I was from a family that left each other on their own as much as was possible. The frequent phone calls and otherwise constant communication Jessie had with her family seemed odd to me at first. The contrast her family's close connections had with my family's extreme detachment could not have brought greater alienation between the two collections of relatives. My parents were once invited to dinner with Jessie's family. However, the two families' feeble attempts at compatibility were basically barren, and they seldom interacted with each other after that.

When severe symptoms acutely dominated my communication (especially when I was ready for the hospital), Jessie would call my mother to report my condition. My mother's dominant yet detached attitude with my poor health was reflected in a phone conversation with Jessie during one breakdown. "She's in her thirties and should be making a living. What is wrong with that girl?" Mother snapped.

Jessie replied, "Don't you realize she is sick? Two is not able to work right now. She has a legitimate disability."

However, for a long time, Mother just did not get it. She clung to memories of my excelling in nearly everything I attempted. Mother lived in persistent denial.

In my mid-thirties Mother retired and moved away to the South and the ocean. While she was away, she chose to continue to plunge herself into a sea of denial. During this time, Jessie accepted sole legal responsibility for making sure I was cared for properly, in and out of the hospital; even if it meant she missed work days. This, combined with her periodic financial assistance, made Jessie essential to my emotional and physical survival. Indeed, it was Jessie who probably kept me off the streets.

Mother returned to my hometown around the time I turned 40. At last, she began to realize and appreciate the weighty responsibility Jessie had regularly performed. It was now my mother's turn to help drive me to medical appointments when I could not. While she began to observe my fundamental needs, she also observed some of the poor treatment I received from the VA. With limited personal knowledge of my disability, she began to read, to educate herself, and gain more understanding of what my mental illness was all about. For a limited time, when I was too sick to work, she provided a generous monthly stipend to pay the bills and allow for a movie or two during the month. This assistance aided me in a major way: I was collecting smaller VA disability checks since I was out of school and no longer getting educational assistance. I will never take that kindness from my mother for granted.

Appalled at the limited amount of disability monies I received, Mother (with Jessie's suggestion) contacted two state senators (who were also old friends) and asked them for help in influencing the VA to increase my disability rating and so enlarge my monthly stipend. She also elicited the help of a lawyer friend who had initially started the momentum of my acquiring enough disability with which to live on independently. I will forever be grateful to this man for his kindness. Without pay, he generously collected an abundance of evidence (letters from past employers, psychiatric evaluations, etc.) indicating I was not able to work. This evidence was sent to the state VA regional office.

Soon after, my VA doctor was directed to perform a formal evaluation with another VA doctor. They both asked me an assortment of questions and prepared an extensive written estimate of the exhaustive symptoms that prevented me from working. I also took a battery of written psychological tests to provide additional evidence of my medical limitations.

In the meantime, Mother assisted me in obtaining Social Security Disability, which provided a small, additional stipend since I had a meager work record. Finally, after a three-year struggle of living off of a small amount of VA disability money along with the help of Mother's monthly checks, and now with SSD, I secured a VA disability rating that allowed me financial independence.

Jessie was appointed my fiduciary by the VA, since I was deemed unable to handle my own money. She was selected to make all major decisions about how I should spend my disability money. This was completely acceptable to me and was warranted since I had never been able to save even during school (when I received VA money that allowed me a small surplus each month). Amazing that I managed to stay out of dangerous debt, even maintaining a modest but acceptable credit rating. Now, it was Jessie who deserved recognition for making sure the bills were always paid. She even enabled me to accumulate a sizable savings account. Having Jessie as my fiduciary has never been a problem since, when it comes to finances, I have much greater confidence in Jessie's judgment than I do in my own.

An increase in my disability rating allowed me to start recovering from some of my guilt over having to depend on my mother for money. However, my guilt over having to live off the government persisted for a considerable time. I was raised with a strong work ethic, and having the government pay the bills was immensely humiliating. I found it necessary to accept money from Jessie, then my mother, and then the government. Between these pitiful gestures, I failed pathetically to fit my desired self-image as a professional into middle or upper management.

My stepfather died in 1994. It happened in his sleep, when he was left to the comfort of his dreams—and my gambler stepfather always had dreams.

Despite their early denial of my mental illness, I love my family. Many families find it too painful to even consider the horrendous, even unspeakable realities of having a significant other suffer serious mental illness. It may be because of love that a family refuses to acknowledge the suffering of a mentally ill loved one.

Therefore, my family was not so unusual in their reaction to my anguish. However, they still had their share of idiosyncrasies. Jessie was the most conventional person I ever befriended and provided a sensible change from former friendships. It is because she seemed so normal and, therefore, so stable that I decided it was time I needed our kind of alliance. She provided the firm foundation I required to maintain solid footing.

Now, it seems that Jessie is beyond being just a friend: It seems she has always been my family. I am, indeed, fortunate she has chosen to be so loyal. For the past 28 years she has made sure I was as comfortable as my mental illness would allow. She has fought battles with doctors and defended me to her friends. From the time I met her and eventually displayed my medical needs, Jessie has been my father, my mother, my brother during times my perceptions left me feeling abandoned by my family. And, her example of loyalty, devotion, and love for her family has provided for me the model required to celebrate how much dysfunctional families such as my own who have not been strangers to chronic denial have always needed each other.

Chapter 15
A DISCIPLINED LIFESTYLE

It was especially easy for Mother to deny my mental illness, especially my lack of success in a career. She had taught me firm self-discipline as a child and I was an easy study. I succeeded in properly finishing weekly chores and was a highly effective student. It was especially difficult for her to accept that such a successful child could grow up to be such an unsuccessful adult. Brother Kenny was also taught about the virtues of hard work, but did not quite catch on until he was married. Then he became a tornado, whirling his way around the community, raising a quality family, owning his own business, and being active in church.

In my childhood home, my stepfather worked his daily eight hours, then spent the evening and weekends claiming exclusive ownership to his recliner. Meanwhile, Mother often put in a good 12 hours a day running her finishing school while making sure Kenny and I earned our allowances. Mother carried with her a personal issue with financial stability and left me with an intense appreciation for those who can keep the budget balanced. This childhood discipline provided a foundation of adult self-discipline.

Where does this leave me in light of my mental illness today? Perhaps the best words for it are "fundamentally functional." I manage enough recovery to navigate through each day, independent from my family but close enough to reassure them that I hold for them a substantial amount of love. I work with a schedule and custom-made charts that remind me daily what is genuinely important to accomplish. On these charts are recorded my daily weight, hours of sleep, computer work, exercise, number of hours of writing, house and yard cleaning, completed reading, meals (along with snacks needed to accommodate my hypoglycemia), and other miscellaneous items.

My disciplined approached to life began with long lists during my last semester of high school. This was about the same time the symptoms of mental mania first wrestled through my body. I felt myself losing control of my days and desperately asked my mother for help. She suggested that I keep my mind clear by listing my goals each day and crossing off each goal when accomplished. However, I soon found myself in a frenzy when I was unable to fit a multitude of written responsibilities into one day. So, my simple lists evolved into complex schedules with special codes to indicate categories and priorities. I found myself feeling great anxiety when everything was not done as planned each day. Certainly, these panics were productive. I did get a lot accomplished. However, the wear and tear on my body and brain were considerable.

Thoroughly frustrated, I once tried to do without a schedule and succeeded in accomplishing nearly nothing. I was too forgetful to remember even important items that needed to be finished. I decided that to be able to utilize my time in a way that enabled me to achieve, I required accounting on paper for every hour at least a week ahead of time.

It was absolutely essential that I live this way while I was in school. What I would study and when I studied was recorded carefully and devoutly followed, hour by hour—with a new weekly plan established every Sunday. Organizing and recording my study schedule a week ahead of time allowed me to approach a college education with more organization and less terror. My schedule would reassure me that, indeed, I was going to complete the necessary study and preparation as planned. I know I must have been tagged as the ideal student who always produced her papers on time, who always had the answers in class, and who was always adequately prepared for her exams (well ahead of time). Who would have guessed the madness behind my management?

Today, with a disability that prevents me from functioning in a competitive work environment, I have found it imperative that I depend on disability checks from Social Security Disability and the Veteran's Administration (which identifies me as a disabled veteran). This has left me financially independent, with an abundance of time to manage. Those early college days of academic/scholastic psychosis that required me to develop a compulsive mind-set, today dictate I continue to follow an exacting schedule and record each day's priorities on my custom charts. This characteristic convinces my doctors that I have a good measure of obsessive-compulsive personality disorder. I carry my written plan in a scheduling book wherever I go, and review it numerous times during each 16 hours of waking time; but never enough times to fully reassure myself that everything will be done. However, at the end of the day, when the last task is crossed off, I usually am fortunate to grasp a glimpse of satisfaction that perhaps the day was worthwhile.

My ultimate goal has been to organize a meaningful life around my mental illness, while keeping this disability under control as much as possible. My greatest enemy is stress. My ability is most closely determined to the amount of stress each day presents. Whatever I can do (or not do) to reduce stress each day while managing to fill each day with meaningful activity determines how successful my every day will be.

I exercise religiously. I complete a collection of stretching exercises each morning. For one-half hour every day I either work out on an exercise machine or swim laps. I also try to walk my dog for one-half hour each day. It is mysterious how the body functions in such a way to reduce despair by some daily exertion. Should I skip more than two days of exercise, my inner supply of endorphins (a body chemical that reduces depression) becomes dangerously low and fails to adequately relieve despair. Depression sneaks into my system.

I have discovered that the medications I absorb induce 10.5 to 11.5 hours sleep each night. Two consecutive nights of much less than that amount of sleep can threaten a spin into mania where I lose control and suffer fanatic activity, including sleepless nights. The ultimate result is hospitalization. Fortunately, the medication Clozaril has significantly reduced the dangers of mania, hallucinations, and delusions—making hospitalization less ominous. Still (to be safe), when I become excessively tired, I try to remember to make sure to rest.

Medications I presently take do not produce euphoria (excessive happiness) for me. However, they do reduce the intensity of my highs and lows, providing a more stable personality. Nevertheless, I drop into a serious depression about four or five times a year, leaving me with the title of "rapid-cycler." This requires a major temporary change, most often increase, in medications; or sometimes, a short-term hospitalization. I do have serious, short-term memory problems that create an inability to effectively handle detail, low tolerance for stress, and chronic paranoia when interacting with coworkers (among other, miscellaneous problems). Therefore, I am prevented from working in a conventional, competitive environment. Also, medications leave me photosensitive to sunlight. More than 15 to 20 minutes of sunshine and I begin to feel shaky. Later, my skin turns ruddy red, similar to a severe sunburn. Therefore, I stay out of the sun and appear a somewhat unhealthy pale.

Twenty years ago it was discovered that I have hypoglycemia (chronic low blood sugar). This requires that I absolutely must have six well-balanced, small meals each day. If I do not eat right, my symptoms (depression, anxiety, even dizziness) are amplified to an intolerable volume. I must omit certain food: mainly refined sugar, white flour, caffeine, and alcohol. I have also found that by drinking 24 ounces of water three times a day (within a 30-minute period after meals) I suffer fewer symptoms. Since the medications I take dictate that I not consume some items (especially alcohol), I am doubly motivated to be selective about what I eat. If I ignored these dietetic restrictions, I would suffer serious and needless symptoms, not unlike those of an unmedicated mental patient. Again, such symptoms could easily result in hospitalization.

Fortunately, my hypoglycemia disappeared in the last five years, primarily because I was so careful with my eating habits.

Now, I can have all the foods (i.e., grapes, bananas, apples, corn, etc.) that I missed for so many years.

Unfortunately, testing has shown that I have serious early onset dementia. This problem has left me finding it often difficult to find just the right word when I need it, and planning projects from beginning to end without tremendous effort (poor executive functioning). I interact for an hour with special computer software three to four times a week to exercise my memory and bring it up to optimum performance.

Maintaining medical necessities (a 30-minute doctor's appointment, a half-hour with a social worker, sometimes an hour with a support group, and a blood test) occupies a considerable amount of time each month. And, just achieving daily necessary personal hygiene requires a substantial part of each 24 hours. Plus, I have to allow time for occasional hospitalizations (usually lasting two weeks a year and requiring another week or two adjusting out of the hospital).

To accomplish it all, I have tried to follow a regular, daily routine. From the time I wake up, there are certain activities that I attempt to perform at certain set times. Of course there is basic, personal hygiene. Then, I complete a full breakfast, a morning breathing and stretching routine plus a worship session (prayer and one-half hour of Bible reading), and one hour of swimming, more grooming, and general housecleaning. All are designed to pour vital endorphins into my brain and clear my mind for as coherent a day as is possible. Then, I check my e-mail. This morning routine takes about four hours to complete. After lunch (during which I listen to positive-thinking affirmations), I may spend an hour working on my memory software program. Then, I may walk the dogs. Then, I try to spend at least two to three hours a day writing. In addition, I try to take vital five-to-ten-minute breaks each one-half hour involving myself in low-stress activities such as light housework (which I find strangely therapeutic), phone calls, and light stretching. Without these breaks (and too often they are neglected when compulsive-obsessive behavior takes over) the stress is escalated each hour, and the rest of my day is barely endured.

All these activities command an abundance of mental, emotional, and physical energy. In the evenings, when I have the stamina, I fit in computer-learning time or struggle through some reading. However, usually I do not have the stamina and I collapse in front of the television each evening to watch two or three hours of favorite shows or videos. Driven by my perilous work ethic, I have taken years to accept the reality that I deserve that much rest each day.

Having some plan to guide me through the day provides the security I need to mentally survive. Structure dictates my activities. My moments are mechanized. My social skills have improved with the help of therapy and medication adjustments, while Jessie (always at ease socially) has served as an adult role model. However, I still find myself preferring to retreat instead of interact with friends or strangers, my ever persisting social phobia.

My physical appearance is critically important to me. This has become problematic in the last ten years since I started taking Clozaril, which is tremendously weight-inducing. I have gained 55 pounds over that time. Whenever I leave the house, I take a last desperate check in the mirror. While I was growing up, Mother edified me (along with her multitude of finishing school students) with the useful information that 90 percent of peoples' opinions of others comes from their first ten seconds of interaction. Fortunately, she also taught me about how to best camouflage extra weight. Knowing I look my best helps increase the courage to face whatever social challenges the day may offer. So do I manage interacting when I pay cashiers, talking to bank tellers, or taking care of errands that I cannot possibly accomplish from the safe distance of a phone call.

Parties have remained difficult but not as impossible as in the past. During such festive occasions I feel like an actor, playing the role of clever conversationalist. I have become accustomed to bracing myself before entering any strange scene, and I usually leave troubled with my performance. A reassuring review from Jessie indicating that I did okay is always welcome. If the evaluation has any negative ingredients, I am left just short of devastated.

Highly structured hospital experiences have reinforced the importance of sustaining a daily schedule. Patients are routinely awakened each day at a set time (usually 6 a.m.), and proceed through planned group sessions, occupational therapy (arts and crafts), and meals. This consistent, predictable performance is not easy for a confused mind. Much credit is deserved by those psychotic patients who, when they exit the hospital, assume personal responsibility to carefully design their days. They, therefore, facilitate longer recoveries.

However, outpatient support groups I have attended have revealed to me that a dismal majority of the seriously mentally ill spend the great bulk of their days sleeping and/or watching TV, while they conscientiously collect monthly disability checks. Crucial exercise is seriously neglected or abandoned entirely. Meaningful activity is nearly completely neglected. Whatever energy that is exerted is in preparing what could only be loosely defined as three meals a day. These devastated victims compound their suffering while they curse their mental disabilities, wondering why they were selected to be so unhappy.

Frequently ending up in hospitals, they just barely maneuver through each scheduled day, sleeping through whatever miscellaneous time is allowed. Usually a rigorous daily exercise program is not part of the daily hospital activity; and patients are not encouraged to engage in rigorous physical exertion on their own. They are given pills and group therapy until their biochemistry achieves a functional measure of balance. These valuable biochemical/social/psychological tools designed to daily cope with their disabilities are provided. However, many patients who leave the hospital discontinue their daily medications and under-utilize skills designed to avoid future breakdowns. What goes wrong?

It is easy to blame the mentally ill for not "trying harder" to stay well. However, that approach is not completely fair. With a serious mental illness, patients are often left considerably incapacitated to do what is necessary to maintain a meaningful measure of health. Telling a psychiatric patient to "shape up and get healthy" is like telling a lame person to "get up and walk."

Fairness dictates that, for these negligent victims of perpetual brain pain, poor outpatient care is a primary culprit—most often inferior to what I am weekly provided by the VA. Once out of the regimented hospital, outpatients are on their own to keep appointments with doctors and groups. Most rely on the state to provide treatment since whatever private insurance coverage is provided soon dwindles (or has already dwindled) to no coverage at all. Whatever state funding that is provided to non-VA outpatient programs depends on whatever state you are in. Some state programs are excellent, furnishing former inpatients with ample low-budget housing and therapeutic support (from psychiatrists, psychologists, social workers, and groups). Other states just barely sustain some kind of medical support, usually involving one monthly 15-minute visit to the doctor to quickly check the effectiveness of previously prescribed medication and prescribe a change if determined necessary. There, the money needed to care for the mentally ill is meagerly legislated. These states present a tragic state of affairs for those who desperately need better medical care. Helping the mentally ill is not a popular political issue, and happy constituents are what politicians need in order to stay in office.

Significant others need to become aware of the monies available to their mentally ill loved ones and pursue these resources. Indeed, not one housing market area in the US exists that a person receiving SSI can afford to rent. The Veterans Administration provides service-connected disability ratings (along with defining these different levels of disability) that allow certain levels of supplemental income warranted by mentally ill veterans. Another financial source is private health insurance. Those with mental illness are most often denied coverage from insurance for the following two main reasons:

1) The "preexisting conditions" clause gives insurance companies the right to refuse to cover anyone who has a verified mental or physical illness when they apply for the coverage.
2) Insurance companies typically put limits (caps) on what

they will pay for. Typically provided are six psychiatric visits per year and 50 percent of the costs of medications or psychiatric hospitalizations.

There are no limits placed on doctors' visits, drugs, or hospitalizations for other medical conditions.

Medicare is the federal health insurance program for many people with disabilities. After 24 months, those who are receiving SSDI qualify for Part A coverage under Medicare. This covers them for hospital care and some follow-up services, hospice care, and nursing facility care. This coverage is free to all who qualify. Part B is optional insurance and costs about $60 or so per month. It covers doctors' visits, lab tests, medical supplies, outpatient services, and other miscellaneous care. Medicare does not cover dental care, eye care, routine check-ups, or medications. If you are mentally disabled you need to be aware of Medicare services you may or may not qualify for.

Because of Medicare's limitations, many who are covered by this public insurance program also carry what valuable private insurance they can find. Inadequate estate planning can result in the loss of SSI and Medicaid for the mentally ill family member when a provider dies. A lawyer who specializes in wills and estate planning can help insure that the loved one's financial security is maximized.

Serious mental illness is a disease of the brain, a physical problem that requires regular competent care and substantial time to produce a meaningful measure of wellness. Since the brain is what is diseased, causing impaired decision-making, telling a patient to "decide to get well" is ludicrous. Again, harsh judgmental requests to the mentally ill to make sensible decisions are not how to get results.

So, what is the answer? Perhaps the fundamental solution lies in a combination of good outpatient care, patience and love from caring family and friends, and faith that some measure of recovery is ahead. All the motivation that can be mustered from significant others to exercise, eat right, and take prescribed medication is vital.

To accomplish this for myself, I have accumulated a valuable, small circle of family and friends who comprise what a social worker would call my support system. In addition, I have ultimately developed a strong dependence on God's love. Managing my life in a meaningful manner has compelled me to engage in the belief that God is there to make each day valuable. And, when hospitalization is necessary, He is there to assist me in obtaining maximum benefit from hospital treatment. My faith in God has also convinced me that, along with His help, I carry a certain amount of responsibility to stay as well as I can. This has enabled me to experience a functional sense of worth, and it is a functional sense of worth that helps me stay out of hospitals.

Prayer is an essential part of every morning. I find it absolutely intolerable not to have daily, quality communication with God. Along with thanking Him for the blessings He has chosen to provide me, I make the regular request that I be guided in making the day full of quality time. Since my decision-making is poor, I pray daily that each 24-hour routine be comprised of a select set of priorities. I want my days to account for something. With God's help, they do. I also end the day with a brief prayer as I lie in bed in the dark; reviewing the day with gratitude, asking where I could have improved, and planning (with God's help) how I can make the next day better.

Thanks to a mother who steered me to church each Sunday, time for God has nearly always been a major priority for me. Without the faith that God is beside me in every daily action I would be a constant, useless package of self-inflicted sorrow. On my desk is a plaque my mother gave me as a daily reminder of how much I can depend on God's help:

> "Lord, help me to remember that nothing is going to happen to me today that You and I together can't handle."

These modest words have enabled me to get through what I believe would have been impossible times. They have convinced me that my disability is manageable as long as I keep my faith alive. Instead of absorbing myself in self-pity, I define my disability as a challenge I have been given to grow in character and contribute to others what I have learned along the way. As self-righteous as that may sound, it is what I believe. I have chosen this path in place of bitterness. Bitterness is a much harder path.

Presently, it is easy to write convictions such as this. It is developing into a good day. I am successively recovering from some depression that has tormented me during the past three weeks. There are other times when I live on the edge and can barely endure my symptoms. It is then I just scarcely survive my disability and (temporarily) fall into self-pity and a greatly reduced awareness of God's power and love. When this worthlessness eventually passes, I rise to receive the relief of another morning, dispensing some new amount of optimism and endurance.

However, despite my capacity to significantly recover, I am not comfortably confident (even on good days) that I am indestructible.

I remain convinced that the pain of the mentally ill is considerably compounded if they do not have God in their lives. I know the daily mountains presented to me would be insurmountable if the Lord did not bless me with the endurance and determination to climb. I have also been endowed with the wisdom necessary to accomplish what I believe is the plan for me, here on earth, to fulfill. I am provided every day in some way the guidance required to help (or prepare to help) the mentally ill. To know why I need to go on living allows me added meaning to my days and tolerable tranquility to my nights. Since so many patients lack the religious background or spiritual experiences that would lead them to God, so many patients suffer without recognizing the potential comfort provided from His crucial assistance to endure life.

Suffering is cruel when it chooses to be present. However, suffering has provided me with invaluable instruction. I have gained priceless lessons in patience, endurance, and compassion that make each day valuable. The understanding that no matter how much I may be hurting there is always someone else, somewhere, who is hurting more—and bearing it—aids me in functioning with a critical measure of biochemical balance. Included in the blessings I have secured, a major degree of peace accompanies my pain. In addition, a profound portion of endurance is facilitated.

I know recovery. Indeed, I choose recovery in place of denial. I recognize recovery as not a destination but a process. A daily schedule carries me through each hour like a continuous, dangling carrot. I'm continually challenged to dare to make my life more important. Instead of fear highlighting my life (fear of failure, fear of relapse, fear of others, and fear of life itself), I have taken steps to facilitate a portion of recovery every day. Every day's worth of tasks is accomplished with discipline though (sometimes) with drudgery.

My recovery has involved gradually changing my attitudes, values, goals, and roles. A desire for increased creativity and spirituality has led me to meditation, organized religion, a 12-step program, self-hypnosis, and daily affirmations. All have helped me along the way to establish a new purpose and identity. After evaluating my assets and my limitations, I have chosen to take on the role of author. I have found, thanks to an innate aptitude to put words together, that I am able to contribute even with the limitations of my illness.

The measure of recovery I experience each day has been more than just an answer to some flippant wish: It has required work. I rise from my bed as early as is possible, stay away from problem foods and drugs, exercise daily, make medical appointments, write, and get as much as possible and is necessary done. My recovery is not a cure. A miracle medication may never appear in my lifetime. However, I can be in the process of a cure. Here, my recovery moves me forward each waking/working hour toward goals that have pivotal purposes.

It may take daily effort to achieve what I define as meaningful, maintaining a ceaseless attitude that involves hope. Sometimes, important goals I set for myself are hard to recognize. Some days are just bad. On bad days, pursuing recovery can be especially difficult. Promising indicators that a meaningful amount of recovery will be there are when I get up in the morning and do not hear voices, or that I am able to remember the day and month and who is president, or that I am better than on my worst day, or that I look forward to breakfast, or that I am glad to remain alive.

It is the good days that advance me most effectively as I

proceed through life accomplishing things. I know I am better when I am working, organizing, playing (especially difficult for me), or loving. It is then I am grateful for some sense of achievement, and always amazed when I manage through what misery comes my way.

Chapter 16
SUGGESTIONS FOR SIGNIFICANT OTHERS

Despite my substantial independent efforts to stay as well as possible, caring people have nearly always played a crucial role in my recovery process. Helping out a seriously mentally ill person is not easy for significant others (usually parents, siblings, spouses, or friends). It can be especially devastating for the patient's family. This results in very confusing relationships with those you would like to see well. You have found you may often not know what you will wake up with: an angel or an ogre.

As a significant other, you soon begin to become acquainted with the deep despair of the seriously depressed; the cycles of highs and lows of manic-depressives; and the scattered communication that schizoaffectives and schizophrenics often display. These troublesome symptoms often require serious attention to achieve meaningful improvement. Most likely the most important thing you can do is make sure the seriously mentally ill person takes the required medication on time each day. Unfortunately, you cannot require this person to take their meds, and many of these disabled have a strong aversion to depositing foreign medical substances into their bodies. The inevitable result to such noncompliance is hospitalization.

Understanding and respect are bywords to follow in living with or near a mentally ill person. When this person is fearful, stay calm. When they are insecure, be accepting. When they are withdrawn, start gentle conversation. When they demonstrate unsound judgment, express relational, common-sense dialogue. When they exhibit a lot of stress, create a calm living environment. When they have trouble concentrating, slow down your speech and use simple sentences. When they are disorientated, present to them a predictable routine. And when they have memory problems, help the person record information. When the mentally ill person demonstrates a lack of self-esteem, emphasize the person's value in any way you can. When they display anger or a major lack of compassion, realize that is a symptom and part of the person's illness (not to be taken personally). If the person expresses a belief in delusions, do not argue about their truth. And when the person is more severely ungrounded in reality, wait for a better time to communicate. (There most often will always be a better time.) Plus, it is often difficult but always important to remember that the disease is not the person.

A summary of what the family may experience within themselves as they cope with a seriously mentally ill person is as follows:

- Considerable confusion and bewilderment
- Denial that there really is mental illness in the family
- Exhaustion for being constantly on call, without an end in sight
- Guilt that a family member(s) is to blame
- Anger over mental illness occurring in the family
- Anger over inadequate mental health services
- Guilt that a family is rarely listened to by mental health professionals
- Extreme apprehension over the potential reactions of others (outside of the family)
- Desire to escape, including moving to another state or country

You will find it tempting to believe there is a good chance the rival mental illness will permanently release its clutch when the mentally ill person shows an occasional measure of recovery. Family and friends can, therefore, not only become a source of refuge but also denial. The fact remains you are dealing with a disease of the brain that, presently, most often has no lasting remedy; though symptoms can be reduced considerably with the right medications. This requires skilled assistance: regular psychotherapy from a social worker, psychologist, or psychiatrist along with the specific attention of a psychiatrist whose credentials are required to adjust medications when necessary.

Should your loved one be a family member, you may be inclined to condemn yourself for providing the genes that created offspring who could ultimately suffer so much. Be kind to yourself. Simply do your best to provide invaluable aid to help your loved one maneuver through life with all the complications mental illness brings; and you have paid the dues required of any caring, significant other.

Granted, knowing you have done your best is much easier said than done. As you witness the transformation of your psychologically afflicted family member or friend from a likeable loved one to a total, often hostile stranger the abuse is often difficult to handle. What do you do when obscenities are directed your way or even when physical abuse is inflicted? You may be tempted to tell the mentally ill person to "get a hold of yourself" or "pull yourself together."

The bottom line is the negative behavior is not a moral issue, it is a medical one. It is not their fault.

Additionally frustrating is that the mentally ill person may choose to exercise complete confidentiality with what goes on between them and their doctor. They have the right to not allow their doctor to disclose what interaction goes on between them. When family and/or friends are not (under any circumstances) able to communicate with the doctor about what is going on with therapy, they suffer a profound inadequacy over what they can do to help.

Temporary legal resources (sometimes involving that the

mentally ill suffer a brief stay in jail before an extended stay in the hospital) may be necessary for your own protection. Should calling 911 and generating initial imprisonment be necessary, additional rapid intervention from you to facilitate hospitalization is crucial. The longer the mentally ill person stays in a frightening prison environment without adequate treatment, the sicker they will become. They often do not understand why they have been locked up and experience terror and confusion. In addition, the mentally ill are often preyed upon by other inmates, suffering experiences of serious sexual and general physical abuse. This may cause the mentally ill prisoner to be placed in solitary confinement. Some prisons provide treatment for the mentally ill. However, basic emphasis is based on management of mental diseases, not recovery. No matter how great the quality of medical care, jails are not the right place for extended provision of such services. Bottom line: Get outside help from a psychiatric facility as soon as possible.

There are essentially two types of hospitalizations: 1) voluntary and 2) involuntary. Voluntary hospitalization is where the mentally ill person agrees to be hospitalized. Compliance on the prospective patient's part makes the outlook much brighter. Involuntary hospitalization is where the mentally ill person cannot be convinced to enter the hospital when the hospital has been identified as the only rational resort. Most states require that the individual be a danger 1) to others, 2) to themselves (suicidal), 3) or to property before they can be hospitalized. Some states recognize a "fifth standard" where loved ones who refuse medication, eat improperly, or (in general) experience rapid deterioration are identified as "dangerous to themselves" or "unable to handle the hazards of their freedom."

It is a terrible thing for a significant other to have to make the decision to have a mentally ill friend or loved one incarcerated without the sick person's approval. However, regardless of how the mentally ill person acts, they are not that person. They are someone else who is in pain and, in spite of themselves, they sometimes may require hospitalization.

Your hospital visits may initially be rejected once the loved one becomes an involuntary inpatient. They may hold angry resentment about your being responsible for putting them in a confined environment and refuse you visits. Do not feel offended or hurt. As the mentally ill person continues receiving hospitalization, you will usually begin to notice a dramatic difference in their behavior. The day nearly always arrives when the loved one receives care sufficient enough to enable them to recognize what is appropriate gratitude for your help.

Hospital treatment will be painfully imperfect. Negative side effects usually accompany the positive effects provided by the medication. This often leaves, once a hospital stay is complete, an improved but still crippled person who needs your patience and love. There will be plenty of times when you will feel estranged from your loved one. However, affection is vital and should be offered whenever it can be comfortably accepted.

Encourage the psychiatrist in charge to institute a team approach. This involves bringing to a common table a member(s) of the family, concerned mental health professionals, and the patient to share insights and opinions concerning his/her progress. All the team members need to be involved with periodic evaluations while the patient is still hospitalized. Some goals that this treatment team might work toward are as follows:

- Getting symptoms under control
- Learning about the specific mental illness and how to maximize recovery
- Learning how to avoid a relapse
- Learning skills needed to live independently
- Finding a place to live
- Returning to school
- Developing necessary job skills
- Improving social skills
- Reducing side effects of the medication
- Stopping consumption of alcohol and/or street drugs

As outpatient treatment takes over when hospitalization does its job (hopefully no later), a new team of mental health professionals needs to become involved. It should meet with significant others as soon as possible. Important items of discussion can include the following:

- Identification and definition of the diagnosis
- Help for significant others to facilitate as much recovery as is possible
- Description of the outpatient treatment plan
- Identification of the most serious symptoms and description of medications being utilized, including side effects
- Stressing the importance of the medical staff listening to the patient so that identifying the appropriate medications is a cooperative effort
- Establishing how often the significant others can meet with the treatment team to discuss the patient's progress
- Determining what aftercare is planned for the patient

Make sure the mentally ill loved one makes their outpatient appointments for therapy and medication adjustments. You will often find yourself sorely disappointed in the community support programs available to you and your loved one. A good community support program will involve the following:

- The necessary number of staff members
- Availability to all who need such services
- Emphasis of involvement by family and friends
- Effective management
- A wide range of coordinated services customized for each person
- Education for the public on matters concerning mental illness
- Access by the client to affordable, community housing
- Consumer self-help and peer support groups
- Job opportunities and job training
- Guidance for the consumer to a network with all important consumer resources (clubhouses, senior centers, appropriate churches, etc.)

- A crisis hotline manned 24 hours by a competent mental health professional

Families and friends need to be successful in working with the community support program to assume the best care possible for their mentally ill consumer. Important suggestions include the following:

- Keep a record of all your activities with the system and make copies. This includes names, dates, and notes of conversations.
- When speaking to mental health professionals, be polite and to the point. If you suspect abuse, contact local mental health advocates to investigate the suspected problem.
- Ask for permission from the mentally ill patient to have access to all medical documents. You customarily must have this permission to know what progress is taking place in the consumer's program.
- Write thank-you letters when appropriate. Also, when appropriate, write letters of complaint. Send such letters to the agency director with copies to all involved. Contact with your legislator or other state officials may be necessary.
- If you do not understand what a mental health professional is telling you, do not hesitate to ask for clarification.
- Keep the patient informed about everything you are doing on their behalf as you work with the relevant mental health professionals. You will find yourself working against a formidable wall if the loved one feels you are sneaking behind their back.
- Don't be afraid of being assertive (but as diplomatic as possible) in your communication to your loved one's caregivers. You are paying for their services (either directly or through taxes), and deserve information and respect. It may be necessary to remind them of that. Your involvement will help get the job done.

241

The mentally ill person will often refuse to take necessary medication when out of the hospital. Or they may just forget because of typical memory problems. The mentally ill person often feels he or she can go it alone, without pills to "pollute" their bodies. It is here that distinct denial of their disability lands many back into the hospital. Remembering to take medications is a serious matter, and there will probably be times you will need to intervene.

Frequently reminding the mentally ill person to take their medication on time may often lead to resentment and resistance. One answer which may be necessary is for you to put the required daily doses in a visible place where you can see if they have been consumed. That way "Have you taken your medication?" will not be a questions regularly resented by the mentally ill individual.

Another valuable thing you can do is keep an individualized list of typical warning symptoms conspicuously displayed (on the refrigerator, etc.), which can often prevent hospitalization. For example, major signs predicting a schizophrenic breakdown can involve confused or delusional thinking, blunted or inappropriate feelings, and/or extreme withdrawal, or hallucinations. A list of symptoms preceding a serious state of mania can involve insomnia, irritability, spending too much money, unnecessary phone calls, euphoria, increased activity, poor judgment, dangerous driving, inappropriate anger, and/or inability to concentrate. Since mania can quickly escalate into delusions and hallucinations, it is vital that it be addressed as soon as possible. Likewise, swift intervention involving referring to a list of symptoms is also crucial with depression. Here, symptoms can involve withdrawal, excessive sleep, nausea, a negative attitude, low self-esteem, suicidal tendencies, fear, aching all over, trembling, and skin problems.

Each mentally ill friend or loved one will have their own, personal set of typical symptoms to keep track of. Both you and the mentally ill individual keeping track of these warning signs may make the difference between a relatively simple outpatient adjustment in medication or an extended hospital stay.

It is vital you regularly remind yourself of the qualities of this person in which you have chosen to invest your time, energy, and often considerable money to make as whole as is possible. You will likely recognize unusual personal, positive qualities in the mentally ill person that deserve your attention (i.e., manic-depressive individuals frequently display high aptitudes in the arts) and feel inclined to nurture these gifts.

Mental illness is not just a family inconvenience; it is a horrible thing to live with. Family members may suffer burnout. Relatives can obtain support for themselves from the local Alliance for the Mentally Ill, local chapters of the American Psychiatric Association, and state and county community mental health centers. Frequently, local newspapers regularly advertise local support groups for those suffering serious mental illness and that also invite family members to attend. NAMI's valuable "Family-to-Family" program provides support groups where significant others can go and receive counsel and direction in dealing with mentally ill related loved ones.

A legal tool that can prove extremely valuable is guardianship. The guardian is assigned by the court to act on behalf of the mentally ill person (called the ward) needing the guardian. Guardianship helps concerned significant others obtain needed medical services without the permission of the mentally ill loved one. Specific statutes regarding guardianship vary from state to state.

You will no doubt soon discover that, especially if the mentally ill person is a family member, medical bills can be overwhelming. It is vital that you become acquainted with the main federal programs that exist to provide disabled individuals financial assistance (Supplemental Security Income and Social Security Disability Insurance, Medicare and other Social Security monthly benefits). Those who are unable to work because of their mental illness are due these same benefits provided to those with other disabilities.

If the mentally ill family member is a veteran, do not hesitate to seek help from the Veterans Administration (VA). You do not need to have a service-connected disability to receive medical care from the VA: Any expenses will be wonderfully minor. However, should you suspect you acquired a health problem or that a health problem was enhanced while you were in the service, you may be eligible for VA monthly disability benefits.

It is time consuming to learn the ins and outs of obtaining Social Security and VA benefits, but investing in the effort is well worth the resulting possibilities.

It is nearly impossible for a mentally ill person to purchase private health insurance. The major reason is the "preexisting conditions" clause, which gives insurance companies the right to refuse coverage for anyone who has a past of mental illness (prior to applying for insurance coverage). Also, with private health insurance nearly all policies place extremely limiting caps on how much they will pay for mental health care.

"Parity" laws that outlaw discrimination against insuring the mentally ill have been rigorously resisted by private insurance companies, which argue that, due to increased costs, premiums would have to increase. However, lawmakers are finding that insurance parity is affordable. A 1998 report concluded that plans utilizing parity with proper managed care could reduce costs of treatment in a major way by 30 to 50 percent. Just around the corner are laws that protect the mentally ill from discrimination by insurance companies that refuse to recognize that serious mental illness is a physiological disease like diabetes or heart disease and deserves equal coverage.

Inadequate estate planning may result in the disabled person losing their Social Security and/or other benefits. When all close family passes away, there is often no one there to take care of the mentally ill left behind. "Surrogate Family" programs have been created to meet this need. Here, mentally ill relatives are provided with a comfortable living environment and receive medical and social services as needed. Also, federal and state benefits are provided as entitled. Many states that utilize this kind of program call it PLAN (Planned Lifetime Services Network), which is sponsored by NAMI. Call Alliance for the Mentally Ill of Wisconsin (800) 236-2988 for more information.

Persuading the mentally ill person to get involved in a church and/or support group can be exceptionally helpful. There, group members usually exchange phone numbers and provide extra invaluable support. Also, providing the mentally ill person some interest in a craft or hobby can often provide the quality time and concentration that helps the sufferer forget about their torment.

Tactfully encourage them to practice good personal hygiene and to eat properly. When anyone eats right and looks good, they naturally feel better. This is especially true of the mentally ill as they endure a delicate biochemistry that demands good health in every other way possible.

Self-isolation has been a byproduct of my mental illness. If it were not for my significant others, I would be a lonely and sad person—and there was a time when that was the case. Now I have accumulated a select few who watch out for my welfare and, indeed, who love me. Subsequently I live with less sorrow and greater ability to make a positive difference in other's lives. Should that sound self-righteous, I offer no apologies. However, I do offer expressions of gratitude that I matter.

PART IV:

CONCLUSIONS AND SOLUTIONS

Chapter 17
FAITH AMID THE MADNESS

I have been able to remain a believer. I can think of many reasons besides memories of a childhood full of closeness to God. However, the best two reasons are: 1) numerous answered prayers and 2) I simply chose to be a believer; even though God chose to challenge me with serious mental illness.

Over and over, I have had specific prayers answered in specific ways that can only result in a deep conviction that God heard and answered those prayers. I rejected the Godless life in which so many of my fellow psychotics existed. It was an abundantly preferable habitat where I perceived a loving God who was on my side. This divine assistance helped me accomplish what often seemed the impossible, as I advanced through life bearing the brutal symptoms of my disease. What a much better place than one where I would have abandoned these beliefs and fought the fight alone.

Church hasn't always provided me the comfort so much of what Christianity promises. However, God did start me out on a reassuring note. Because I was raised in my family's church of choice, I welcomed the Lord as a comforting companion. He knew I was plagued by frequent depression. He knew I lived on the outside of conversations, afraid others would become offended by the deliberate distance created by my fears. It always felt like God protected me from a hostile planet. Sunday church services enabled me to endure each week that lay before me. I could survive the anguish of life thanks to blessings God provided. God appreciated my devotion and always granted me a way to make it to another Sunday.

During my years at home my stepfather, mother, my brother, and I joined in family prayer each evening. However, we were not what could be called a devout family according to our strict church's standards. My stepfather finally agreed to join the church when I was in my mid-teens to appease my mother's regular prodding. However, he seldom attended services. What close social contacts my family nurtured were few and mainly other than church members.

When mental illness struck my family's collective peace of mind, their faith (especially my mother's) was significantly enhanced. Many families find their religious faith challenged when mental illness strikes a family member. They often find God an easy source to blame for their family's misfortune. They also may seek other sources on which to place blame: mental health professionals are faulted for not having a cure, the mentally ill person is made a target, and often family members blame themselves for creating the mental illness.

My disease was unexpected and devastating like most serious mental illnesses. When symptoms first occurred in my late teens, it was during a time that everyone shared only optimism about my future. I made the transformation from "Outstanding Senior Girl" to a stranger whose behavior was bizarre. My family began to live in constant anxiety, moving from crisis to crisis. It was just a beginning for them. They would be given more emotional challenges than they ever thought possible.

When serious mental illness attacked my spiritual awareness, the comfort of church vanished for me. Church leaders appeared to glare at me from the pulpit with accusing stares. I was terrorized as they seemed to gaze into my soul, aware of my every weakness. I soon began to dread attending services. They were no longer a haven from the cruelties of the world. It even became painful to pray as I isolated myself in my room, kneeling alone in quiet desperation. My despondent pleas to heaven brought no comfort. My heart bled a profusion of fear and anger. How could God allow this turmoil to afflict me? My urgent questions only left me with more terror. I became convinced that God knew my despondent heart and was angry at my every doubt. How else could he allow me to suffer such a spiritual collapse?

My sickness matured. However, I still managed to continue to attend some church services and to struggle with daily prayer. Those worshiping around me gradually appeared more and more false and cold, while church leaders appeared to persist judging the quality of my presence. I became sure they despised me and, refusing to accept my bundle of transgressions, certainly desired that I immediately leave the chapel. I eventually decided to discontinue regularly attending church. Then, additionally burdened with the heavy conviction that I must be guilty of serious sin, I believed not even God's perfect love allowed me forgiveness.

An all-time spiritual low was to accompany one early major mental breakdown. I had locked myself in a rented room and desperately prayed and read scriptures from the Bible. For my trouble, I was given frightening hallucinations that I could not suppress. Demons invaded my small living space, and I felt people could see through the walls and witness my hopelessness. Finally, I reached a desperate moment when I questioned the existence of God. It did not logically follow that my sincere religious activity could be accompanied by such grotesque pain and fear. However, the moment passed and I immediately withdrew my doubts, petrified my maimed mind could even accommodate such thoughts. Soon after that, my pain was interrupted as I was escorted to a hospital where I suffered through a limited measure of recovery. However, my religious struggles continued.

My faith was tested again and again during my sorry medical history. It was during my 25 plus hospitalizations that I became most aware of how isolated lives became without a belief in and reverence for God. I witnessed bitter psychiatric patients groping through a variety of hellish, Godless abysses that left them no peace. I knew my own hell but was, nevertheless, nearly always lifted to a measure of security that an outside, divine source was providing some relief and harbored a measure of hope. I found it a comfort to sometimes request prayers from others, and I was convinced they helped.

Psychiatrists call it religiosity when a mental patient dwells on religion. With nowhere else to turn, a good number of patients do become desperately religious. Religiosity is a legitimate clinical term that has accented psychiatric medicine for years. Freud saw religion as a social neurosis since there was no valid reason to believe in God. It can be argued that many desperate patients seek God with such an abundance of zeal that they appear extreme in their exaggerated efforts for comfort. Mental health experts insist it is detectible where a reasonable approach to God ends and an unrealistic exercise of faith begins. It would likely be legitimate for a therapist to question as symptomatic deeply reverent prayers for guidance in choosing what shoes to wear each day or whether it was a good time to take a bath. However, repetitive pleas to heaven that the gnawing pain of psychosis be removed could be considered a valid religious activity.

Likewise, the Bible reports occasions where demons and evil spirits possess individuals. There were also angels that brought comfort to personalities described in the Bible. If then, why not now? Still, psychiatric medicine has traditionally discounted reports of demons, fears of being possessed by evil spirits, and accounts of visits from angels as everything but the real thing. They instead diagnose these spirits as symptoms of serious mental instability rather than genuine and frightening visions straight from the lower inferno. Likewise, these angels are identified as other than authentic positive beings appearing after appeals for comfort.

Clinical cynicism such as this pervades mental hospitals everywhere and can easily create spiritual doubt in the heart of even the most pious patient. Substantial spiritual confusion can occur for the mentally ill, who often find it difficult to detect the difference between a legitimate spiritual experience and a psychotic/pathological experience. It seems to be the accepted norm that if you speak to God, you are praying. However, if God speaks to you, you are schizophrenic. It is vital you do not allow yourself to feel guilt, say the therapists. It is easy to forget trying to become a more ethical person that requires a degree of guilt as a motivator. Indeed, it is a remarkable thing when religious persons who are treated for mental illness still maintain a sense of ethics and their faith in God. Religion's connection to recovery cannot be underestimated. Famed psychiatrist Carl Jung identified the absence of religion in patients' lives as the chief cause of psychological disorders. Research shows that those who do keep their faith are better able to stay out of mental hospitals.

Fear and apathy caused me to stop attending church regularly in my mid-twenties. This period lasted about three years. I also harbored doubts that left me with a multitude of questions about the validity of the church of my youth. When I finally again decided to more actively engage in worship, my childhood religion began to again provide some comfort.

While religiosity permeated much of my communication with my church congregation, my mother (500 miles away) also did not escape my religious zeal. One Sunday I wrote a letter to her filled with excessive religion. It was my assumption that I was contributing to her life by communicating credibility in her choice of business: a finishing school and model agency. It is important to realize that this letter was the product of serious and intense concern, not meant to be taken lightly. Though it was probably peculiar to Mother, it was not peculiar to a victim of mental illness who suffered from delusions of grandeur and a surplus of religiosity. What follows are brief excerpts from this lengthy discourse:

Dear Mother,

Today is Sunday and I've felt inclined to ponder on beauty, fashion, and how these concepts fit into a religious framework. In the process, I have begun to devise a personal philosophy of fashion: the proper perspective in which to view the fashion world and the way in which to apply its influence to everyday life. It is, more or less, what I view as the "ethics of fashion."

There are those of certain ethical persuasion who would view fashion as pertaining only to frivolity, extravagance, vanity, and even vulgarity. They see the fashion world as a mire of greed, excess, and self-indulgence.

During His day, the Savior's appearance supported the principles He taught: humility and unselfishness. He knew it was important to be a living example of what He advocated; so He dressed in the most suitable, and generally acceptable, simple attire of His time.

What we should ask ourselves when we ponder, "What do I wear?" is, "What principle will I be communicating to others by my attire?" If by not bathing enough we are offensive and communicating unseemliness to others, then we are exemplifying a wrong principle. By staying well groomed and tastefully and modestly dressed, we communicate important positive principles of cleanliness, dignity, and order. I find it fascinating that it is simplicity in fashion that endures.

The point of it all is the Lord would have us take the time and effort to groom and dress properly knowing full well that, as we first consider loving and serving Him, what is "proper" will take care of itself. Sometimes this may require extra training. However, when final decisions of how to look are made in the framework of the Lord's teachings, the ultimate in good taste is always achieved.

Believe it or not, there have been times when zealous little me has questioned whether a finishing school and model agency was important or even especially good. Today, I'm convinced that such enterprises can provide a valuable service to those who suffer from insecurity, self-doubt, and despair...because they were never taught principles of dress, grooming, and social graces; or because, somehow, those principles became distorted along the way.

Love Two

"Who cares?" was the question of the moment. The most likely answer was probably only me. My inclination to ruminate (excessively preoccupy myself with pointless themes) was typical to me and symptomatic of a serious psychiatric problem.

Mother never answered my letter.

Rumination also revealed itself in talks I was assigned to give in church. One talk went on and on about the psychological advantages of the messages gleaned from the Sermon on the Mount. My points were well taken. However, my preoccupation with mental health and its consistent link to specific scriptures was, at the very best, tiresome.

My obsession with time management crept into another talk assigned to me as I crawled along whatever religious roads were provided me. Religiosity reared its persistent head as I identified and defined a link between making the most of the time given us each day and being obedient. The following excerpts from this talk continue to both interest and amuse me:

Early this year, I tried a new approach to accomplish my church responsibilities, which are basic to us all, even if we don't have a specific church calling.

My spiritual goals to accomplish daily were as follows:
- Morning and evening prayer (15 minutes)
- Scripture reading and meditation (45 minutes)
- Write in a journal (15 minutes)
- These activities took a total of minutes a day (8¾ hours per week).

My weekly spiritual goals were as follows:
- Attend all church meetings (5 hours)
- Have a weekly, spiritual get-together
- (11½ hours per week)
- Engage in at least 2 hours per week to the poor, sick, or lonely

All my spiritual activities added up to 18½ hours per week. Subtracting 8 hours per day to sleep and 4½ hours per day to washing, dressing, and eating, I was left with 50¼ hours per week for work, exercise, social activities, and play.

I continued this sermon with even more detail on how I would fit my spiritual responsibilities into a 24-hour day. I feel certain this message was at the very best grueling to all but me. Indeed, compulsive-obsessive me found the whole exercise of detailing my time commitment to God a fascinating undertaking.

I was basically tolerant when it came to other's imperfections except when it came to gossip, my most despised vice. I made a serious attempt to eliminate it from my conversation and discourage it in others. No doubt, I was inspired to despise this imperfection because I was so easily its target; often bearing the stigma of mental illness like a crimson "M." Though I made every attempt to keep my mental illness to myself, it was most often impossible to hide frequent hospitalizations. Consequently, my disability would often become general knowledge. As the painful target of frequent vicious gossip, I made it my job to discourage this hateful vocal activity in every way possible, and never be the one to generate the damage it developed. As a journalism student in undergraduate school, I championed the cause of privacy and made sure all campus news stories I wrote did not reveal their sources when "off the record" was requested. To me, privacy was sacred. I despised the national tabloids that revealed the most intimate (most often the most incorrect) information about famous personalities. I sympathized with those who found it necessary to trade their fame for a tarnished reputation.

Despite uncertainties, I remained a devout and diligent member of my childhood church until I turned 30 years old. I then found I harbored too much skepticism to continue with this religion. After a rigorous search of the community, I found another faith I was comfortable with. It provided a traditional, Biblical approach to Christianity along with an appealing amount of ritual. Most attractive, I could put a main emphasis of worship on the individual's personal relationship with God, not as much on church structure (the focus of my childhood church).

Understanding the genuine meaning of grace, that God recognized my sins and at the same time forgave them all if I repented (and sincerely tried not to repeat the transgression)—no matter how many times I failed—was an initial struggle for a few years in my newfound church. My first church had put a primary emphasis on works where repentance often required excommunication and lengthy sacrifice to be reinstated; including diligent prayer, regular visits to church leaders, and dependable church attendance.

Therefore it was understandable that I found grace, providing absolute forgiveness without so much consequence from the church itself, a difficult notion to grasp. However, though this overwhelmingly generous viewpoint initially eluded me, after talking to pastors, reading relevant material, and earnestly praying for understanding, I eventually began to grasp this miraculous phenomenon of grace. I maintained these beliefs in my heart, convinced of my grateful responsibility to God to live an obedient Christian life. These concepts created a crucial foundation for my new faith—and marked the beginning of a more rational comprehension of God's love for me.

Thirty-nine years of serious mental illness and my occasional struggle with the concept of a loving God have caused me to occasionally ponder why the Savior suffered and why I must suffer in my life. Such moments of reflection have allowed me to reach my own brand of understanding about suffering. I have come to accept that this earth accommodates an abundance of it. Wars, hunger, disease all find their way into countries and cultures. I do not completely understand why there is so much hurt for some, but I believe it is there for a purpose. When it invades a life, it can be entertained with bitterness or with courage. It can cause a person to crumble or to grow in character. I have come to accept this suffering as a part of a grand and divine plan that I will one day completely understand.

Prayer is an essential part of my every morning, which has now become a comfortable time to communicate with God; and, typically, my prayers are answered. During the brief interludes when my prayers are considerably below the quality I try to sustain, I am usually so psychologically sick I cannot concentrate on prayer, or reading, or just about anything that requires deliberate mental effort. However, when I am blessed with sufficient mental health, I secure a strong awareness of God's specific plans for me: very likely periodic suffering while exercising the necessity to manage my health with caution. My answered prayers have left me convinced that God is taking care of me. I have selected this path in place of bitterness and believe it is ultimately good for my health. In return for my faith, God has blessed me with the endurance and determination necessary to help reduce the pain of those who suffer mental illness and bring hope to the mentally ill. So have I gratefully discovered my own direction—my destiny.

My faith has provided me with the capacity to be keenly aware that God has always known my suffering and that His love has always been there to generate answers to my prayers. Life was never meant to be easy for me, but I could have known worse. Indeed, I now have the medication Clozaril, which sustains a critical measure of comfort and sanity. My prayers focus mainly on the specific ordeals of each day as it comes rather than recurrently wrestling with the overwhelming trials of a skeptical medical future; asking each morning what His will is for me that day and praying for the ability to fulfill my part.

God's decision to shower my life with an abundance of blessings keeps me unwilling to waste much time speculating on what an alternative existence would have offered me. My todays are so much better than my yesterdays: I have so many more days of gratitude than of misery. I am thankful the world of psychiatric medicine has discovered new ways to provide me longer periods of comfort. I occasionally dare to speculate about a time when a true cure for serious mental illness arrives. It will be like having Christmas every day of the year. This will be the greatest gift of all, and worthy of the celebration of a song I wrote that applauds such a Christmas. Following are the lyrics:

Make It Last All Year

People goin' shoppin',
Buyin' lots of things.
Downtown stores are hoppin'
With sales the season brings.

Though there's too much buyin',
There's also lots of cheer.
Give me Christmas every day.
Make it last all year.

258

Lots of people suffer
In almost every land.
If I had it rougher
Perhaps I'd understand.

But still there's something I can do
To make my message clear.
Give me Christmas every day.
Make it last all year.

I know I can't save the world.
I know there's only one
Who can save what matters
And He's already come.

So make a wish for peace, my friend
And sing a song of joy.
Say a prayer all war will end
Then buy another toy.

For givin' makes the holidays,
Not the hate and fear.
Give me Christmas every day.
Make it last all year.

Today, Christmas may come just once a year while, through it all there are people who look out for me. And, there is a loving God who always knew my endurance. He provides for me the gift of a functional reality, as He blesses me each day with my own brand of awareness.

Chapter 18
LUCK OR LOVE —
SUMMING THINGS UP

After a current total of 39 years of serious mental illness, highlighted by over 25 hospitalizations with the ultimate diagnosis of schizoaffective disorder, life has presented a serious series of challenges—accented by an assortment of blessings.

I averted the hospitals of the 1950s and 1960s when the mentally ill were placed in asylums referred to as "snake pits." My first hospitalization occurred in the early 1970s when positive reforms were beginning to take place on mental wards.

My mental disability was determined "military service connected." Therefore, my hospitals were almost exclusively run by the Veterans Administration (VA) and so provided care without cost. Whenever I was placed in a private hospital, it was provided by the VA as transitional care until a bed on a VA psychiatric ward became available. Most mentally ill struggle to obtain any funds from biased insurance companies and health plans and, ultimately, cannot afford satisfactory care in private hospitals. These patients end up in seriously inferior state mental hospitals, often receiving miserable treatment. When state patients are discharged, they are also frequently put in state outpatient programs that are poorly staffed, providing treatment that often quickly lands them back into state hospitals.

My service-connected designation also provided me with funds from VA vocational rehabilitation to pay for my undergraduate work while the GI Bill paid for my graduate work; without my having to work part-time, which didn't work before the military. And, so my family and I were saved the disastrous costs of both the medical attention I required and the higher education I desired.

I can only suspect it was more than luck that shock therapy never assaulted my body. Frequently feared by patients, it carries with it an abundance of reassurance from doctors and staff. Their story is that the procedure has been tempered and does not carry the torment it once did. When a patient seems hopelessly depressed, not benefiting adequately from medication, shock therapy is most often a quick proposal. My depression responded just well enough to medication to avoid this treatment. After witnessing the lethargic behavior and short-term memory problems of those who were victims of shock therapy, I became convinced it was to my profound advantage that I escaped this dubious remedy. I had occasion to read, witness, and hear from patients that the side effects of shock therapy can be permanent short-term memory loss with depression returning in a short time. I was lucky enough to be informed of the dangers of shock therapy before I gave up and crumbled under depression. Fear of shock therapy increased my motivation to fight the dominate despair.

Out of a total of 25 or more VA hospitalizations, only a very few were what I recall as disasters. (There may have been more than a few that my memory has preferred to overlook.) One medical fiasco was due to an incompetent staff that expressed every negative emotion, neglecting compassion. Other devastating hospital stays were unsuccessful due to psychiatrists who made painfully poor decisions about my medication. Early hospitals presented distinctive arenas of agony. However, as the number of hospitalizations built up I became stoic to the suffering I witnessed again and again. Still, I could only, in the early years of disease, fear my new surroundings: caldrons of seething emotions threatened at any time to boil out of control. I fortunately, always, soon left these psycho-pharmaceutical nightmares within two weeks. Though my VA psychiatric units were never ideal, they were most often adequate, occasionally exceptional, and always without cost.

I endured being placed in seclusion only once. Like certain other new patients who presented the possibility of dangerous behavior (to themselves and/or others), I was placed in isolation (complete with padded walls and bare mattress). My suicidal symptoms prompted the doctor to have me locked in this tiny room with no way to leave but by way of the magic key possessed by a staff member who had nearly no idea what lonely desperation was churning inside of me. I could hear the cries of other nearby patients also in seclusion rooms. Their devastating moans communicated a profusion of suffering. A simple need like visiting the bathroom became a basis of major anxiety for me and my fellow solitary shut-ins; a need that was most frequently postponed to the point where finally patients found it necessary to relieve ourselves without the luxury of a toilet. Ultimate humiliation accompanied this biological necessity, one I fortunately never needed to endure since my isolation was not long-term.

I have suffered restraints only once. This occurred during my second hospitalization and after being inoculated with a mystery medication that left me unconscious. Upon awakening, I became aware of a bandage around my head and my hands tied to my bed. I was told I had suffered seizures that had caused a head injury, and that it was required I be tied to my bed to prevent further harm.

Currently, the National Alliance for the Mentally Ill is calling for a national investigation regarding the wrongful deaths associated with the use of involuntary restraints and unnecessary mental torment associated with seclusion in mental hospitals. The goal is to eliminate the use of both these extreme measures. Ironically, the greater the reduction in restraint and seclusion, the greater the reduction in staff injuries. Such extreme measures are solidly indicative of treatment failure.

I escaped the horror of tardive dyskinesia, in which antipsychotic medications would have caused me to lose control of, most typically, my facial muscles (resulting in chronically grotesque expressions). About 5 percent of those who are treated using antipsychotic drugs suffer from this side effect. It is especially common among medicated mentally ill women. And worse, this condition is most often irreversible. I recall during my first few hospitalizations seeing patients who suffered this side effect (mainly schizophrenics), and how much their frightening expressions enhanced my already existing fear of mental wards. Though I have had more than my share of antipsychotic medications, my face has remained unaffected. Fortunately, the new antipsychotic medication I now take, Clozaril, carries with it minimal danger for tardive dyskinesia. A few other, newer antipsychotics such as risperidone, olanzapine, aripirazole, and ziprasidone also carry much less risk.

Recalling the sad collection of veterans with whom I have shared hospitalizations and outpatient treatment, I can only acknowledge that I was, most often, in a better place. I was no stranger to suffering. Hallucinations (both auditory and visual) and delusions (fantasies that others, especially famous persons, were infatuated with me) were not foreign to my conditions. Usually, however, once I was medicated for a short time (two to three weeks), the hallucinations disappeared, and my ability to cognate (make sense) usually became fairly good. I would bounce back fairly fast to a functional existence.

My pain was real and continuous, primarily consisting of acutely desperate and exhausting mania (often involving visual and auditory hallucinations), severe depression (profound sadness), paranoia (intense fear), and the side effect of extreme muscle spasms (most often located in my neck). However, I most often possessed the presence of mind that enabled me to practice more than acceptable personal hygiene. Attention to appearance is most often less than acceptable with the seriously mentally ill. Keeping clean and visually respectable is usually not a priority when you are hearing voices and seeing demons.

It was my mother's early attention to my public image that enabled me to usually escape "appearing" mentally ill. An expert on the subject of appearances, she was always there during my upbringing (when not running her finishing school) to provide good advice concerning how I visually and verbally presented myself to others. Therefore, instead of manifesting the disheveled appearance of the typical mentally ill patient, I projected an image that proclaimed a reasonably healthy-minded individual. This was sometimes to my disadvantage: Doctors often underestimated the seriousness of my condition. Also, my reasonably normal appearance resulted in impressive, though illusive job interviews that usually secured employment. I repeatedly landed jobs I couldn't consistently perform. Still, a respectable appearance sustained in my mind and heart a sense of dignity for which I will always be grateful.

I was never the victim of rape from other patients or staff. Sexual abuse, ranging from lewd language and advances to rape, is often no stranger to women who frequently spend much time inside psychiatric wards. In a VA mental hospital where men dominate the population, it is a particular disadvantage to be female. I most often feared physical/sexual assault on wards where I was not locked in my room at night in order to make frequent night checks more convenient for the staff. My trepidation resulted in a sense of absolute helplessness and complete dependency on God's protection. One night, I awakened to see a male patient urinating next to my bed. I cried out and a staff member quickly removed the culprit and locked my door. Offensive language that often involved gross X-rated descriptions was also not unusual as patients verbalized their sexual confusion. Otherwise, I was kept safe from the nightmare of this lewd abuse.

Some psychiatrists have presented therapy (involving both medications and verbal exchange) that was often considerably less than ideal, often bordering on incompetence. However, I was the victim of outright cruelty from only two psychiatrists. The first was a rigid military doctor (a colonel) who believed pulling rank and reprimanding me was effective therapy. And, I will never forget the second barbaric doctor who severely chastised me for the simple offense of not being able to sit still, even though the very medication he prescribed for me created the side effect of extreme restlessness. I can hear his angry demands that I sit in my chair, "Sit still right now," while he interrogated me. I recall the helplessness I felt, truly being unable to sit still in a chair for even a few seconds.

Despite a collection of mediocre-to-bad doctors, today I enjoy therapeutic prosperity from treatment by a psychiatrist who is close as possible to ideal. As Director of Mental Health at the local VA clinic, she replaced many questionable mental health professionals. Due to the complications of my diagnosis, she has agreed to accept me as a personal patient. Her abundance of compassion has convinced me she is fully committed to securing as much recovery as possible for me. During our weekly appointments, she demonstrates an intensity of support that is constantly demonstrated through simple gestures such as leaning forward and making direct and earnest eye contact as she listens. And she *always* listens. Her questions are consistently relevant, indicating that she bothered to review my medical file since our last visit (a simple practice that is too rarely ignored). This VA psychiatrist has enough confidence in me and dedication to my welfare to reveal to me her cellular and home phone numbers. I have been careful not to abuse this privilege, and I breathe easier than I ever have, convinced that I have a legitimately caring psychiatrist. Displaying ardent concern for the patient is the one most useful thing a psychiatrist can do. My present psychiatrist is an expert at demonstrating this type of humanity, a benevolence I have learned to never take for granted.

An excellent psychiatric nurse and support group complement this psychiatrist's care nicely, enabling me to prevail each week.

Regarding work: Despite my inability to continuously hold a job, I have never been hungry or without a roof over my head. Unfortunately, this is not the case for the one-third of all homeless people who are severely mentally ill. That means the rest of the seriously mentally ill who live in the community reside with their families or in other types of housing. Many end up in prison. Mental health advocates estimate 159,000 mentally ill individuals are jailed at any given time just to wait for psychiatric hospital beds— not for breaking laws. Presently, there are less than 70,000 publicly funded psychiatric beds, down from 500,000 in the 1960s.

How I have always escaped the dangers of the streets and the jails is a blessing that bewilders me. We see them huddling over steam grates, carrying on energetic conversations with invisible comrades, wearing filthy and torn clothing, defecating and urinating on sidewalks, and threatening passersby. They are indeed victims: that is, victims of suicide or violent crime, more often the casualty than the criminal. Women are the most frequent targets of an abundance of abuse in these hazardous habitats. Studies have shown that 22 percent of women who suffer untreated schizophrenia have been raped. These women also suffer suicide rates 10 to 15 times greater than those of the general population. An uncanny and unrealistic sense of safety most always prevailed in my disabled mind during my psychotic breaks. However, there were dangers that I was able to mysteriously avert. Unaware of traffic or other hazards, I could have been left dead in some alley or seriously injured; perhaps permanently disabled with an additional, physical handicap. However, when I did not have the presence of mind to hospitalize myself, there was always someone there to make sure I was put in the safety and care of a hospital when it was needed. Then, once again stabilized on a new collection of medications, I would be discharged from the hospital. And, again, I would be functional enough to secure housing and adhere to an outpatient program where I could independently stay for a lengthy time on my medications and make all medical appointments; necessities God provided that kept me safe from the perils of street life.

Creating a career was traumatic. I eventually learned how the stigma created by others' awareness of my mental illness would render me emotionally unemployable; so I mainly chose not to volunteer that information to potential employers. The paranoia of the possibility of my coworkers discovering my mental illness manifested itself to me in every competitive work environment and left me consistently alienated. My ability to make clear and timely judgments was severely impaired by a combination of symptoms from my disability and side effects from my medications. Since I could never build up enough seniority to warrant meaningful promotions and pay raises (I survived each job for only about a year before finally succumbing to the overwhelming stress), my income was always severely limited. I was acutely aware of my vulnerabilities in the workplace. It was inevitable that I would eventually experience a full-blown breakdown while on the job. When it happened, it happened BIG. As I bounced from coworker to coworker, engaging in rapid, manic discourse, it quickly became clear to the staff something was really wrong with me. Roommate Jessie was called to drive me home, and I was hospitalized the next day. I can only pay tribute to Jessie and my mother for their selfless financial assistance that combined with my limited income when no other sources were available. It most likely kept me off the streets.

Today I live in a house with a yard and trees and roommate Jessie, who is there during medical emergencies while still respecting my privacy. Again, with current disability benefits, I have a good life. Many serious mentally ill patients cannot maintain employment or are so disabled and alone they are not able to complete the routine tasks of everyday living or afford the necessities that make life reasonably comfortable. Being able to afford houses or apartments of their own becomes a silenced dream. These seriously mentally ill are so isolated they need to be monitored and therefore require living in transitional housing (when it is available). In each house, the patients manage as a group, supervised by a mental health professional(s). These guided patients share household responsibilities such as cleaning, shopping, and cooking. This structured living keeps former hospitalized patients on their medications and in the doctors' offices for regular scheduled appointments. Such simple benefits are major privileges in the world of mental illness.

Though suicide was an option I twice attempted, I fortunately failed twice. Both times, life had become unbearable, and the only solution to my misery seemed to be to take my own life. About four years into my serious symptoms, my treatment had been only slightly successful. My endurance for pain had always been limited, and the sweet retreat of death seemed the only achievable answer to ending my suffering. I was not alone. As much as 90 percent of all who commit suicide suffer from mental illness. What is even more tragic is that the mental illness is in most cases eventually treatable.

Many believe the mentally ill do not hurt, that they exist in another world where everything is comfortably counterfeit. Such outsiders see mental illness as a break from reality, not involving pain but rather an escape from pain. I am here to witness that psychological pain is real pain, both physical and emotional. Though not easy to explain, it is assuredly most often a part of mental illness. Sometimes it starts with the head, then often travels down the body to result in an overall physical agony.

Besides definite physical suffering, there is mental/emotional anguish, where depression, anger, and/or fear are prevalent. Perhaps it can be explained by comparing the suffering of mental illness to a gamut of negative thoughts and feelings that trap themselves inside the psyche. They then frequently insist on escalating until they often turn into terrifying hallucinations (demons, spiders, etc.) and delusions (grandiose self-concepts, and confusing perceptions regarding relationships).

For those who suffer bouts of mania (extreme hyperactivity), it is often impossible to sleep or even sit still. These individuals often go for days, even weeks, pacing the floor, unable to sleep, in a general state of agony. Consequently, suicide is all too often considered the only viable alternative. With manic-depressives, about 15 to 20 percent successfully commit suicide; and it is estimated that about 10 percent of all schizophrenics commit suicide. Indeed, suicide is not uncommon to all serious mental illnesses.

The two times (about a year apart) I attempted to take my life are clear in my memory. I just hurt too much. I decisively lay down, consumed a handful of aspirin, and waited to die with great anticipation. Today, I feel fortunate I failed to succeed with both suicide attempts. Instead, I achieved what could be called an aspirin hangover, creating a level of misery that caused me to regret failing to finish the job. I am left with the clear conviction that suicide is not an acceptable answer to ending any psychological pain. Shortly after my second attempt, I happened to read about two scientific studies of many who had near-death experiences. All descriptions of dying were incredibly similar, extremely positive, and considerably convincing. However, a major exception involved those who attempted suicide: They were made to feel all the pain they caused those they left behind. Today, I am convinced that if I had succeeded in ending my life, not only would my loved ones have suffered, but this ultimate gesture would have, to my great torment, displeased God.

My health habits were superior to most psychiatric patients I have encountered. Having been raised in a religion that instilled in my young mind the importance of not consuming caffeine, tobacco, or alcoholic beverages, not consuming these hazardous substances (along with street drugs) created a passion for good health. Serious exercise was introduced to me in my late teens: I enrolled in a Red Cross swim class and earned certification to teach swimming. I was required to develop the physical fitness that enabled me to swim an initially vigorous quarter of a mile without stopping. This initiated a lifetime of diligent exercise that developed into frequent, intense workouts in whatever swimming pool I found available. As a result, endorphins (chemicals typically introduced to the brain during exercise that reduce depression) were frequently presented to my suffering biochemistry. During each workout, the water surrounded me with a welcoming blanket of comfort, which ultimately made daily exercise comfortably addictive.

I have never suffered from terrible hunger. My excellent physical fitness united with a decidedly inferior diet during the early years of my mental illness. (I just chose not to eat right.) However, today I benefit from regular meals that keep my biochemistry functioning to the max. Proper nutrition was not always conveniently available and my knowledge of the importance of the proper food to fuel my demanding biochemistry was too often meager. Though I ate when I was hungry, I frequently failed to fix regular (well-balanced) meals. When I joined the military, I was relieved from the responsibility of cooking and was provided adequate, even appetizing nourishment. However, the military did not instill in me the habit of preparing my own meals. Once out of the military, I was back to a poor daily diet, even inferior to my eating program before I entered the military service.

My best daily menus were those I learned when in

undergraduate school. I had decided I was going to learn to cook well. I was successful for four years. Starting graduate school ended my culinary zeal. I finally got the point: I did not like to cook. When I was ultimately diagnosed with hypoglycemia (low blood sugar) in 1979, I began to take my diet much more seriously. A balanced diet significantly diminished my symptoms of serious mental illness—and I was desperate to feel good. When I followed the proper diet, I felt markedly better. Consequently, though the problem of hypoglycemia left me around the age of 45, it provided the important motivation to eat wisely. This has reduced or eliminated a variety of other health problems. Despite the advantages of this disorder, several of the medications I have taken over the ensuing years still have created the disadvantage of increasing appetite. Therefore, staying at my ideal weight has remained a significant and ongoing challenge.

Street drugs were never a problem for me as they are for many others who self-medicate to relieve the pain of mental illness. Such drugs successfully tempt many of the mentally ill who live in desperation for the temporary relief these substances provide. No matter how much relief results from street drugs and from alcohol, the typical trade-off is eventual descent to a depression that only causes increased craving and more self-mediation.

Schizoaffective disorder (somewhere between manic depression and schizophrenia) is my most recent and most obviously correct diagnosis. It has taken doctors more than 25 years to identify what is really wrong with me. I have lived with the diagnosis of manic depression most of my life. However, it has become plain, primarily due to improved diagnostic references that doctors now depend upon, that I have always been schizoaffective.

The correct diagnosis has enabled me to receive more effective care. This new, more serious label of schizoaffective disorder makes more sense than my former, defined more functional, bipolar classification. It has become apparent over the years that I cannot make a reasonable living working in the stressful and demanding psychology/sociology of a competitive work environment. Today, I am able to write two to three hours a day in the privacy of my home, with ten-minute breaks each hour to reduce the stress that builds up from the intensity of my efforts. The rest of my attempts at a productive day involve elementary tasks such as housecleaning and simple errands. It all produces a wear and tear on my psyche that requires a considerable measure of rest during my evenings and overnight. Even with my limited amount of daily activity, I am still uncomfortably susceptible to the anxiety that accompanies my efforts to make life have value.

However, my original diagnosis of schizophrenia presents itself as an overstatement. Though my breakdowns have frequently supported the diagnosis of schizophrenia, they have been limited in their duration. Also significant has been my ability to perform in a reasonably utilitarian manner each day. It has just been unlikely that a schizophrenic could function as effectively as I have managed to function.

Therefore, I have existed somewhere between the abysses of bumpy pain presented by bipolar disorder and the chronic/intense confusion of schizophrenia. This has left me susceptible to the mood swings of bipolar disorder while also no stranger to the sustained hallucinations and delusions of schizophrenia. It was never my expectation that I could not have a career. My struggle with college carried with it the assumption that I would be able to earn a good living. My doctor's awareness of my inability to make a reasonable living has provided for me a necessary monthly disability check. Despite the pride that was always a part of my family, where it was important to earn what bounty came my way, I have swallowed (sometimes choked) on my self-respect and grown grateful for disability checks.

My current medical care is better than it has ever been. With better medication and dramatically improved weekly care from a doctor and a social worker (and periodic support group) my former daily anguish has been dramatically diminished. Though my diagnosis is serious, during the past four years I have been saved from the blatant pain characterized by my medical history primarily thanks to a fairly new medication.

Clozaril requires biweekly blood tests and visits to the doctor. The blood tests identify any reduction in white blood cells as well as a reduction in my body's immunity, a possible (but not likely) critical side effect. My white blood cell count has stayed normal and so I have been able to remain on this medication. The yearly costs to the VA for Clozaril and the care required to dispense it properly (including the blood tests) is about $22,000. Without the VA paying the way, this large sum would have left my family financially crippled. My medical history clearly shows that without Clozaril I would be more frequently hospitalized.

Three non-VA programs have also provided valuable support. I have attended weekly 12-step programs. Though originally the 12 steps were the central tenets of Alcoholics Anonymous, nonalcoholics are now able to benefit from 12-step, self-help programs such as Emotions Anonymous (for those with psychological problems) and Overeaters' Anonymous (a great help in keeping my weight manageable despite the wait-gaining side effects of some of my medications). Maintaining a focus on the 12 steps that guide program members, I have been able to grow in character and in my capacity to do for others. In addition, it is impossible to avoid making friendships with people who attend meetings that make them better people.

Two other meetings outside of the VA that help sustain me through the week are both spiritually based: I sporadically attend church on Sunday and a class that focuses on Christian topics during the middle of the week. This religious activity, like my activity in a 12-step program, helps feed my social-spiritual needs.

Jessie, a rare friend and roommate, keeps an eye on me and cautions when I begin to display classic warning signs that are predictors of breakdowns. Between her regular workday as a schoolteacher and her other daily obligations, she manages to watch me carefully. When any signs occur that warn of a breakdown (such as excessive talking, the extreme physical activity of mania, or the immobility that severe depression brings) Jessie has me call the doctor to request an extra appointment for a possible medication change, extra verbal therapy, or even hospitalization. There have been those times Jessie found it necessary to miss work teaching school and drive me to the hospital.

Appointed by the VA as my fiduciary, Jessie handles my financial affairs. I have full confidence in Jessie's good judgment and integrity and find myself with a reasonable savings account for the first time in my life. This trust characterizes our relationship. Indeed, for me, having experienced the loneliness from the stigma of mental illness, ostracized and alienated by a society that too often refuses to provide critical compassion and care, Jessie's friendship is unquestionably an extraordinary blessing.

Crucial to my mental health was an upbringing highlighted by a faith in God. My mother's Sundays involved about four hours of church. This ritual consistently embraced my upbringing, along with Mother's insistence that the four of us share family prayer each evening. So I was provided a foundation of faith in God that managed to sustain me through childhood depression. This faith has also carried me through 39 adult years of serious mental illness despite the suffering I ultimately endured where, at times, I felt completely separated from everything—even God.

Unlike so many of the mentally ill, I never retreated into a lasting cynicism. During the crucial times when I suffered some skepticism and self-doubt, my mother would remind me that I could pray and God would listen; that He loved me enough to continue to provide comfort. I believed her.

My religious background provided a basic understanding of Christ and, therefore, a role model that I could always hold onto when I did not know what to do with myself. Having observed an abundance of mentally ill patients, I have witnessed the spiritually afflicted (those who have not recognized the love of God in their lives) are most inclined to paranoia and least inclined to a reasonable amount of recovery. Also, these patients' families typically lose patience and dissociate themselves from their difficult, mentally ill relatives. I escaped the pain of this kind of abandonment: I never felt my family, a Christ-based collection of kin, was ashamed of me.

The longer I live the more I am convinced it has all been more than luck. God has preserved for me a multitude of blessings, a massive gesture from a loving God as opposed to the serendipity of plain luck. God's love or just luck? Decide for yourself from the following:

- I just missed the misery of the "snake pits" of the 1950s and 1960s. My first hospitalization occurred in 1974, when mental hospitals were beginning to reflect some major and positive reforms.
- I decided to join the military to finance a college education. This decision resulted in a master's degree and ample, necessary medical care—without cost to me or my family.
- I have been able to avoid shock therapy.
- Most of my hospitalizations were positive experiences.
- Only once did I endure seclusion.
- I was involuntarily restrained only once.
- I escaped tardive dyskinesia, an horrendous side effect of antipsychotic medications, and typically nonreversible.
- Despite symptoms that caused frequent hospitalizations, hospital stays were usually brief (two weeks).
- Most often, I was able to maintain a presentable appearance, resulting in a significant, meaningful measure of dignity.
- I was never a victim of rape, in or out of the hospital.
- Only two psychiatrists who treated me did so with outright cruelty.
- I currently benefit from outstanding psychiatric care, involving an excellent psychiatrist, social worker, and support group.
- Though I have experienced a shaky career, I have never been a victim of the streets; always managing a roof over my head and never knowing hunger.
- I was unsuccessful in my two attempts at suicide and am now convinced that this kind of escape is wrong.
- I have nearly always found it important to practice good health habits; exercising regularly, maintaining an adequate diet, and avoiding alcohol, tobacco, and illegal drugs.
- I am now correctly diagnosed with schizoaffective disorder, which enables me to benefit from the extremely effective medication Clozaril.
- I benefit from the loyalty of a roommate and friend who keeps a cautious eye on me, identifying when I need to

have extra medical attention.
- My family instilled in my young mind a faith in God and confidence that His love would always pull me through.

Consequently, through it all, I have remained convinced that love (especially God's love), not luck, has kept me alive, reasonably balanced, and able to reach substantial goals. And, therefore, as far as I can remember, from an unkind childhood prone to depression; to an adolescence where my first serious symptoms emerged; to an adulthood where I quickly became no stranger to psychotic breakdowns; it has most often been my belief that maintaining maximum mental/physical well-being is a responsibility I have to a loving God. This God gave me a body, biochemically crippled but capable of managing whatever measure of endurance is required to engineer through my daily struggle for optimum health and meaningful productivity. I awaken each day with the awareness that my prayers are answered and grateful that those prayers have kept my faith in God intact.

Sustained with the realization of why I populate a space on this earth, I am provided a daily reason for remaining conscious. I believe I was meant to bring knowledge, comfort, hope, and self-esteem to victims of serious mental illness who courageously awaken every day without knowing the torment that day will bring. My hope is that I do this while generating compassion and respect from healthy, significant others. In turn, I am provided with an abundant measure of fulfillment and accomplishment, knowing it was always more than luck that enabled me to survive the life chosen for me. It could only have been God's love that ultimately left me convinced my story is important enough to tell—and God's love for the mentally ill and their families and friends who hunger for a clear and complete understanding only those who have been there can reveal.

Index

acetaminophen, 111
Advanced Individual Training (AIT), 56, 195
aggression, 104, 115, 165
agitation, 77, 78, 103, 137
Alliance for the Mentally Ill, 243
ambivalence, 35–36, 203
American Board of Psychiatry and Neurology, 81
American Psychiatric Association, 243
Americans with Disabilities Act (ADA), 204
"Analysis," 36
anger
   displays of, 147
   manic, 66
   stress and, 108
   symptoms of, 216, 236, 242
   toward authority, 58, 60
antianxiety drugs, 98
antidepressants
   pets as, 19–20
   side effects of, 109–110, 111
   for treatment of depression, 98
   see also specific types
antipsychotics
   prescribing, 103
   side effects of, 99, 109

.

Breinigsville, PA USA
14 April 2010
236110BV00001B/80/P